Self-Made Women in the 1920s United States

Self-Made Women in the 1920s United States

Literary Trailblazers

Matthew Niven Teorey

LEXINGTON BOOKS
Lanham • Boulder • New York • London

Published by Lexington Books
An imprint of The Rowman & Littlefield Publishing Group, Inc.
4501 Forbes Boulevard, Suite 200, Lanham, Maryland 20706
www.rowman.com

86-90 Paul Street, London EC2A 4NE, United Kingdom

British Library Cataloguing in Publication Information Available

Library of Congress Cataloging-in-Publication Data Available

ISBN 978-1-7936-2832-9 (cloth)
ISBN 978-1-7936-2833-6 (epub)

Contents

Acknowledgments

I thank Tara Demers for her unwavering love and support. She inspires me to try to be better every day. I thank the many teachers I have had, starting with my wonderful parents Toby and Juliette, for challenging and guiding me intellectually and emotionally. I thank my sisters, Carol and Marilyn, as well as my colleagues and the students I have had the pleasure to work with at Peninsula College. Finally, I thank all those at Lexington Books that helped edit and publish this book.

Introduction

Counter-Narratives
and Reimagined Selfhoods

The 1920s was a pivotal decade in the cultural history of the United States. Historical scholar Paula Fass goes so far as to contend, "American culture was remade in the 1920s."[1] I believe the main impetus for this overhaul was society's obstinate adherence to repressive attitudes and institutions that subjugated people based on their gender, class, race, ethnicity, sexual orientation, or religious beliefs. Completely fed up, members of maligned groups voiced their displeasure and took purposeful action against the norms and traditions that underpinned long-standing inequalities and injustices in the United States. Their participation in protest marches and adoption of convention-defying lifestyles prompted historian Frederick Lewis Allen to attest in 1931, "A first-class revolt against the accepted American order was certainly taking place during those early years of the Post-war Decade."[2] Allen bore witness to increased demands for civil rights and cries for human acknowledgment, a big step toward altering the nation's policies and remaking its very identity.

In this large-scale revolt, women stepped to the forefront. They acted individually and collectively to fight for greater political power, social status, economic independence, sexual freedom, and artistic recognition. In particular, the words and actions of young, white, middle-class feminists formulated a new American narrative, one meant to inspire women like them to forge empowered selfhoods and initiate meaningful change in mainstream society.

Authors played an important role in writing this counter-narrative. Pulitzer Prize-winning poet Edna St. Vincent Millay expressed the defiant, self-aware conviction felt by many women in the Roaring Twenties when she wrote in her poem "I know my mind and I have made my choice":

Not from your temper does my doom depend;
Love me or love me not, you have no voice
In this, that is my portion to the end.[3]

1

Millay disregarded the edict that women obey their designated role of silent and submissive objects under male control. She represented women who spoke up and pursued emancipation from outdated social rules. These women not only chose to partake in the vital activities of modern culture like earning their own paychecks and dancing to hot jazz in nightclubs, but they also changed the culture itself by demanding the right to vote, taking charge of their own sexuality, and defending the underserved and unwanted.

As Millay's poem suggests, the ability to know one's own mind and the strength to make one's own choices are central to a woman's efforts to gain self-determination and gender equality. Despite social pressures, she must not be subsumed by male voices or tempers. I should note that a sizable portion of these women also had to withstand the crushing weight of racism, classism, or homophobia, in part because the leaders of the feminist movement during the 1920s focused on the rights and interests of middle-class, heterosexual, white women. Nevertheless, the feminist ideology they promoted awakened the consciousness of all types of women, including women of color, immigrants and their daughters, lesbians and bisexuals, and the working poor. This ideology influenced contemporary fiction, tales written by talented authors that entertained and encouraged every woman to claim her portion of the rights and privileges of modern life.

Unfortunately (but predictably), little attention has been paid to women's writing from the 1920s, as the bulk of literary scholarship has privileged male writers, chiefly members of the Lost Generation. Groundbreaking novelists like Jewish immigrant Anzia Yezierska and African American Nella Larsen were excluded from the literary canon for years and have only recently begun to gain the respect their work deserves. Although recent scholars have analyzed literary compositions by individual female authors, my study takes the novel approach of comparing how multiple authors from different backgrounds used a range of media—fiction, poetry, stage plays, film scenarios, blues lyrics—to identify and counter the aggressive forms of oppression women faced during the twenties.

This book considers famous and forgotten woman-authored texts from the Jazz Age, examining important identity shifts their protagonists undergo and contextualizing the message of female empowerment within 1920s culture. Of the eleven authors I discuss, some names may be familiar, such as playwright and actor Mae West, blues singer and songwriter Bessie Smith, author and activist Dorothy Parker, or poet and famed salon host Gertrude Stein. Other names may not be as familiar, like poets Djuna Barnes and Amy Lowell, Hollywood screenwriter Josephine Lovett, or novelists Anita Loos, Mourning Dove, Anzia Yezierska, and Nella Larsen. To select each author, I used three criteria: her main works were available to a mass audience in the

1920s, her works feature female protagonists who confront onerous gender restrictions, and her works express a distinctively twenties style. By no means am I conducting a comprehensive study of this period. Notable writers are briefly mentioned or left out entirely, not because they are unworthy but because I intend to scrutinize just a few representative texts that complement each other and explicate several core societal problems besieging women.

I bring literary works into conversation with one another, many for the first time, to compare their presentation of different approaches 1920s women could adopt to carve out a place for themselves in the male-dominated world. In addition to gender, I consider the important role race, class, and non-binary sexuality play in the women's fight for self-actualization and the stories they tell. This study reveals multiple ways the authors' female characters defined emancipation as they struggled to be recognized as intelligent, passionate, self-governing human beings. Although fictional works may not carry the same weight as historical accounts of actual women's lived experiences, these stories' familiar settings, relatable characters, and engaging plots resonated with audiences who craved role models that bespeak strategies for exerting control over their lives and maximizing their future prospects.

The authors I have selected composed counter-narratives to the "moral policing"[4] of the time. They understood that, in spite of the era's rapid social changes, conservative attitudes lingered. Their opponents favored gender roles that exerted tight controls over a woman's freedoms and kept her out of the public sphere. In 1922, sociologist and feminist Elsie Clews Parsons called for an end to "the American concept of chivalry,"[5] which attempted to confine women to two roles, submissive wife or powerless prostitute. Parsons knew a concerted effort was needed to combat the male conception of woman as an economic commodity and passionless servant, "a depersonalized, and, sexually, an unresponsive being." My point is that the progressive counter-narratives by Mae West, Bessie Smith, Dorothy Parker, Gertrude Stein, Djuna Barnes, Amy Lowell, Josephine Lovett, Anita Loos, Mourning Dove, Anzia Yezierska, and Nella Larsen reflected a growing nation-wide effort, especially among young people, to break free of outmoded attitudes about women and unreasonable restrictions on their behavior.

One reason I juxtapose different creative visions is each author offered her own version of femininity and success. Together, the stories show that a woman's personal and professional goals interact with numerous components of her public status, such as stability in a professional career, acceptance into mainstream society, and freedom as a sexual being. Another reason to connect these literary works is to examine contrasting reactions to male domination and bourgeois culture's moral hypocrisies. For example, some protagonists negotiate the tension between oppression and freedom by defiantly standing up to every injustice regardless of consequence, while others pretend to acquiesce, gaining power and profit by subverting the rules without detection. Because 1920s society "physically, emotionally, and spiritually restricted their rightful autonomy,"[6] the latter group "achieved some measure of freedom by disguising defiance to look like conformity."

What the protagonists have in common is an unbreakable internal fortitude and the ability to express a unique subjectivity, as each signals how a woman with progressive beliefs could succeed in the modern milieu. The characters learn to claim ownership over their selfhood and assert some control over their environment, fearlessly inserting themselves into the public sphere. Because the actual achievements of accomplished women in the 1920s were not as widely known, these works of fiction were a revelation for female audiences who restlessly wanted a different role but had begrudgingly accepted the misogynistic prohibition against personal and professional fulfillment, a set of ambitions and desires lauded in men but demonized and suppressed in women. The authors, in line with contemporary feminist leaders, hoped to propel "a change in the meaning of 'woman.'"[7]

It seems obvious to label the authors I have chosen as feminists because their writing highlights a woman's strengths, contributions, and value in deliberate contradiction to gender stereotypes and sexist mandates. The term itself did not appear in popular dictionaries until the 1910s, but by the 1920s "feminism had become an accepted term for beliefs in and movements for women's emancipation."[8] I am aware that feminism was then (as it is now) a loaded and debated term that "resists boundaries."[9] Also, not all of the authors I discuss considered themselves feminists, though "for a woman in the 1920s, putting pen to paper was, consciously or not, a feminist act."[10] In any event, this study will sometimes refer to the eleven authors or their ideas as feminist to indicate that they intentionally contested systems of male power and chauvinism to affirm female agency and self-respect.

To guide my use of the term, I turn to Nancy Cott's three-part definition of feminism and its goals: (1) replacing sex hierarchy with sex equality, (2) identifying a woman's subordinate position as socially constructed and not predestined by nature, and (3) encouraging a woman to see herself as not only an individual with personal subjectivity, but also a contributor to a social group who must participate in a "community of action" to initiate meaningful societal change.[11] An example of these three elements at work, the suffrage movement rallied diverse groups of women to engage in unified public action so they could change an institutionalized limitation of women's citizenship and put them on equal footing with men.

After women won the vote in 1920, however, the woman's movement splintered.[12] Lacking a shared definition of womanhood and a uniting political issue, many women with progressive views embraced individualism and focused more attention on personal liberty than group concerns, which created a crisis for feminists.[13] The movement's leaders supported women who struck out on their own to attain the prerogatives and rights automatically afforded men, but their depleted ranks left them vulnerable to attacks from conservatives, including women who fiercely opposed feminism and vigorously condemned the progressive agenda. Anti-feminists worked to convince other women that "the ideals of liberalism—that a person be self-governing, self-autonomous, self-determined—applied only to men."[14]

This study analyzes fiction that forcefully opposed this attitude, rejecting the limited and diminished roles women were given within "the patriarchal family."[15] The protagonists give readers permission to disregard traditional obligations and work toward individual goals. Moreover, the characters build a non-patriarchal family, winning the support of like-minded female friends who helped them assert a strong sense of self. They are fictional, but by mimicking the thoughts, feelings, abilities, and desires of actual women, the protagonists reminded readers that they were not alone. The authors spoke to and for the voiceless, including those who felt invisible because of class, race, or sexual orientation.

It is important to note that no single feminist voice could accurately represent the diverse and complex experiences of all women. In addition, works of fiction necessarily reduce the complexity of real people's lived experiences to tell an efficient, coherent story. Nevertheless, talented writers can identify common needs and desires among women, inviting them to see themselves and their struggles in the fictional characters. Thus, the cadre of authors I have selected gained popularity and respect in the 1920s for their authentic dramatizations of pressing societal issues. Their stories created a sense of community for readers, and their female characters modeled how women could devise unique and self-assured identities in an inhospitable world.

THE MODERN WOMAN

Women of the Roaring Twenties entered public life in a number of distinct ways. Younger women gravitated to the flapper aesthetic, which was built upon a display of impetuous rebellion and self-liberation. To strike the proper flapper pose, though, a woman had to immerse herself in consumerism and mass culture. Critics considered the flapper a superficial performance that focused entirely on image, notably short skirts or pants, bobbed hair, make-up, and cigarettes. However, it was also an attitude. The flapper had to exude joy and energy, living life fully by burning the candle at both ends as Edna

St. Vincent Millay promoted in her 1922 poem "First Fig."[16] Moreover, this persona relied on an independent, forthright spirit, one that spurred a woman to venture out of the home to find gainful employment, as well as openly express her sexuality. Flappers resisted the feminist label, but they subscribed to a feminist ideology and incorporated it into their behavior. Self-aware, they seized ownership over their bodies, their image, and their role in society.

Some feminists that scorned the flappers claimed the older label New Woman, a cultural phenomenon that started in the 1880s. Like the flapper, the New Woman wanted freedom of movement and control over her finances and sexual satisfaction, but she worked from the inside out, an approach more grounded and practical than the flapper's ostentatious displays. The New Woman fostered an image of self-discipline, intelligence, and professional decorum. She set long-term career goals and coordinated prudent activism for progressive socio-political change.

The authors discussed in this book gave their protagonists either the New Woman's sensible self-refashioning or the flapper's rebellious flair, yet all wanted the reader to liberate herself from male governance, choose her own appearance, and join the larger world at the same level with men. It is the common interests of the flapper and the New Woman that cause me to align them under the broader heading modern women. The modern woman wanted equality for her gender and freedom for herself. This vision caused an upheaval in conservative circles because it incited women to demand and fight for "the right to self-expression, self-determination, and personal satisfaction."[17] In the novels, poems, stage plays, blues songs, and film scenarios of the eleven authors I have chosen, the protagonists tackle imposing obstacles from conservative authority figures, attaining personal freedom and, to some degree, gender equality through individual strength, self-assurance, intelligence, creativity, ambition, guile, and hard work.

My argument is that these works were read and enjoyed by large audiences in the 1920s because they confirmed and expanded women's understanding of empowered femininity and posed multiple routes that might lead them to the American Dream of being who and what they wanted (and deserved) to be as full members of modern society.

I have organized the chapters in terms of each literary work's connection to one of five key routes to social achievement and self-love: economic independence, sexual empowerment, racial inclusion, lesbian pride, and political activism. Anzia Yezierska, Anita Loos, Mae West, Josephine Lovett, Nella Larsen, Mourning Dove, Djuna Barnes, Amy Lowell, Gertrude Stein, Bessie Smith, and Dorothy Parker took on these difficult issues knowing the enormous resistance they faced, based on the demeaning assumptions about the modern woman firmly held by many across the nation. These authors could not ignore the need for major cultural change, recognizing the impact their writing might have on the understanding and development of a woman's identity as a complete human being and her standing as an equal member of society. The protagonist in each story was a fictional creation, but female audiences cared about her and wanted to follow her example.

Because not every woman shares the same vision of personal empowerment and public success, each chapter compares perspectives from multiple authors, except for Dorothy Parker whose impact I believe warrants its own chapter. The first two chapters focus on how women operate as individuals, overcoming society's deterrents to design discrete identities. Chapter 1: Economic Independence: creating a New Self investigates how Anzia Yezierska's novel *Bread Givers* and Anita Loos's novel *Gentlemen Prefer Blondes* portray a woman's campaign to become a professional who earns her own living. The main characters are disciplined, practical, self-made entrepreneurs that forswear the cliques of silly romantic girls looking to compete with each other for a man to whom they can become dependent. Yezierska's protagonist Sara Smolinsky and Loos's protagonist Lorelei Lee are markedly different women—Sara is stubbornly outspoken and forthright while Lorelei hides her maneuvers behind a façade of dizziness and compliance. Yet, neither protagonist accepts second class status as a mere male accessory or domestic servant, which was often the case for wives in the real world. Instead, the characters devote themselves to being mentally strong, so they may acquire independence and financial self-sufficiency, Sara through her brave resolve to bust into the male-controlled system and Lorelei through her sly manipulation of that system from within.

Yezierska and Loos advanced a vision of individual selfhood that was based on a woman's capability and determination. Their protagonists acquire the necessary education, be it formal or self-directed, to secure a professional career that satisfies their ambitions and protects their freedom and self-esteem. Chapter 2: Sexual Empowerment: Freeing the Sensual Self continues this theme of a woman's personal liberty and public image, but it turns from gaining a professional position to expressing a heterosexual identity. Like Sara and Lorelei, the protagonists of Mae West's notorious Broadway play "SEX" and Josephine Lovett's Oscar-nominated film scenario "The Dancing Girl" are confident women who must endure society's scorn to succeed. Each character exhibits her sensual selves honestly and authentically, rather than suppressing it to gain society's approval and win a husband. West's protagonist, prostitute Margy Lamont, and Lovett's protagonist, jazz baby Diana Medford, are comfortable in their own skin as they strive to disconnect a woman's reputation, as defined by men, from her moral character and public identity, which she defines for herself.

As in the novels discussed in the first chapter, the plays by West and Lovett demonstrate that the subservient, domestic identity required by polite society is not healthy or fulfilling. This outcome is made clear by antagonists Clara and Ann, who surrender themselves to Victorian "true womanhood" and become hypocritical, possessive, corrupt, and self-destructive. On the other hand, protagonists Margy and Diana, like Sara and Lorelei, claim ownership over their body and its function in society. Whereas Sara and Lorelei control their labor as a source of financial independence, Margy and Diana legitimize their erotic desire as a source of personal satisfaction and mastery of their public persona. They genuinely like themselves and maintain a cheerful, optimistic outlook despite society's disapproval. Margy and Diana rehabilitate their public image, rebelliously undercutting the sexual objectification of the male gaze and championing a woman's sexual subjectivity and agency.

Moving beyond the issues women faced as individuals, the next two chapters focus on issues that minority women faced as members of groups that were doubly marginalized. Chapter 3: Racial Hybridity: Healing the Torn Self addresses a type of rebellion and rehabilitation that was foreign to Margy and Dianna. Race was a contentious issue in the 1920s, and the biracial woman was abused from both sides of the color line. To rebuff these attacks, the African American woman joined her sisters and brothers to broadcast their voices by way of a cultural movement, the Harlem Renaissance, and physically fight for their rights in the streets of major US cities. Less visible were Native Americans, yet they too battled to procure opportunities and assert their personhood. Like the white women analyzed in the first two chapters, African Americans and Native Americans sought economic independence and sexual freedom; however, they had the added challenge of racist dehumanization.

Chapter 3 explores how Nella Larsen's novel *Passing* and Mourning Dove's novel *Cogewea: The Half Blood* wrestle with dilemmas connected with being biracial in a segregated and discriminatory society. Larsen's protagonist Clare Kendry and Mourning Dove's protagonist Cogewea McDonald can pass as white, necessary for acceptance into mainstream society, but they recognize the white mindset as oppressive and corrupt. Just as white characters Sara, Lorelei, Margy, and Diana refuse to compromise their desires and identities in the face of unjust abuse, Clare and Cogewea will not minimize or conceal their Otherness. Instead, they embrace it as part of a hybrid identity, reaffirming their ties to a non-white heritage while also claiming the rights associated with whiteness, rights that should be available to all. Standing strong against intense scorn, Clare and Cogewea rehabilitate their Otherness as the foundation for a cohesive multicultural selfhood that celebrates the unique beauty and strength of an undervalued culture. The characters in the stories from all three chapters model a powerful, integrated self, one that replaces intolerance and division with inclusion and cooperation.

Chapter 4, like chapter 3, focuses on how developing a positive group identity helps women find themselves and grow as individuals. Chapter 3 analyzes the efforts made by women of color to construct a strong identity and insert themselves into the world. Chapter 4: Lesbian Pride: Decoding the Erotic Self scrutinizes the efforts made by four authors to openly express a proud lesbian or bisexual selfhood. Blues singer-songwriter Bessie Smith and poets Djuna Barnes, Amy Lowell, and Gertrude Stein did not shrink from the sensual voice and sexual experiences of women who love women, using explicitly erotic descriptions and embracing female desire without the shame, guilt, dishonor, or regret that society typically heaped on the "fallen woman." The poetic and blues lyrics speak out against the cultural dispossession and personal diminishment perpetrated by the homophobia pervasive in mainstream society.

Like the works in the previous three chapters, the characters in these lyrics display unique public identities that reject the tyranny of restrictive gender roles. Instead of encoding queerness within heteronormative situations and language, the lyrics liberate important aspects of the lesbian experience and voice, encouraging these women to assert dominion over their own personhood and proclaim it publicly. The songs and poems sound a feminist call for mutual respect and unity, encouraging female listeners and readers to build ties of trust, support, joy, and love with other women. Barnes, Lowell, Smith, and Stein portrayed women who, like the characters discussed in the first three chapters, confound patriarchal expectations by affirming their autonomy as they enter the public sphere and press for equal footing with men.

The event most associated with gender equality in the 1920s was the passage of a constitutional amendment that prohibited the discrimination of voting on account of sex. This triumph demonstrated the power and influence women can have, especially when they unite around a single cause. Enfranchisement was a win for all women, yet white feminists ultimately failed their Black sisters, as voter suppression excluded women of color from voting for decades. Nevertheless, feminists did demonstrate that political activism and organized women's movements were effective mechanisms to bring about needed social breakthroughs. While chapters 1 and 2 focus on a woman finding success through her reaffirmation of an individual identity and chapters 3 and 4 focus on a woman finding success through her rehabilitation of a group identity, Chapter 5: Political Activism: Asserting the Creative Self probes the benefits and limitations of activism to women individually and collectively. The chapter's subject is Dorothy Parker's stories, poems, essays, and personal life. Unlike the other chapters, I spotlight a single author because of her significant cultural importance and the volume of her creative output.

Parker, an activist herself, provided a strong voice for the political involvement of not only middle-class, white women, but also women of color and the poor. She penned satiric feminist attacks against misogynistic belittlement and exclusion of women; plus, she wrote scathing criticism of racist and classist attitudes. Her counter-narratives rebuked stereotypes, offering an alternative vision of women as independent thinkers and actors in the public sphere. Probably the most famous female author of the twenties, Parker was respected by the male cultural nobility, yet her subversive writing was beloved by feminists. Thus, it is no surprise that her work has never gone out of print and her name remains synonymous with an era of lively, sarcastic wit, as well as consequential changes to women's lives and identities.

Not only does this book analyze the social and cultural issues raised by these authors, but every chapter also reflects on their act of storytelling. The texts are artistic creations, so I view them through the lens of critical literary analysis. Chapter 1 discusses how narrative perspective in *Bread Givers* and *Gentlemen Prefer Blondes* gives voice and agency to the protagonists and the readers, women toiling to support themselves financially and emotionally. Chapter 2 explains how staging and performance of a play like "SEX" or a film scenario like "The Dancing Girl" assists in the development of female characters and feminist themes. Chapter 3 examines the role of setting in the novels *Passing* and *Cogewea* as both an important geographical location and a symbol of segregated spaces in which one's choices either reinforce or destabilize the hierarchy of whiteness over Otherness. Chapter 4 highlights language use in poetry and blues lyrics, noting the aesthetic beauty and social power in the works' rhythms and melodies. Chapter 5 returns to narrative point of view, analyzing how Dorothy Parker's use of perspective and tone determined whether her protagonists would gain the confidence to stand up for themselves and fight for social justice or shrink into themselves and give up. It is clear which role Parker and her fellow feminists hoped their readers would adopt.

The 1920s was a time of tension between freedom and oppression, a conflict that provoked women to seek significant improvements in themselves and their society. Spurning an unacceptable vision of their womanhood that bound them to outdated stereotypes and traditional roles, the modern woman laid claim to the rights, freedoms, and opportunities all humans deserve. A courageous group of authors contributed to this effort by observing the culture closely, examining their own personhood carefully, conceiving of empowered female identities, and writing a modern narrative into the public consciousness.

Jazz Age trailblazers Anzia Yezierska, Anita Loos, Mae West, Josephine Lovett, Nella Larsen, Mourning Dove, Djuna Barnes, Amy Lowell, Gertrude Stein, Bessie Smith, and Dorothy Parker employed creativity and eloquence to delight the imagination and arouse the social conscience of their audiences. These impressive women did not achieve all their feminist goals, work that continues a century later, but they alerted the general population to the sins of the patriarchy and provided examples of gender equality and women's self-actualization that inspired a generation.

NOTES

1. Paula Fass, *The Damned and the Beautiful* (Oxford: Oxford University Press, 1977), 3.

2. Frederick Lewis Allen, *Only Yesterday: An Informal History of the 1920's* (New York: Harper, 1931), 73.

3. Edna St. Vincent Millay, "I know my mind and I have made my choice," *Poetry: A Magazine of Verse* 37, no. 1 (October 1930), 2.

4. Christina Simmons, *Making Marriage Modern* (Oxford: Oxford University Press, 2009), 7.

5. Elsie Clews Parsons, "Sex," in *Civilization in the United States: An Inquiry by Thirty Americans*, ed. Harold E. Stearns (New York: Harcourt, Brace, 1922), 317.

6. Angela Latham, *Posing a Threat* (Middletown: Wesleyan University Press, 2000), 2.

7. Elizabeth Francis, *The Secret Treachery of Words: Feminism and Modernism in America* (Minneapolis: University of Minnesota Press, 2002), xxi.

8. Francis, *The Secret Treachery of Words*, xv.

9. Nancy Cott, *The Grounding of Modern Feminism* (New Haven: Yale University Press, 1987), 4.

10. Peter Childs, *Modernism* (New York: Routledge, 2000), 98.

11. Cott, *The Grounding of Modern Feminism*, 4.

12. Lantham, *Posing a Threat*, 9.

13. Francis, *The Secret Treachery of Words*, xiv.

14. Kim E. Neilsen, *Un-American Womanhood: Antiradicalism, Antifeminism, and the First Red Scare* (Columbus: The Ohio State University Press, 2001), 2.

15. Neilsen, *Un-American Womanhood*, 1.

16. Edna St. Vincent Millay, *A Few Figs from Thistles* (New York: Harper and Brothers, 1922), 9.

17. Fass, *The Damned and the Beautiful*, 23.

Chapter One

Economic Independence

Creating a New Self

Women of the 1920s perceived that economic self-reliance was essential to gaining personal autonomy and public respect. Like previous generations, they were pressured to find a husband and make a home; however, many considered a different life, choosing to enroll in college and embark on a career. In fact, the 1920s was "a high point for women's education,"[1] as "female students represented 47 percent of the student body in colleges and universities." Graduates entering the workforce, though, "were relegated to positions thought to be best suited to women . . . [and] made far less money in these positions than men."[2] Undaunted, professional women set an example of earning their own living and running their own lives.

This chapter focuses on two novels published in 1925: the sober and earnest *Bread Givers* by Anzia Yezierska (1880–1970) and the farcical and viciously ironic *Gentlemen Prefer Blondes: The Illuminating Diary of a Professional Lady* by Anita Loos (1889–1981). Although each author took a decidedly different tack to presenting the values and identity of the career woman, both championed working-class women's efforts to gain financial self-sufficiency and professional standing.

Yezierska was a Polish immigrant striving to attain the American Dream. Her immigrant protagonist, Sara, embraced a New Woman (and a New World) identity of hard work and self-sacrifice in order to make herself into a person worthy of respect. The novel *Bread Givers* was well received at the time, partly due to Yezierska's fame in the 1910s for her essays that described New York's working-class Jewish community and for her best seller *Hungry Hearts* (1920), a collection of short stories about immigrants struggling to find their place in the U.S. One of these tales won the Edward O'Brien Best Short Story award for 1919, and the collection was turned into a Hollywood film in 1922. Audiences were fascinated with the trials and tribulations of the "sweatshop Cinderella," admiring her desire for advancement. Yezierska, a respected public figure, had a vision of America as a place where anyone, including a poor, immigrant woman, could become independent and self-reliant.

Loos, herself a bit of a flapper, composed a protagonist, Lorelei, that embraced the flapper identity of freedom and public performance as she manipulates gullible millionaire men to fund her extravagant lifestyle. Loos, a smart and accomplished novelist and screenwriter, meant *Gentlemen Prefer Blondes* as a criticism of women like Lorelei and the men taken in by their charms. However, audiences appreciated the character's mental toughness and shrewd approach to life and relationships, lauding her as a hero rather than a villain. Originally published as short sketches in *Harper's Bazaar*, the book version immediately became a best seller that led to a popular film in 1928. The book was praised by respected authors William Faulkner and Edith Wharton, the first woman to win the Pulitzer Prize in 1921, who dubbed Loos's work "the great American novel (at last!)"[3] and Loos herself "a genius."

Yezierska and Loos, disturbed by the sexism at the time, invited female readers to undertake extensive re-envisioning of their personal and economic identities. The efforts of their young protagonists to make something of themselves mirrored an increasingly feminized youth culture in the United States, which "probably gave young women a greater sense of cultural inclusion and presence"[4] than they had ever known. Spurning the passive role of a sexualized body to be desired or a commodity to be exchanged, many young women secured gainful employment and became valued consumers, often the primary target of a newly professionalized and culturally influential advertising industry. Moreover, those who obtained a white-collar job exerted some authority over the means of production. Women were surging into the public sphere, heeding modernity's call to fully realize their personhood.

My analysis of *Bread Givers* and *Gentle Prefer Blondes* highlights the qualities of two vastly different approaches women could take to attain financial independence and personal liberty. I will discuss ways the novels follow the bildungsroman model to show how the protagonists overcome societal limitations to acquire white-collar employment and middle-class respectability. I will also examine how the main characters develop their own sense of professionalism and narrate the creation of their own self-identity. The stories depict a key component of my overall thesis, that a career promoted empowered femininity and assisted women in seizing full membership in society. However, before unpacking the novels by Yezierska and Loos, I want to give a little cultural and literary context for the role women were compelled to play in the years leading up to the 1920s, namely, the doting and submissive wife instead of the capable employee and self-governing individual.

A "LITTLE GOOSE"

Sara and Lorelei had grand plans, educating themselves to escape the lower class and wrest control of their lives. Initially, they put their bodies to work, but the professions and social standing they wanted depended on their cleverness. The men in the novels, though, treated these ambitious, talented protagonists as nothing but bodies, existing to serve male needs as an attractive public accessory and a domestic drudge. While the young women looked to the future, to a career and a partnership marriage, the men clamoring for them looked to the past.

Building on centuries of misogynistic cultural attitudes, late-nineteenth-century male scholars and scientists added biological determinism to their justification of the oppression of women and other non-dominant groups. In 1890, one of America's leading evolutionary biologist Edward Drinker Cope professed that recent scientific discoveries proved white men had an innate rationality and superior intelligence. He defended men's position at the head of families, businesses, and governments as an inalterable law of nature, a circumstance that "cannot be otherwise, nor ought it be otherwise."[5] The famed biologist warned against the "fraud" of sex equality, asserting that women who wanted to usurp male roles represented "a disease"[6] to human society. Cope added that "a spirit of revolt" brewing among "masculine women" must be squelched to avoid a serious disordering of nature. Beyond the role of affectionate helpmates, women simply "don't count."[7] No outlier, Cope led a throng of male authority figures who institutionalized chauvinistic beliefs that denied women equal status and professional self-determination.

Of course, there were feminists at that time who criticized the hypocritical contention that sex segregation in the workplace, and other public situations, somehow protected women and improved their lives. Several notable fiction writers dramatized the moral destructiveness of the male-controlled marketplace for a mass readership. For example, female author George Eliot argued through her popular novels that "masculine economies pose gendered threats to women, who are often exchanged as objects or hoarded as prized possessions."[8]

Renown female authors at the turn of twentieth century created protagonists that glimpsed self-fulfillment but had trouble overcoming entrenched social mores. One major limitation a woman faced was the expectation that she marry and assume a subservient role. Kate Chopin presents a wife in "The Story of an Hour" (1894) who dies immediately after losing her independence, the "possession of self-assertion which she suddenly recognized as the strongest impulse of her being!"[9] When Chopin's protagonist Louise Mallard learns her controlling husband has died, she is overcome by an unfamiliar appreciation for freedom. After years of faithful service to another, she gladly embraces "a long procession of years to come that would belong to her absolutely." Unfortunately, just as Louise begins to enjoy her newfound autonomy "like a goddess of Victory," her husband unexpectedly arrives home alive, causing her to suffer complete heart failure. Metaphorically, the woman is broken hearted to have lost the "monstrous joy" of governing her own finances and selfhood.

A contemporary of Chopin, Charlotte Perkins Gilman conveyed the destructive consequences of conventional marriage in "The Yellow Wallpaper" (1892). The short story portrays a woman mentally and emotionally abused by the men in her life, her free will and humanity unfairly confiscated. Unlike her husband John, the woman in the story is unnamed, nothing more than a servant to other people's needs as wife, mother, sister. Misdiagnosed as having neurasthenia, itself a dubious nervous condition, the woman is forced to endure bed rest and isolation in a former nursery, reducing her to infant status. Similar to many women at the time, Gilman's protagonist is denied a true sense of self-worth, something men could gain, in part, through a career. Her husband John attains public respect as a medical doctor, his authority and dignity bolstered by the ability to support and, thus, rule his family. Throughout the story, John routinely belittles his wife's intellectual and emotional needs, denigrating her as a "little goose"[10] and "little girl." He tears away her creative talent and self-esteem, until she loses her sanity. At the end of the story, she finally succumbs to her helpless confinement, another madwoman trapped in the prison of the Victorian vision of ideal womanhood.

These stories demonstrate that men were expected to be independent, the boss and breadwinner, while women were constrained as dependents, refused any measure of power or respect. Gilman raised this concern in her 1898 feminist treatise *Women and Economics—A Study of the Economic Relation between Men and Women as a Factor in Social Evolution*, stating, "We are the only animal species in which the female depends on the male for food, the only animal species in which the sex-relation is also an economic relation. With us an entire sex lives in a relation of economic dependence upon the other sex, and the economic relation is combined with the sex-relation."[11] Positioned as sex objects, ornaments, or domestic servants, women of this era experienced economic disenfranchisement. They lacked the means and opportunity to be anything other than a leech on male production and trade, as Olive Schreiner protested in her 1911 book *Woman and Labour*: "Again and again in the history of the past, when among human creatures a certain stage of material civilization has been reached, a curious tendency has manifested itself for the human female to become more or less parasitic."[12] Without access to employment, women had little choice beyond subservience, a role that suppresses feelings of societal usefulness and self-fulfillment.

Gilman and Schreiner affirmed that this dependency was neither necessary nor acceptable. Schreiner argued for men to "give us labour and the training which fits for labour!"[13] Gilman bypassed men entirely in her 1915 utopian novel *Herland* by depicting an all-female community whose success illustrates the constructed-ness of gender roles and debunks patriarchal attitudes and assumptions. Individual achievement and mutual support ensure that no woman is a parasite. The novel echoes the hope Gilman expressed in *Women and Economics* that "the present century is witnessing the beginnings of a great change."[14] If a woman is to possess her own labor and its rewards she must reject "the power and will of another."[15]

Women of the 1920s embraced this precept and seized access to the public sphere. They followed Mary Wollstonecraft's advice that a woman "must not be dependent on her husband's bounty for her subsistence during his life, or support after his death—for how can a being be generous who has nothing of its own? or, virtuous, who is not free?"[16] Wollstonecraft declared in her 1792 treatise *A Vindication of the Rights of Woman* for women to be allowed to become "physicians as well as nurses," professionals who can be "supported by their own industry." As twentieth-century suffragists marched to get the vote and jazz babies boldly danced and drank in nightclubs, professional women entered male-identified careers and became the bosses of their own lives. In 1929, V.F. Calverton went so far as to assert that a "woman's economic independence has been a far more important item in her emancipation than her political enfranchisement."[17] Voting, while vitally important, occurs only once a year, but earning a salary reinforces a woman's agency on a daily basis and provides her a greater presence in the community, which spurs change to oppressive gender and class roles.

Chopin and Gilman presented middle-class, white protagonists who are destroyed by societal pressures. Yezierska and Loos, however, presented resilient working-class protagonists, one a Jewish immigrant from Eastern Europe. Their 1920s characters do not go mad or drop dead; they get up when society knocks them down, posing a more optimistic future of independence and self-government. Rather than a doomed wife, Sara Smolinsky fits the mold of the New Woman, a female role model that had emerged during the Progressive Era of 1890–1920. This controversial female figure chose to leave so-called domestic bliss for higher education and white-collar employment. Needless to say, the New Woman had to endure attacks on her body, her character, and her spirit as she strove to fulfill the same dreams and aspirations that men were lauded for pursuing. The feminist paragon was a "soberly dressed woman who seeks to make the most of her intellectual capabilities, to receive adequate training so that she may contribute actively to society and, in return, maintain her life in independence."[18] This description perfectly fits the appearance and attitude of Yezierska's protagonist. Like Yezierska, Sara comes of age in the decades preceding the Roaring Twenties, making her slightly old-fashioned in the eyes of a flapper, like Loos's protagonist Lorelei Lee. The New Woman paved the way for the flapper generation of the 1920s to flaunt an even bolder identity of freedom and subjectivity, as more women openly rebelled against traditional attitudes and conventions.

It must be said that economic independence was not available to every would-be New Woman or flapper, particularly women of color. However, the 1920s did see a sharp increase of women engaged in skilled work, enabling the New Woman to acquire "money and a room of her own,"[19] which author and feminist Virginia Woolf in 1929 deemed necessities for women to grasp control their lives and speak their minds. This shift meaningfully advanced "women's economic and creative freedom, intellectual and aesthetic growth, productivity and self-esteem."[20] Authors of Jazz Age literature led the charge, creating characters that fearlessly stepped outside the accepted norms and called attention to a whole generation's eagerness for liberation and self-actualization.

PULLING ON ONE'S BOOTSTRAPS

The novels by Yezierska and Loos celebrate the working-class woman's assertion of public selfhood by utilizing the bildungsroman, a heralded literary tradition that tells a young person's coming-of-age story. The bildungsroman's protagonist, typically a young man, undergoes difficult character growth as he overcomes his initial conflict with society and its values to find a place for himself within that society. Using first-person point of view, the protagonist describes his journey to material success, emotional maturity, and moral enlightenment. Toward the end of the nineteenth century, Horatio Alger penned a highly popular series of rags-to-riches novels. He popularized the myth of the self-made man, which was central to Western manhood and the American Dream. Alger's Ragged Dick character escapes poverty as a boy through hard work, determination, courage, and patronage by a rich businessman who recognizes his potential. As a result, the young man secures a professional career and a middle-class identity.

Following this general model, Yezierska and Loos featured disadvantaged female characters who remake themselves as a means of acquiring economic independence. The novels' protagonists Sara Smolinsky in *Bread Givers* and Lorelei Lee in *Gentlemen Prefer Blondes* ignore familial and societal expectations as young girls to construct autonomous identities that empower them to realize their ambitions and succeed in the public sphere as adults. Each begins her journey alone, initially engaging in physical work to acquire a sustainable income and maintain a private residence—Sara through hard labor in a laundry and Lorelei as a mistress to a rich businessman. Through determination and sacrifice, they attain professional careers and middle-class respectability. Sara and Lorelei also resist traditional marriage, turning down offers women were told to want. They focus on their careers, and then locate partners who allow a woman to be her own boss.

These characters were meant to inspire women to assert themselves and enter the public sphere. Independence, though, did not necessitate isolation. Reading the tales of Sara and Lorelei reminded career-focused women that they were not alone in the battle for economic equality and social justice, echoing the efforts of activist groups like the Women's Joint Legislative Conference (WJLC). The WJLC took on the cause of working women and helped them tackle a variety of daunting obstacles: "Created in September 1918, the WJLC initially propounded an aggressive agenda of labor legislation, only to face internal tensions and the strong opposition of a counter-network of Republican state legislators, businessmen, and members of the National Woman's Party."[21] The WJLC fought to improve women's wages and working conditions through legislative and legal means; plus, they encouraged women to break into professional careers, so they could actualize their own potential and act as role models for others.

Sara and Lorelei realize that their professional aspirations demand a practical, focused, and unromantic approach to employment and self-creation. Fed up with their fathers' restrictions, these characters leave home as teenagers to make a life for themselves in the masculine work world. Sara dedicates herself to the long, difficult road of becoming a teacher, which begins by accounting for every cent she earns because she is paying for rent, food, and school on her own. The position and identity that she wants entails years of self-development, which compels her to forgo any romantic entanglements. When a brief bout of unrequited puppy love causes a pre-teen Sara significant hurt and humiliation, she commits to tedious work in a box factory and forgoes girlish dreams of romance: "I stamped forever love and everything beautiful out of my heart."[22] While adult Sara will regain a sense of beauty and love, young-adult Sara must fashion a hardened individual personhood, separate from a man.

Despite needing to climb out of poverty, Sara consciously refuses to sell her ambition for the hollow promise of a fairy-tale life as a wife and mother. This position is bolstered by her married sisters' miserable households, which reflect their surrender to social convention in relationships that cause a denial of self and a descent into domestic slavery. Sara, on the other hand, sticks to her plan of making herself into "a person." In other words, she strives to achieve the "male 'American Dream' of individual freedom, personal identity and material prosperity of her own,"[23] which was typically withheld from women.

Lorelei, on the other hand, welcomes romantic entanglements, as long as it is wealthy married men that she entangles. Success for Lorelei requires she not allow herself to feel romantic about the men or the relationships. Instead, she is practical, warning herself not to fall in love and, thereby, lose her power over a rich patron: "I always seem to think that when a girl really enjoys being with a gentleman, it puts her to quite a disadvantage and no real good can come of it."[24] Lorelei overturns "male sexuality's colonizing power"[25] by maintaining a professional attitude toward her liaisons and the income she earns through the labor of her body. A type of businesswoman, she is always in control of her relationships and her own priorities, asserting that a man "kissing your hand may make you feel very very good but a diamond and safire [sic] bracelet lasts forever."[26]

Lorelei's role as the mistress of a married man is different from the role of a traditional wife. She remains independent, living in her own apartment and controlling her own finances. Her earnings may depend on men, but her personal liberty and free will establish her more as an employee than the customary "kept" woman or housewife. In fact, one might argue that Lorelei is self-employed, contracting her labor as she sees fit. For instance, she and only she owns her body, remaining sexually inactive unless she is properly compensated. Furthermore, she lives outside the confinement of the domestic sphere before and after she marries, declining a honeymoon and pushing her dull millionaire husband to focus on his own interests so she has free reign to produce her film scenarios and associate with a man she finds more alluring.

SELF-MADE WOMEN

Sara and Lorelei share similar goals of income acquisition and self-government, yet they clearly have very different approaches, which gives them contrasting relationships with their authors. Sara follows the traditional path of the self-made man, rising from poverty through hard work, formal education, and sexual restraint. In addition, she also must challenge patriarchal restrictions from the larger society and from within her family. These experiences and personality traits match those of Yezierska. Like her protagonist, the author was a Jewish immigrant with an overbearing Orthodox father. She struggled to escape poverty in New York and oppressive pressure from the Jewish community against a woman's autonomy. Yezierska trusted that a woman's route to personhood included choosing education and independence over romance and family obligations. Therefore, Sara leaves home in defiance of her father's dictate that she gives her wages to him until he finds the man who will pay him a fat dowry to purchase her in marriage. One can see defiance and self-confidence in this portrait of Anzia Yezierska:

Sara represents Yezierska's strength and determination, as well as her ultimate desire to achieve self-fulfillment even at the expense of her womanly duty to family. She mirrors Yezierska's personality as an "aggressive, dynamic, demanding and forceful" person who "sought and created a satisfying, self-directed career."[27] Rather than being a commodity and a slave to father or husband, Sara asserts ownership of herself and pays for her own living space in a boarding house. She lives by herself, doing exhausting physical work in a laundry so she can attend night school, obtain her high school diploma, and, later, a college degree. She gains confidence with each achievement, which leads to renting higher quality accommodations, winning academic awards, and realizing her career ambitions.

Figure 1.1. Anzia Yezierska
Drawn by Emily Klein

Lorelei, on the other hand, gains wealth without grueling physical labor, formal education, or sexual restraint. She appears intellectually impoverished, evident in her misspellings, ignorance of history and literature, and lack of analytical skills. She represents all that her clever and accomplished author Anita Loos hated about the stereotypical dumb blonde. Loos hoped her book would expose mainstream society's absurd devotion to silly, beautiful women at the expense of intelligent, capable women. Nevertheless, Lorelei claws her way out of the working class and attains the respected position in Hollywood that Loos craved. The ruthless Lorelei, born Mabel Minnow, attends a trade college in Little Rock, Arkansas, to become a stenographer until she murders her boss-turned-lover in a jealous rage. Convincing an all-male jury to acquit her transforms Mabel from a minnow to a shark, causing her to change her name to Lorelei, the alluring but dangerous siren of German legend, and leave the little pond of Little Rock for the dangerous ocean of Hollywood to become an actress.

After she attracts the attention of a wealthy Chicago businessman, Lorelei moves to New York and installs herself in a luxurious apartment as his courtesan. She appears pliant and obedient to male admirers, but she actually earns a living on her own terms. She gives or withholds sex and public companionship if his gifts (i.e., salary) of jewelry are not expensive enough. After being treated to a lavish trip across Europe, Lorelei discards her "sugar daddy" and becomes the wife of a different wealthy man. Marriage, however, does not compel her to become servile or domestic. On the contrary, Lorelei maintains her financial, social, and sexual freedom.

Loos does not like that Lorelei's power is sexual and her motives selfish, or that she relies on and even feeds into gender stereotypes. For Loos, the fact that even the smartest, most world-wise men preferred "a witless blonde . . .was palpably unjust."[28] Her satirical novel attempts to exact a measure of revenge on these blondes and the great men who are bewitched by them, writing in the introduction that Lorelei is "a symbol of the lowest possible mentality of our nation."[29] Nevertheless, the character is far from the weak, obedient, helpless, passive persona she presents to her male admirers. Her "brains" and "education" may be euphemisms for sexual appeal and experience, but Lorelei uses her power strategically to remain independent and exert complete control over the most rich, powerful, and intelligent men she meets. One

Figure 1.2. Anita Loos
Drawn by Emily Klein

can see in this portrait of Anita Loos the author's trepidation about a woman of intelligence and integrity struggling to break into the male-controlled professions.

For all their differences, Sara and Lorelei both refuse to be deterred by the economic limitations placed on women, using an unwavering faith in themselves to gain financial self-sufficiency and become their own bosses, which made these novels appealing to female readers in the 1920s. Sara, the New Woman, disrupts attitudes of male superiority and female subordination to achieve self-reliance and create a public self that is equal to any man. Lorelei, the flapper, exploits the expectations and assumptions associated with traditional gender roles, thereby reversing the power dynamic within her sexual relationships. Society may consider her dependent, as a "kept" woman and later a wife, but she retains ownership over her sexuality and her identity, much like the prostitute-protagonist Margy Lamont in Mae West's Broadway play "SEX" featured in chapter 2. In short, Lorelei and Sara exemplify two approaches to the creation of a socio-economically empowered self, previously the exclusive purview of men.

|

A WOMAN'S PLACE

Yezierska's protagonist Sara frequently hears the command, "Woman! Stay in your place!"[30] from her tyrannical father in *Bread Givers*. Reb Smolinsky believes women exist only to engage in devoted, selfless service to men. Fashioning himself a scholar of Judaism, Reb asserts to his wife and four daughters that the Torah requires obedience and submission because "only through a man has a woman an existence. Only through a man can a woman enter Heaven."[31] Because he spends his days studying his holy books instead of earning a living, Reb charges his daughters to hand over all their wages to him until he can sell each into marriage like a piece of property. Defiant, Sara denounces her father and his beliefs, causing him to call her a blasphemer and attempt to beat respect for the patriarch into her. Sara quickly decides that Old-World dogma and misogynistic bullying will not stop her from achieving her dream—making herself into *a person*.

Not everyone was glad that Yezierska had made a name for herself as "one of the more prolific and popular American writers of the first half of the twentieth century."[32] Despite her novel's mainstream appeal, *Bread Givers* was not well received in the Jewish-American community. Yezierska's conservative Jewish father had contempt for her writing, her success, and her abilities; to him, a woman's work was worthless unless it directly served her husband's needs. In addition, reviews in *The Menorah Journal* attacked the book and the author. Clearly, Yezierska "could expect no support at all from the Jewish establishment."[33] Yet, she was not alone. She joined a rich tradition of Jewish immigrant authors on either side of a "generational conflict within the Jewish community."[34]

The novel repudiated "the gendered experience of Judaism,"[35] which dictated the absolute authority of fathers, brothers, and husbands. Those in the community that kowtowed to tradition considered a figure like Reb a prophet and a hero. In the novel, many of his Jewish neighbors commend Reb's renunciation of his landlady for her inability to understand the incalculable spiritual wealth he provides everyone. He has the adoration and respect of his community and his wife because "he encapsulates the Jewish collective spirit which has allowed them to survive generations of persecution."[36] For women in the twenties, this persecution was ongoing as Jewish and Christian leaders castigated the New Woman and the flapper for abandoning her duties as a wife and mother. The religious and social authorities commanded that employment be restricted to traditional domestic roles, afraid higher education and professional careers would make women unfit to manage their household, resulting in the inevitable disintegration of Western civilization.[37]

Reb demoralizes Sara's sisters, forcing each to compromise her ambitions and accept his vision of her selfhood and her future. Reb is not only patriarchal, as he eradicates any autonomy or self-respect these young women try to generate, but he is also selfish and hard-hearted, since the husbands he sells his daughters to are cruel, petty, and domineering. Even worse, Reb blames the women for their misery, refusing to consider any flaw in his own motives or matchmaking abilities.

In the first chapter, a ten-year-old Sara observes the exhaustion of her sister Bessie for shouldering the responsibility to support the entire family, an obligation that impoverishes her financially and spiritually. Reb, who studies the Torah instead of working, proudly calls Bessie the family's "burden-bearer."[38] His eldest daughter toils selflessly so the family can pay for rent and food, yet she recognizes the crushing weight of this duty. She wishes she could escape "slaving to choke myself in the dirt," crying out, "I want to live while I'm yet alive." However, her father drives away the man she wants to marry because he wishes to own her labor. Sara watches Bessie "sink into herself as if all the life went out of her heart and she didn't care about anything anymore."[39] When Reb does sell Bessie to an insensitive widower, she must take on an even heavier burden, assisting in his fish peddling business and raising his six children.

Reb squashes the dreams of Sara's next oldest sister Fania, who wishes to marry young poet Morris Lipkin. Fania loves Lipkin and his verses about the crush of poverty and the transcendence of love, but her father berates the boy's creativity and suggests, hypocritically, that Lipkin's bookishness is a crime against society and his daughter. When the young man visits the family's apartment, Reb humiliates him, acting as if he does not exist and treating him like "an unwanted ghost"[40] instead of a person of substance and value. After her dream is dashed, Fania only wants to escape her father's tyranny and accepts the first man who offers her father a generous dowry. It turns out this seemingly wealthy clothing dealer continually gambles away his income and abuses Fania. This betrayal causes Sara's sister to lose her youthful innocence and idealism as she becomes bitter, materialistic, self-important, restless, and lonely.

The third sister Mashah loves beauty, foregoing lunches to buy nice hats and dating an accomplished concert pianist. Although it is her boyfriend's rich Gentile father not Reb that separates them, Reb immediately takes advantage of the opportunity to sell his daughter to a seemingly wealthy diamond dealer. Resigned to a life of ugliness and misery, Mashah demeans herself to accommodate this selfish man. When Sara visits the couple, she is ashamed that her sister must beg her husband for money to purchase milk for their young children. Mashah feels imprisoned, ground down by poverty and hopelessness. Her youth and self-worth have been used up by a husband who calls her "nothing but a worn-out rag. . .. With your worn-out face, nice clothes would be wasted on you."[41] This treatment infuriates Sara, but she soon realizes the pointlessness of her ire since Mashah will not defend herself. Unlike her sisters, Sara's dreams do not depend on finding the right husband and investing her whole self in him. A New Woman, Sara refuses to stay in a woman's assigned place as her father commands.

The New Woman trained herself to "think and feel 'as a man,'"[42] so she might succeed in the public realm. Threatened, men in authoritative roles attacked "the respectability and legitimacy of the New Woman."[43] As they feared, "the more politically radical of the New Women" rallied other like-minded women to their cause, for they wanted to "forge a network of women reformers and social innovators into a singularly effective political machine."[44] Feminist activists and social work pioneers like Jane Addams and Lillian Wald established settlement houses where educated women shared knowledge with poor women and helped them locate employment, unionize, and strike an acceptable balance between work and family. The goal was to provide a practical pathway to individual success, which would eventually lead to reforming the patriarchal attitudes and institutions that held women back.

In *Gentlemen Prefer Blondes*, Lorelei takes a different approach to navigating difficult patriarchal waters. Unlike the chapters devoted to Sara's childhood, Lorelei summarizes her background in a few paragraphs. When explaining how she was acquitted of murdering her predatory boss Mr. Jennings, she reveals that she used men's denial of a woman's agency against them without their knowledge. In addition to applying her sex appeal to influence the judge and jury, Lorelei leans on their assumption that women are empty-headed slaves to their emotions, testifying: "I had quite a bad case of hysterics [sic] and my mind was really a blank and when I came out of it, it seems that I had a revolver in my hand and it seems that the revolver had shot Mr. Jennings."[45] With tears in their eyes for a woman that represents their vision of a sister or daughter, the jury agrees that it was the revolver not a simple, helpless girl that shot and killed the man. Based on her performance in court, Lorelei decides to pursue a career in the cinema.

This belief that performing a traditional version of femininity gives a woman the best chance at success in a male-controlled society sharply contrasts with Sara's decision in *Bread Givers* to acquire professional employment and respect by muting her femininity, or at least society's stereotype of what form femininity must take. From a young age, Sara acts as a young man would: working physically demanding jobs, dedicating herself to her education, and supporting herself. Her "masculine" approach is further highlighted by two failed attempts to be accepted by female co-workers and fellow college students as one of the girls. Her inexperience with choosing feminine clothing and putting on make-up results in ridicule and humiliation. Therefore, Sara feels shame for briefly adopting a "false face"[46] and configures an authentic self that honestly represents her values, her goals, and her personality, a self she can love.

Lorelei, on the other hand, deftly uses the guise of society-sanctioned femininity to subvert male expectations. As the subtitle (*The Illuminating Diary of a Professional Lady*) of the novel indicates, the protagonist trades her performance on the silver screen for a performance in real life as "a professional lady." Instead of struggling to overcome the stereotype that women were "scatterbrained, unable to concentrate on the business at hand in the office, too temperamental and emotional for the impersonal world of work,"[47] Lorelei plays to that stereotype, empowering herself from within her gendered role and participating in public life without male resistance. While Sara becomes a teacher of immigrant children, Lorelei becomes a "teacher" of philandering men, instructing them on how to pay for a woman's attention and accord her personal agency. Lorelei exploits her admirers' assumptions of her helplessness by weeping crocodile tears to get what she wants. Her methods may cause a feminist's skin to crawl, but she secures an autonomous identity, sustains monetary self-sufficiency, and seizes social power over rich and respected men.

EARNING ONE'S DAILY BREAD

Sara and Lorelei not only commandeer professional employment and financial independence, but they also expose the morally corrupt and hypocritical nature of gender roles that place socio-economic restrictions on women.

The title to Yezierska's book, *Bread Givers*, is invoked frequently by Sara's mother and sisters to bemoan the deficiencies of their male providers. Not allowed to earn their own living, these women depend on the productivity and generosity of men, who are often either unable or unwilling to give women what they need, choosing instead to spend their earnings on themselves, as Mashah's husband does, or give it away to Jewish charities, as Sara's father does. Sara resists her father's bullying, claiming that in America "women don't need men to boss them"[48] because they can earn their own living and rule their own lives. A woman can become a person in the world and act as her own bread giver.

Although leaving home is relatively easy, finding employment and developing one's selfhood are more difficult tasks than Sara assumes, made additionally challenging by landlords that refuse to rent to single women, employers who assume women cannot or will not persist in a difficult job, and cafeteria servers who unfairly give female workers smaller portions of food than male workers. For Sara to make herself into a person, she must leave her father's household to develop her determination, self-respect, individuality, and self-sufficiency. She needs a room of her own, as a symbol of her self-possession and a location for self-examination and personal growth. Entering her own door in a boarding house helps Sara birth a new selfhood, claiming, "This door was life."[49] As Virginia Woolf proposed, a woman cannot become the person she wants to be without her own space and the ability to shut the door on the misogynistic attitudes and gendered expectations of the outside world. At first, potential landladies turn Sara away, assuming a single woman will use the room for indecent purposes. However, she asserts herself, demanding the landlady see her as a tenant and a person. Of course, it is Sara's ability to pay a month's rent in advance that convinces the woman. In a consumer society, personhood, like any other possession, is transactional. Sara's $6 for rent allows her to purchase not only the appearance of personhood, but also the reality of her self-assurance and independence.

The fact that a woman bars Sara's success shows the damage internalized sexism can do to a woman's self-identity, her relationship with other women, and her ability to withstand objectification and invalidation. Yezierska calls attention to this form of sexism, especially rampant in the life of working-class women in the 1920s. For Sara, the simple act of buying lunch reveals that society believes male workers should receive more and better food than female workers. She complains to a female server and a female supervisor about her inadequate helping, but because the practice is normalized these women ignore her appeal. When they state that they have given Sara a fair portion, she wishes she could shout her disapproval, but she feels "too trampled to speak."[50] She realizes other restaurants will treat her the same way, so she chooses to go without lunch. Experiences like this cause many women to doubt their abilities, compromise their identities, disconnect from other women, and hate themselves.

While Sara initially makes do with a single room in a boarding house, Lorelei has a whole apartment to herself. When her benefactor, Chicago's button king, makes the occasional trip to New York, she must admit him to the flat, but she can close her bedroom door and her sexuality to him if she chooses: "I told him. . . I had quite a headache and I had better stay in a dark room all day and I told him I would see him the next day, perhaps."[51] Just as Sara studies in her room, Lorelei contemplates the best strategies to serve her ambitions. She uses her beauty and sexuality to purchase a comfortable life instead of marrying, adorning herself with the appearance of class and respectability while waging and winning a capitalist battle.

Lorelei may appear to have internalized patriarchal attitudes, but she actually "knows that women are marginalized and exploited by patriarchal power."[52] She adeptly reverses this exploitation through her gendered performance of obedient subordinate and sex object. First, she recognizes the unequal cost on a woman's reputation and future when an "improper" love affair becomes known: "a gentleman never pays for those things but a girl always pays."[53] Second, she understands the need to preemptively manipulate and trick men under her influence because a gentleman of power and privilege often attempts to deceive "a girl" and exert his sexual authority until he tires of her. Mr. Eisman is fooled by her performance, showing the reader that Lorelei adheres to a deeper truth when she states, "money was not everything, because after all, it is only brains that count."[54] Her schemes succeed because of her cleverness and boldness, such as keeping her fiancée's letters in case she needs to blackmail him or quarreling with a man she entices on her cross-Atlantic trip so she can keep the uncut diamonds he hoped would grant him sexual favors.

Lorelei feels her mercenary approach is justified since men hold much of the social power and an attractive, gullible girl soon becomes an unwanted old maid. Her behavior, may not be foolish or a betrayal of feminism, but rather empowered, even subversive. She acts as a spy in the camp of self-important, lecherous men, using their interest in (and low opinion of) a beautiful blonde woman against them. To emphasize that she is merely playing a role, Lorelei follows the request of a British military officer to spy on a U.S. government official, who turns out to be the former prosecutor in her murder case. Lorelei eagerly undermines male superiority from an individual and an institutional standpoint, suggesting just a bit of the damage that can accompany misjudging a woman's ability and treating her unfairly.

PROFESSIONAL RESPECTABILITY

Yezierska and Loos present protagonists who, in building a professional persona, act as a bridge between feminist rebellion and the conservative status quo. Sara uses determination and Lorelei uses shrewdness to avoid or overcome the pitfalls that crush the dreams of many downtrodden and desperate women. Yet, neither seeks to dismantle the existing societal structures; they merely want to remove the obstacles barring women from achieving self-determination. For Sara, after becoming a self-supporting teacher with an apartment of her own, she reconciles with her disapproving father, recognizing the traits she shares with him and the value of understanding and honoring some elements of her Jewish cultural heritage. Lorelei may not share the conservative values of her millionaire husband, but publicly she plays the part of dutiful wife. She allows his continued efforts to censor risqué films to distract him from her own activities. Both characters carve out a role for themselves without upsetting the established order.

Yezierska and Loos followed the Alger model where success means upward mobility and middle-class respectability.[55] Their protagonists are outsiders playing by the rules set by society's insiders. Sara capably functions in the traditional male role and insists that the system's promise of merit-based advancement provide her the opportunities it provides a man with the same talents and determination. Lorelei appears to function in the traditional female role, but she exhibits beauty and performs inferiority to manipulate men's ingrained misogyny, so she may gain the financial benefits and personal freedom she desires.

To gain acceptance into the upper echelons of the dominant culture, Yezierska faced an additional obstacle. As a Jewish immigrant, she was "a young woman in a world where ambition was the path to Americanization and ambition seemed designed for men."[56] The author contested the staunch nativism of the time. The anti-immigrant frenzy during World War I culminated in the Emergency Quota Act of 1921 and the National Origins Act of 1924. This legislation aimed to close U.S. borders to "undesirable" ethnic groups from southern and eastern Europe, as well as Asia and Africa. The National Origins Act was significant to Jewish people in Europe because they could no longer look to the United States as a refuge to escape anti-Semitism and, in the following decade, "the maelstrom of Nazism."[57] In addition to restricting immigration, "the quota systems in colleges and universities, hospitals, and law firms, limited—or eliminated—Jewish entry."[58] Faced with discrimination and disdain, Jews of the 1920s sustained their own communities and supported each other, with men as the family's decision-maker and voice.

Yezierska acted as "the voice of the voiceless"[59] by arguing that "Jewish women" had the ability to succeed in the public sphere as an individual and should be allowed to seek the American Dream of higher education, professional employment, economic self-sufficiency, and personal self-realization. In Yezierska's short story "How I Found America" (1920), the female narrator rebels against the domination and dehumanization of immigrant women. Instead, she asserts the value of her own mind, "Does America want only the work from my body, my hands? Ain't it thoughts that turn over the world?"[60] Family is not antithetical to the Dream, but, like men, women cannot permit it to compromise their ability to secure satisfying work through their own efforts and talents. Thus, a woman's highest duty is to herself, not to a husband or even children. Like Sara, the narrator in "How I Found America" fights for a romantic idea of America: education, opportunity, and respect for every person, along with the encouragement to develop her best self. Yezierska stories argue for women to be extended the same opportunities as men without unfair gendered expectations.

In *Bread Givers*, Sara refuses to be passive or see herself as inferior when she has the intelligence, energy, determination, and creativity to fulfill her own ambitions. Called *"Blut-und-Eisen"*[61] (blood-and-iron) by her parents, she is bull-headed, industrious, thrifty, and opinionated. These traits help her overcome soul-crushing poverty. In the first chapter, 10-year-old Sara is to go into business for herself, quickly turning a profit on the twenty-five cents she borrowed from a neighbor. Her bold self-assertion and fearless self-expression enable her to enter the public sphere, earn an income, and provide for her family. Even the most meager profit makes Sara feel "richer than Rockefeller"[62] because she is also earning her first taste of independence and self-reliance, which assures her a definite sense of personhood.

Sara works as a wage slave to earn a college degree. Women at universities were no longer a novelty in the 1920s, but it was expected that women would treat the experience as merely an opportunity to find a suitable husband, so any employment after graduation was meant to be temporary until the young woman "began her true vocation, that of wife and mother."[63] Sara, however, represents women who procured economic independence and then built a family without sacrificing their career or their identity. Sara's hard work pays off when she finally becomes a professional, accepting a position as an elementary schoolteacher. She adopts what educational reformer John Dewey called a "professional spirit" in a 1913 essay, which to him "means intellectual awakening and enlightenment."[64] It is a revelation to Sara when she gains insight into her humanity, learning reason and self-control.

Sara's position gives her entry into the middle class. She finds an upscale apartment in a prominent neighborhood by going to a housing agent's office, glad not to have to squabble with narrow-minded landladies. In addition to the solitude, privacy, and cleanliness of her new space, Sara loves the objects and routine of a middle-class identity, absorbing attacks from her family. She weathers her sisters' criticism that she turned her back on her family to become a "new-found stylish lady."[65] She brushes aside her impoverished mother's comments about her new clothes and her "princess" demeanor, choosing instead to gift her mother several newly minted twenty-dollar gold coins. After the mother dies, Sara's persona of respectability is further attacked when her father's new wife sends an accusatory letter to the principal of her school, criticizing her for not supporting them. Sara withstands this abuse and maintains her professionalism. Later she does choose to support her father, but on her own terms, which releases her from hating her father and her lower-class origins. Furthermore, she has found a way to be incorporate the Jewish elements of her identity into her American personhood.

Loos also put a premium on female professionalism, disparaging her own "idiot heroine"[66] in *Gentlemen Prefer Blondes* as anything but respectable from a moral or an intellectual standpoint. Part of the issue is that the zero-sum-game of capitalism "placed women like Lorelei and Loos in competition with one another."[67] Hence, if Lorelei's idiocy and superficiality wins, then Loos's aptitude, imagination, and substance must lose. Lorelei's access to the American Dream prompts Loos to feel envy as well as resentment for her unearned success. Loos, like Sara Smolinsky, succeeded by developing her brains and doggedly fighting her way into the male-dominated society. Lorelei, however, is resourceful in a different way, using male desire to situate herself in respectable society without the need of intellect or hard labor. Her prosperity may undermine the feminist effort in some ways, but Loos's protagonist enters high society because she has the mental toughness and emotional fortitude to climb "an obviously corrupt ladder."[68] She is more a cut-throat capitalist than a passive victim, which may lead Lorelei to be, as her name suggests, a predator of men.[69] For Lorelei, sexuality is merely a tool of her trade, and once she has earned a profit she leaves the wealthy man behind without a second thought.

Throughout the novel, Lorelei explains that she can accept attention and payment from men without forfeiting her body or mortgaging her self-respect. The men, competing with each other, make donations to her with no guarantee of sexual payment. Since the terms of the exchange are unspoken, what the men receive for their offerings is completely up to her. Thus, Lorelei, not a man, sets the price of gaining or just glimpsing her companionship, and by refusing to invest emotion into these relationships she does not consent to men purchasing or possessing her. They may not realize it, but these captains of industry and social leaders have had their masculine economies of power, possession, self-interest, and desire supplanted by Lorelei's economy of acquisition-seduction where she is the capitalist and men are the commodities.

As I mentioned earlier, the novel's subtitle indicates that Lorelei considers herself a "professional lady." Lorelei's public appearance is as a traditional woman, one that is domestic, chaste, and submissive, but she makes it her business to force her gentlemen admirers to submit to her will. For instance, she privately accepts a pay-off to leave a rich young man alone while she publicly appears reformed and old fashioned. Moreover, she ingratiates herself to high society by participating in conventional rituals like hosting a debutante coming-out party. Such a stunt is meant to shape her public identity, putting the critics and doubters in their place. Lorelei cultivates a carefree appearance, seemingly a passive observer of her life who is carried by circumstance from one situation to another. The reality, though, is that the daily work required to maintain her lifestyle demands perception and perspicacity in real-world situations that have taught her professional skills like risk assessment, competitive self-interest, and dispassionate decision-making.

Success in this role as a professional lady suggests she, like Sara, applies a professional spirit to her work. Lorelei has awakened to how the male world functions, that her gentlemen friends succeed in business and politics largely because they only appear to follow the rules of propriety, honesty, and fairness. So, she plays the female image they have constructed against the reality they desire. This deft sleight of hand, making the men think they prevail when actually she has used them for her benefit, helps Lorelei expand her sphere of influence from the boudoir to the film studio as a producer. Her manipulation of male-imposed gender roles is encoded in the book's last paragraph, "And so I am very happy myself because, after all, the greatest thing in life is to always be making everyone else happy."[70] Lorelei gets what she wants, while the men think she has given them what they want.

The process of becoming a professional requires Sara and Lorelei to reconfigure their identities, their public personae, and their relationships to tradition. Sara acquires self-determination by severing traditional ties to family and culture. This process hardens her, which the college dean explains is essential for her to enter the professional world, "All pioneers have to get hard to survive."[71] When Sara's mother dies, she mourns but does not to follow the Jewish tradition of rending her new, expensive professional outfit. Even as Sara assimilates into the dominant culture, she must admit to being a lot like her father. Her boyfriend Hugo helps her see that she shares Reb's hunger for knowledge and learning, as well as his strong sense of self and his iron-willed devotion to a set of beliefs, albeit different ones.

In the end, Sara discovers there is room for both new and old cultural characteristics in her personhood. She actually starts this process earlier in the novel when she uses prayer to find the "infinite peace"[72] that helps her survive self-doubt and loneliness as she completes her college degree. As a professional living in her own apartment, Sara enjoys having a quiet personal space, something her father claims for himself in the family's tiny apartment so he can study the Torah. She realizes it is a similar passion that fuels her fight for freedom as she escapes poverty and becomes a professional.

Lorelei also reconfigures her relationship with male authority figures to fulfill her ambition as a professional lady. She has a hard-hearted determination and never compromises her autonomy for a lover or a husband, but, unlike Sara, she cloaks it with the softer, more traditional powers of femininity. With her youthful beauty, sexual power, and ruthless machinations, Lorelei dominates men, taking control in every relationship with a man. Loos may not like Lorelei's methods, but she surely appreciated her protagonist's ability to control her own life and those in her sphere, earning what she needs from Gus and Piggy before becoming the head of Henry Spoffard's wealthy family and usurping Henry's authority for her own purposes. One could say that Lorelei "moves in the economic order from the position of worker to that of capitalist; from selling her labor to selling the signs of her labor."[73] She does not compromise her goals of material prosperity and self-determination for sentiment or romance; instead of being possessed by men, Lorelei possesses her husband's wealth and her lover's affections.

NARRATIVE SELF-CREATION

Sara frequently reiterates the goal of becoming "a person," making it a mantra that feeds her determination to progress along a proud but lonely path of ambition and self-discovery. She quickly learns that self-creation requires experience and self-awareness, strategic planning and meaningful action. Jumping through the hoops of a formal education, Sara finds that she, not a middle-class male professor, is her own best teacher, so it is up to her to analyze the challenges of professional life and apply the lessons she learns. Lorelei also claims to be self-taught, evident in seemingly absurd but strangely accurate comments like, "I seem to be thinking practically all of the time" and "it is only brains that count."[74] Rather than being carried away by emotion, she often tasks herself with thinking up schemes to acquire the financial and social capital she covets. Strategic and fierce, Lorelei enlists the help of her friend Dorothy to "take advantage of everybody we meet,"[75] capitalizing on men's weaknesses and exploiting the assumption that a beautiful blonde woman is simple-minded and gullible. Learning from experience, the protagonists announce the self-sufficiency they want. They narrate to 1920s readers two methods of using strength of will beat the men at their own game, Sara in the role of self-made man and Lorelei in the role of professional lady.

The autonomy of these empowered women is underscored by their first-person point of view. Sara and Lorelei act as the authors of their own stories, choosing which of their intimate thoughts and feelings to share, and how to frame their victories and their failures. These narrator-protagonists own their personhood and their voice from start to finish, composing an identity of competence and a narrative of success. Neither woman bows to a man, including a narrator who might not understand her motivation or respect her linguistic performance.

In fact, Lorelei does not even bow to an author, succeeding despite Loos's disavowal of her protagonist as an exemplar of "human stupidity."[76] The story is told through Lorelei's diary entries, not an omniscient narrator or a mediating editor, which gives the character the power to persuade readers to respect her strength of personality and not discount her capability. Although there are mistakes in her writing, Lorelei only appears to misunderstand her circumstances, choosing to obscure a higher level of competence and self-awareness behind a façade of incomprehension and compliance. A depth of understanding frequently peeks out of Lorelei's writing, such as being amused that she can convince her conservative husband to let her appear in the type of film he is trying to censor, remarking contemptuously, "So I even talked him into that."[77]

The use of first-person narrative encourages readers to care about and root for these protagonists. Readers appreciate characters they can identify with, and young women reading these novels in the 1920s particularly appreciated characters who escaped the dependent roles that family and society compelled them to accept. Sara's narration remains optimistic, despite her father's continual commentary that women were worthless in the eyes of men and God. She is spurred on by her goals, particularly the American Dream of individual opportunity and socio-economic success. Lorelei, a true flapper, declares to her readers that she does whatever she wants, which involves sexual liberation and getting away with murder. Loos did not intend her character to be a role model for young women, but flappers appreciated how she simultaneously embodied and undermined a delicate, submissive femininity. By confronting unjust accusations and enjoying risqué jokes and stories, Lorelei is more like Loos than the author might want to admit.

First-person point of view permits the reader to experience these characters' struggle to fulfill their ambitions. For example, a ten-year-old Sara relates,

> "More and more I began to think inside myself. I don't want to sell herring for the rest of my days. I want to learn something. I want to do something. I want some day to make myself for a person and come among people. But

how can I do it if I live in this hell house of Father's preaching and Mother's complaining?"[78]

Of course, the characters' control over the narrative also grants them the ability to shape it. Lorelei admits there are things she has left out of her diary, as well as euphemisms like her humorously cryptic statements about time spent alone with her benefactor: "we really do not seem to do practically anything else but the same thing."[79] By writing their selfhood into existence, these narrator-protagonists exert control over their life choices, their public identities, and the society in which they succeed.

Each narrator takes a unique approach to storytelling. Sara is brutally honest, while Lorelei obscures the truth behind a masquerade of refinement and ignorance. Sara represents one group of 1920s feminists who battled the patriarchal social order directly, voicing their opposition to hierarchies and actively prying open the doors to political access, economic independence, and social equality. Lorelei, on the other hand, represents another contingent of feminists who sought social and sexual power by employing a more indirect or covert approach. Loos herself wondered if her audience was ready for a direct assault on the status quo, reportedly scoffing at the tactics of feminists in later decades and stating, "women always knew they were more intelligent than men, but that in the twenties they were smart enough not to let men know it."[80] Nonetheless, Loos's satire is anything but conciliatory, aiming to alter gender relations and power dynamics. Thus, some feminists consider *Gentlemen Prefer Blondes* "a touchstone of early twentieth century feminist rhetorical indirection" and Loos's feminist critique as "radical though coded."[81] Like Lorelei's duplicity, Loos's satire is subversive, exerting female autonomy and authority over powerful men without their knowledge, an oblique attack on sacred male beliefs about women and about themselves.

On the surface, the narrative has a simple, light, fun quality, with Lorelei seemingly coopted by society's binary and hierarchical gender identities. Beneath the surface, *Gentlemen Prefer Blondes* unseats male power and privilege through the use of "covert female power."[82] Scholar Jason Barrett-Fox elucidates Loos's feminist rhetoric by playfully re-writing the famous metaphor of poet and feminist activist Audre Lorde about the rebel using the master's tools to dismantle the master's house: "Lorelei doesn't use the master's tools to tear down the master's house; she uses the master's tools to occupy the master's house, while he cheerfully sets up a tent on the lawn."[83] Using men's expectations and assumptions against them, Lorelei can only be defeated if the men reverse themselves, abandoning their objectification and possession of women's bodies and their dismissal of women's intellect and personhood.

DISILLUSIONED STRENGTH

The 1925 novel that has received the most scholarly attention is *The Great Gatsby* by F. Scott Fitzgerald. This iconic bildungsroman presents the rise and ultimate destruction of a young man who believes he can emerge from lowly origins to gain self-fulfillment through wealth and status. In the novel, James Gatz remakes himself as Jay Gatsby to compete with society's elites, people who look down their nose at him for thinking that his wits, hard work, and force of character should allow him entrance into their ranks. Gatsby chases the "grotesquely flawed"[84] mirage that is the American Dream, and he ultimately turns the woman of his dreams into just another possession, a rare gem for him to own and display. Gatsby builds an audacious home, believing the ecstasy of "the orgastic future"[85] is his birthright. Although America's socioeconomic shortcomings corrupt and destroy Gatsby, he also fails through a lack of self-awareness and a limited understanding of the values and norms that underpin society. Of course, Gatsby's castles-in-the-air are Fitzgerald's, an author who "willfully (almost naively) crossed over in his narrative into a world of illusion" and "reveled in delusion."[86]

Unlike Fitzgerald, female authors Yezierska and Loos had few illusions about modern culture or the American Dream. They clearly understood the corruption at society's core and created protagonists who triumph because they are self-aware and willing to co-opt the prejudices encountered by ambitious women in the 1920s. Like Gatsby, Sara and Lorelei are bold, but these women do not seek to impress and win a mate, nor do they hold Gatsby's "child-like fantasies concerning the past."[87] These female characters do not buy into society's norms and attitudes as Gatsby does; they merely play the game so they may integrate into the social structures, gaining a professional position while maintaining a truly independent spirit.

Gatsby's disillusionment makes Fitzgerald's novel a tragedy. Yezierska and Loos, however, take disillusionment for granted. As a romantic, Gatsby's dedication to the rules lead to his demise. Conversely, Sara and Lorelei are pragmatic and they cleverly use the American Dream as a tool to rise above the injustices of male-dominated society. For them, self-actualization in the public and the private spheres is the ultimate prize, not wealth, power, or mastery over an "orgastic future." However, these women do acquire the wealth and status necessary for self-determination. They use mainstream society's reverence of individualism and competition without succumbing to it themselves. They also demonstrate that women, particularly single women, are not doomed to dependency; they can succeed as professionals and manage their own money just as well as any man.

NOTES

1. Ana M. Martinez Aleman and Kristen A. Renn, *Women in Higher Education: An Encyclopedia* (Santa Barbara: ABC-CLIO, 2002), 11.

2. Joyce G. Webb, "The Evolution of Women's Roles within the University and the Workplace," *Forum on Public Policy* 5 (2010), 2, accessed December 17, 2021, https://files.eric.ed.gov/fulltext/EJ913097.pdf.

3. Susan Hegeman, "Taking Blondes Seriously," *American Literary History* 7, no. 3, (1995), 525.

4. Liz Conor, *The Spectacular Modern Woman: Feminine Visibility in the 1920s* (Bloomington: Indiana University Press, 2004), 226.

5. Edward Drinker Cope, "Two Perils of the Indo-European," *The Open Court* 3, no. 127 (January 30, 1890), 2070.

6. Cope, "Two Perils of the Indo-European," 2071.

7. Cope, "E. D. Cope to Julia Cope, March 27, 1888," KIC Document 53, American Museum of National History Library.

8. Lana L. Dalley and Jill Rappoport, *Economic Women: Essays on Desire and Dispossession in Nineteenth-Century British Culture* (Columbus: Ohio State University Press, 2017), 7.

9. Kate Chopin, "The Story of an Hour," *The Kate Chopin International Society*, accessed March 30, 2021, https://www.katechopin.org/story-hour.

10. Charlotte Perkins Gilman, "The Yellow Wallpaper," in *Herland and Selected Stories*, ed. Barbara H. Solomon (New York: Signet, 1992), 168, 173.

11. Charlotte Perkins Gilman, *Women and Economics: A Study of the Economic Relation Between Men and Women as a Factor in Social Evolution* (Boston: Small, Maynard & Co., 1898), 5.

12. Olive Schreiner, *Woman and Labour* (Leipzig: Bernhard Tauchnitz, 1911), 76–77.

13. Schreiner, *Woman and Labour*, 27

14. Gilman, *Women and Economics*, 6.

15. Ibid., 7.

16. Mary Wollstonecraft, *A Vindication of the Rights of Woman* (Project Gutenberg, 2001), accessed Dec. 17, 2021, http://www.gutenberg.org/ebooks/3420.

17. Victor Francis Calverton, "Careers for Women—A Survey of Results," *Current-History* 29 (1929), 638.

18. Patricia Marks, *Bicycles, Bangs, and Bloomers: the New Woman in the Popular Press* (Lexington: University Press of Kentucky, 1990), 205.

19. Virginia Woolf, *A Room of One's Own* (Orlando: Harcourt, 1989), 4.

20. Erika Dreifus, "A Room of Anzia Yezierska's Own," *JBooks.com: The Online Jewish Book Community,* 2009, accessed Dec. 17, 2021, http://jbooks.com/interviews/index/IP_Dreifus_Yezierska.htm.

21. John McGuire, "From the Courts to the State Legislatures: Social Justice Feminism, Labor Legislation, and the 1920s," *Labor History* 45, no. 2 (2004): 225.

22. Anzia Yezierska, *Bread Givers* (New York: Persea, 2003), 88.

23. Francisco Jose Cortes Vieco, "The (Mis)Education of 'The American Girl' in Europe in Anita Loos's Gentlemen Prefer Blondes," *Revista de Estudios Norteamericanos* 19 (2015), 30.

24. Anita Loos, *Gentlemen Prefer Blondes* (New York: Liveright, 1998), 56.

25. Jason Barrett-Fox, "Rhetorics of Indirection, Indiscretion, Insurrection: The 'Feminine Style' of Anita Loos, 1912-1925," *JAC: Journal of Advanced Composition* 32, no. 1 (2012): 221.

26. Loos, *Gentlemen Prefer Blondes*, 75.

27. Alice Kessler-Harris, Introduction to *Bread Givers* (New York: Persea, 2003), xxvi.

28. Loos, *Gentlemen Prefer Blondes*, xix.

29. Ibid., xxi.

30. Yezierska, *Bread Givers*, 16.

31. Ibid., 137.

32. Bettina Berch, *From Hester Street to Hollywood: The Life and Work of Anzia Yezierska* (New York: Sefer International, 2009), 15.

33. Berch, *From Hester Street to Hollywood*, 147.

34. Gay Wilentz, "Cultural Mediation and the Immigrant's Daughter: Anzia Yezierska's Bread Givers," *MELUS* 17, no. 3 (1991–1992), 33.

35. Victor Seidler, *Jewish Philosophy and Western Culture: A Modern Introduction* (London: I.B. Tauris, 2007), xiii.

36. Wilentz, "Cultural Mediation and the Immigrant's Daughter," 36.

37. Susan M. Cruea, "Changing Ideals of Womanhood during the Nineteenth-Century Woman Movement," *ATQ: 19th century American literature and culture* 19, no. 3 (2005), 202.

38. Yezierska, *Bread Givers*, 39.

39. Ibid., 51.

40. Ibid., 74.

41. Ibid., 150.

42. Carroll Smith-Rosenberg, "The New Woman as Androgyne: Social Disorder and Gender Crisis, 1870–1936," in *Feminism: Critical Concepts in Literary and Cultural Studies*, ed. Mary Evans (New York: Routledge, 2001), 161.

43. Smith-Rosenberg, "The New Woman as Androgyne," 172.

44. Ibid., 164.

45. Loos, *Gentlemen Prefer Blondes*, 32.

46. Yezierska, *Bread Givers*, 183.

47. Margery Davies, *Woman's Place is at the Typewriter* (Philadelphia: Temple University Press, 2010), 84.

48. Yezierska, *Bread Givers*, 137.

49. Ibid., 159.

50. Ibid., 169.

51. Loos, *Gentlemen Prefer Blondes*, 41.

52. Linda De Roche, *The Jazz Age: A Historical Exploration of Literature* (Santa Barbara: ABC-CLIO, 2015), 104.

53. Loos, *Gentlemen Prefer Blondes*, 41.

54. Ibid., 154.

55. Ana-Isabel Aliaga-Buchenau, *The Dangerous Potential of Reading: Readers & the Negotiation of Power in Nineteenth-Century Narratives* (New York: Routledge, 2004), 24.

56. Kessler-Harris, Introduction to *Bread Givers*, vii.

57. Hasia R. Diner, *The Jews of the United States, 1654 to 2000* (Berkeley: University of California Press, 2004), 201.

58. Diner, *The Jews of the United States, 1654 to 2000*, 3.

59. Kessler-Harris, Introduction to *Bread Givers*, x.

60. Anzia Yezierska, *How I Found America: Collected Stories of Anzia Yezierska* (New York: Persea, 1991), 121.

61. Yezierska, *Bread Givers*, 20.

62. Ibid., 22.

63. Nicole Neatby, "Preparing for the Working World: Women at Queen's during the 1920s," *Historical Studies in Education* 1, no. 1 (1989), 54.

64. John Dewey, "Professional Spirit Among Teachers," *American Teacher* 2 (1913), 116.

65. Yezierska, *Bread Givers*, 247.

66. Loos, *Gentlemen Prefer Blondes*, xx.

67. Melanie Benson Taylor, *Disturbing Calculations: The Economics of Identity in Postcolonial Southern, 1912–2002* (Athens: University of Georgia Press, 2008), 110.

68. Taylor, *Disturbing Calculations*, 112.

69. Hegeman, "Taking Blondes Seriously," 534.

70. Loos, *Gentlemen Prefer Blondes*, 165.

71. Yezierska, *Bread Givers*, 232.

72. Ibid., 220.

73. Hageman, "Taking Blondes Seriously," 543.

74. Loos, *Gentlemen Prefer Blondes*, 3, 154.

75. Ibid., 41.

76. Ibid., xxi.

77. Ibid., 160.

78. Yezierska, *Bread Givers*, 66.

79. Loos, *Gentlemen Prefer Blondes*, 99.

80. Molly Haskell, *From Reverence to Rape: The Treatment of Women in the Movies*, 3rd ed. (Chicago: University of Chicago Press, 2016), 44.

81. Barrett-Fox, "Rhetorics of Indirection, Indiscretion, Insurrection," 225.

82. Ibid., 240.

83. Barrett-Fox, "Rhetorics of Indirection, Indiscretion, Insurrection," 239.

84. Kimberly Hearne, "Fitzgerald's Rendering of a Dream," *The Explicator* 68, no. 3 (2010), 189.

85. F. Scott Fitzgerald, *The Great Gatsby* (New York: Charles Scribner's Sons, 1953), 182.

86. Benjamin Hart Fishkin, "F. Scott Fitzgerald and the Pain of Exclusion," in *Fears, Doubts and Joys of Not Belonging*, ed. Benjamin Hart Fishkin, Adaku T.

Ankumah, and Bill F. Ndi (Bamenda: Langaa Research & Publishing Common Initiative Group, 2014), 113.

87. David Noskin and Angela Marshalek, "Applying Multiculturalism to a High School American Literature Course: Changing Lenses and Crossing Borders," *The English Journal* 84, no. 6 (1995), 84.

Chapter Two

Sexual Empowerment

Freeing the Sensual Self

Women destabilized gender roles to obtain greater economic and social opportunities in the 1920s. However, when they entered public life, women were expected, even commanded to present themselves as respectable ladies and refrain from brazenly parading their sexuality. Judged on their outward appearance, women felt tremendous pressure to conform to social conventions conflating their moral character with their reputation. Conservative social leaders attacked those who publicly repudiated sexist directives, calling on the public to shame them into compliance. In Anita Loos's 1925 novel *Gentlemen Prefer Blondes*, professional mistress Lorelei Lee succeeds, in part, because she can veil her sexuality behind euphemism and a projected image of innocence and compliance, fooling her moralistic fiancé into believing she is an "old-fashioned girl."[1] Although it was widely acceptable for men to view a woman as a sex object, she was not supposed to display herself that way. Nevertheless, flappers and feminists flouted social norms dictating they perform a repressive ideal of femininity.

The standard bearers for the sexual revolution were white, middle-class, and heterosexual. They, by and large, agreed with the dominant view that racial minorities, immigrants, lesbians, and the poor were undesirable if not inferior. Women outside of the mainstream who were seeking control over their own sexuality, particularly women of color, had the added challenge of being stereotyped as dangerously hypersexual and possibly subhuman by the dominant group. They experienced different norms of femininity, and their own community pushed them to be exceedingly genteel and respectable in public. The fear was that a salacious woman in their ranks might throw a shadow of disrepute over the whole community and damage its efforts at upliftment and full citizenship. Women of color pushed back against this repressive form of racial solidarity to express themselves and their sexuality freely. Authors leading the charge for unfettered self-expression of non-white women will be analyzed in chapters 3, 4, and 5.

This chapter focuses on two white authors, Mae West (1893–1980) and Josephine Lovett (1877–1958), who sharply critiqued the virgin/whore dichotomy and championed mainstream women's sexual self-actualization. Their fictional works best known in the twenties are West's notorious 1926 Broadway play "SEX" and Lovett's risqué 1928 film scenario "The Dancing Girl." In each story, the protagonist expresses her sexuality proudly and separates her moral character, which she can control, from her public image, which she cannot. I will explore how these works use three 1920s archetypes to denote a woman's sexual choices and the social consequences: the unrepentant rebel, the opportunistic conformist, and the repentant conformist. First, though, I will provide a little literary and cultural context.

TRUE WOMANHOOD

West and Lovett, like Anzia Yezierska and Anita Loos in chapter 1, took a step beyond the previous generation of authors by depicting self-actualized and autonomous female characters. Feminists of that earlier generation, such as Edith Wharton, Charlotte Perkins Gilman, and Kate Chopin, drew attention to the limitations placed on white, middle-class women, but their courageous, talented protagonists fail to attain a full sense of self and pay a significant personal price for their rebellion. In Wharton's novel *The House of Mirth* (1905), protagonist Lily Bart's disruption of traditional gender restrictions proves unacceptable to the cultural elites, and the young woman's desperate grasp at liberty quickly leads to social condemnation, poverty, unhappiness, and premature death.

Lily is a potent example of a turn of the century woman trapped by the need to publicly display "the Victorian idealization of women's nature and domestic roles."[2] Wharton objected to essentializing women and confining female behavior to a narrow range of permissible virtues, namely, chastity, piety, domesticity, and submissiveness. Normalized gender stereotypes drove women to feel they would be failures to themselves, their family, and their community if they sought a role in the male-dominated professional world or chose to be sexually active before marriage. To climb out of poverty, Lily must adopt a limiting and false identity to broker a marriage to a rich but old-fashioned family. Percy Gryce is not the right type of man for a clever, self-possessed woman who has a mind of her own, but financial security depends on her performance of Victorian-era norms. She swallows her pride and self-respect to present a fiction of herself as a demure, religious, compliant young lady.

However, Lily cannot separate the masquerade from her true selfhood, a skill Lorelei Lee masters a generation later. The corrupted self-identity is so dissatisfying that Lily sabotages her own prospects. Marrying Percy would free her from financial worries, but she understands it would also deny the deeper human need to stimulate and sustain "a kind of republic of the spirit."[3] It is this spirit, this access to a woman's inalienable rights of life, liberty, and the pursuit of happiness, that drives 1920s characters like Lorelei and the protagonists in West's and Lovett's plays to actualize their full potential.

Wharton and progressive activists at the beginning of the twentieth century pointed out how "the cult of true womanhood structured the worlds of private and public, the home and the workplace, the family and the professions; how it helped to maintain class- and race-based hierarchies of power; and how it justified women's exclusion from participatory democracy."[4] This ideology was ridiculed by 1920s feminists, but the unenlightened continued to assume that a limited, inferior role must be a woman's natural destiny, the only suitable way to fulfill her obligation to the proper functioning of society, as well as her best option for a comfortable life. In addition, many men took advantage of this particular vision of womanhood, seeking to wed a woman who would be their possession or servant, rather than an autonomous human being who could stand up to her husband and also stand with him as an equal partner.

Popular woman-authored novels in the 1920s, including Wharton's later work, depicted contemporary marriage as "a legal form of bondage."[5] This unequal business arrangement gave men the power to deny a wife access to a career and control over her own sexuality. Yet, marriage rates were rising, due partially to the interest in compassionate marriages, which were based on love and promoted sexual equality between the partners. Of course, women with privilege were most able to choose when or if they married, who they married, and why they married, as "access to education and jobs meant that middle- and upper-middle-class white women were under less pressure to marry, were better able to leave unhappy marriages, and had access to a greater number of positive role models for living autonomously."[6] Marriage manuals provided these women sexual advice, such as the goal of mutual orgasm, so couples would "meld equality for women with sexual intimacy as the essential cement of modern marriage."[7]

Attitudes about women's sexuality were undergoing dramatic changes by the beginning of the Jazz Age, yet the remnants of the true womanhood ideology lingered. It is important to remember that "behind the noise of the

'Roaring Twenties'"[8] attitudes by and large remained "deeply conservative." Across the nation and over the radio airwaves, social and religious leaders expressed concerns about the impact increased sexual freedom was having on women's moral character and public image. Conservative voices loudly defended traditional values, which continued to disenfranchise women and fend off reforms to sexist social norms. The hope was to assuage a cultural schizophrenia that accompanied what anti-feminists feared would be disruptive and disorienting shifts in gender roles and sexual identities. Despite this clamor to reestablish restrictive customs, progressive women were not dissuaded from activating their sexuality or inserting themselves into the public sphere.

The conflict was further complicated by national advertising campaigns. Instead of separating a woman's reputation from her personhood, sophisticated publicity strategies sold a nation on the supremacy of the external, tying a woman's appearance and reputation to the quality of her character. For example, advertisements identified and rebuked a consumer if she had bad breath, dandruff, or body odor, which the ads called the most "damning, unforgivable social fault."[9] Not using hygiene products damned the woman featured in a 1929 ad as "a pathetic figure," whose moral failing reduced her to ranks of the unwanted and alone. Major corporations played on people's insecurities and basest desires, packaging an ethic of superficiality in the guise of self-awareness and social responsibility. Success required looking good, and a desirable veneer must be paid for.

By elevating image over substance, consumerism and mass media undercut the feminist message of not letting appearance or reputation determine a woman's identity or worth. For instance, advertisers taught the modern man that he could procure the coveted façade of authority, good judgment, and respectability only if he invested in the proper automobile, the proper mouthwash, and the proper wife. Even before the consumer boom of the 1920s, Thorstein Veblen recognized women were being treated as consumable objects, asserting in his 1899 treatise *The Theory of the Leisure Class: An Economic Study of Institutions* that "the institution of ownership has begun with the ownership of persons, primarily women."[10]

Unlike the feminists, who criticized the commodification of women, the flappers eagerly bought into the consumer ethos, rehabilitating the bad-girl image to promote their rebellious independence and sexual availability. Regardless, both feminists and flappers "suffered a vigorous assault"[11] from men and women policing the social order. Women who disregarded the social conventions about sexual discretion and restraint were condemned as a "whore." This derogatory and devastating label was meant to reassert male control and apply unjust constraints on a woman's thoughts and actions. Conservatives claimed they were protecting "the patriarchal family and the nation itself"[12] from "radical" self-governing women who had the audacity of wanting to vote in elections, become working professionals, dance the Charleston, wear makeup, or enjoy recreational sex. The mere threat of a damaged reputation, resulting in alienation from family and community, pressed women to conform to socially prescribed behavior.

Those who defined their own womanhood engaged in an intense "debate over women's sexual and social autonomy that raged throughout the first third of the twentieth century."[13] Unlike the flapper, who freely displayed her sexuality, embraced consumer culture, and did not identify as a feminist, the New Woman was more modest as she joined feminists working for political and social rights. Nevertheless, "the sexual discourse of the 1920s," for feminists and anti-feminists alike, "transposed the New Woman into a sexually freighted metaphor for social disorder and protest." New Woman and flapper were deemed symbols of sexual openness and equality. The New Woman modeled how a woman could discard the misogynist view of femininity, taking control of her life and her sexuality. Her "criticism of sexual repression was part of a larger feminist critique of male supremacy and a commitment to ensuring that women would be able to lead full self-actualized lives."[14] The New Woman decried the sexual double standard that unfairly restricted and punished her for doing the same things that were allowable and even praiseworthy for a man. In particular, she undermined society's demand that a woman protect her reputation by hiding her eroticism and restraining her sexual activity.

EMPOWERED SEXUALITY

Economic independence helped 1920s women resist outdated gender roles and sexual taboos. Earning a livable wage offered women, particularly white, middle-class women access to public life and self-esteem. As a result, they developed the autonomy to live by their own rules and seize access to the male domains, including sexual subjectivity.

Technological breakthroughs also played a role in women claiming their sexual selfhood. From the beginning of the century to the 1920s, the number of Americans who owned cars jumped from a few thousand to tens of millions.[15] "By 1920, it was more common for families to have an automobile than indoor plumbing."[16] Car culture offered women greater mobility and sexual privacy. Access to automobiles crossed socio-economic, racial, and cultural lines, as did parents' fears about what young people did in cars. Girls and boys went joyriding, a term filled with sexual innuendo. They could travel unchaperoned to a dance or a secluded lovers lane, and they could be unexpectedly delayed when the car "accidentally" ran out of gas or broke down.

During this time, popular songs noted the sexual potential of the automobile, such as "On the Back Seat of the Henry Ford" (1916), "Riding in Love's Limousine" (1920), "I'm Going to Park Myself in Your Arms" (1926), and "Tumble in a Rumble Seat" (1933). Some towns passed laws against intercourse and even kissing in cars, and Henry Ford intentionally built smaller cars to discourage sexual activity. However, as novelist John Steinbeck jokes in *Cannery Row* (1945), "Most of the babies of the period were conceived in Model T Fords."[17]

In addition to the automobile, prohibition provided an opportunity for women to claim their "right to sexuality and personal liberty."[18] Many people opposed the government's legislation of morality through the eighteenth amendment, as well as "the puritanical streak in 1920s culture."[19] Consequently, the long-standing taboo against young women entering saloons did not apply as strictly to the nightclubs and speakeasies springing up across the nation. These were places where women could let their hair down and be themselves, for "some New Women had advocated drinking as a kind of defiant assertion of self."[20]

When women entered jazz clubs, they left their inhibitions at the door. "The transgression of drinking alcohol [at nightclubs] also went hand in hand with the growing demand by many women, especially younger women, for greater sexual autonomy."[21] Lois Long, famed writer for *The New Yorker* in the 1920s, frequented nightclubs and "used her column to flaunt the drinking habits and adventures of young women like herself who no longer felt bound by Victorian notions of feminine propriety."[22] The flappers and "jazz babies" of all ages felt emboldened by Long's example to dance in short skirts, drink alcohol, and engage in petting parties with men late into the night.

Of course, couples were doing more than petting. "This innovative leisure culture was meant for men and women to enjoy together, and it ushered in a new frankness about sex and romance."[23] The modern woman knew that sexual freedom required control over her fertility, the separation of intercourse and reproduction. Increased access to contraception gave women more sexual freedom. Feminists argued that every woman had a right to control her body and proposed that sex was an important form of a woman's self-expression and personal development, boosting an ethos of female desire and gratification that was gaining prominence in popular sex manuals. Calling women to speak and act in defiance, a new wave of authors, including Mae West and Josephine Lovett, trumpeted the importance of women's sexual liberation.

Another industry that significantly influenced 1920s culture was the cinema, a medium in which both West and Lovett thrived. By the end of the decade, motion pictures were openly celebrating female liberation and the sexually self-possessed woman. The majority of moviegoers were women, many of whom idolized handsome leading men like Rudolph Valentino and identified with on-screen female characters that were socially outspoken yet morally upstanding, at least by feminist standards. Audiences saw that the modern woman in popular films "demanded equality on the sexual as well as the sociopolitical front."[24] Actors portrayed the female fantasy of an ordinary girl escaping the drab domestic life her mother endured to live on her own, meet interesting men, dance on tables, and wear modern dresses. Young viewers attended these films because "the liberated, modern stories and stars captured this image [of a freethinking and progressive America], giving it both substance and glamour. . . . These stars, ordinary and extraordinary at the same time, could represent a point of resistance to local class oppressions and traditional sexual taboos."[25] Movies were "more unbridled, salacious, subversive"[26] before censorship efforts intensified with the institution of the Production Code in 1930. Even then, West, Lovett, and other unrepentant rebels promoted female eroticism and sexual equality by depicting "women in control of their own powerful sexuality."[27]

These technological and cultural advances encouraged many strong, independent women to break from their parents' Victorian values and society's sexual double standard to find new outlets for their sexual energy. Led by the younger generation of flappers and jazz babies, the intrepid group of modern women recast their image as rebels who replaced social pretense and sexual repression with personal choice and experimentation. Only then could they fulfill Anzia Yezierska's call to "make yourself for a person"[28] and either happily remain single or marry a man who would allow his wife to be her own boss.

Asserting ownership over her sexuality, the modern woman demonstrated that a free and public expression of her sexuality was not synonymous with being promiscuous. This attitude defied the virgin/whore binary that forced women to make an unfair choice men were not asked to make: to separate themselves from either their sexuality or public respectability. "The majority of women involved in the New Woman movement believed that sexual identity and behavior should not be linked with public respectability. Sexual activity should not destroy a woman's reputation."[29] Freely expressing her sexuality without sacrificing social acceptability, the modern woman was no more a whore than her male dance partner, or her male sexual partner for that matter. (Note: a discussion of lesbians and bisexuals who struggled with social acceptability in the 1920s can be found in chapter 4.)

"THE DANCING GIRL" AND "SEX"

One of these liberated women, Diana Medford, is the protagonist of the popular 1928 film "Our Dancing Daughters," written by Josephine Lovett and starring Joan Crawford in her breakout role. Lovett herself enjoyed a brief stint acting on stage and screen before she began a long and productive career writing screenplays and film scenarios for major directors and female stars, such as Greta Garbo, Marlene Dietrich, Lillian Gish, Mary Pickford, and Gloria Swanson. Many of her scenarios included sexually suggestive material that made the censors uneasy but earned a profit at the box office and garnered Lovett an academy award nomination. The scenario for "Our Dancing Daughters," originally titled "The Dancing Girl," was adapted from a short story Lovett published in the Hearst newspapers in 1927. She was extremely serious about contesting stereotypes, made plain by her expression in this portrait.

The first half of the film introduces Diana as one of three main female characters, each a flapper who advances a different approach to female sexual identity as it relates to her values and social persona. "Dangerous" Diana openly expresses her sexuality without compromising her self-respect. She wants society to allow her

Figure 2.1.   Josephine Lovett
Drawn by Emily Klein

to be herself, particularly her enjoyment of wearing revealing clothes, dancing to jazz, drinking alcohol, and flirting with men. Diana's friend Beatrice is more reserved and self-conscious after engaging in pre-marital sex with someone in their social circle. She worries about her image and hides the truth so society will not reject her, though she is honest with her fiancé Norman. Diana's rival Ann adopts the false image of traditional womanhood to fool a wealthy and old-fashioned suitor, Ben. Although Ann enjoys drinking, dancing, and flirting, she pretends to be chaste, pious, demure, and domestic in order to wed Ben, a source of financial security but not someone she loves. Unlike Ann, Diana does love Ben, but her rejection of public modesty and submission causes him to choose Ann instead.

In the film's second half, Diana despairs at the unfairness of cultural conventions, but she refuses to change. Bea is devoted to her wedding vows, but her husband's unfounded jealousy and distrust about her sexual past damages their relationship. Conversely, Ann immediately drops her fake Victorian propriety and domesticity once she is married, disregarding her vows and daring husband Ben to stop her. She frequently attends parties, drinks to excess, and makes love to her former boyfriend while enjoying her husband's wealth and status. Ben soon realizes the horrible mistake he made by misjudging both Ann and Diana. On the night Diana leaves for an extended stay in Europe, Ben confesses his love for her and his belief in her as a person. Ann confronts them, accusing Diana of being in love with Ben and committing to making his life miserable. In a state of drunken self-congratulation, Ann accidentally falls down a flight of stairs to her death. In a coda to the story, Diana returns from Europe after two years and marries Ben.

It should be noted that Diana has the means to flout Victorian propriety and sexual self-denial on principle. Unlike Ann, her family has money, so it is not an economic necessity for her to act meek and sell herself into marriage. The cost to Diana of standing on principle is a ruined reputation, which means stigmatization and social alienation but not financial ruin. Nonetheless, it still hurts when Ben rejects Diana and Norman shuns Bea. By acting "free," these women are classed as irremediable and labeled whores. Diana, however, refutes being branded as a sex worker and seeks to redefine what should be considered respectable.

Actual prostitution was hazardous and dehumanizing, yet it did offer an income, plus a small measure of sexual liberation and social independence. Some have argued that prostitutes were at the forefront of 1920s feminism, as they "won virtually all the freedoms that were denied to women but are now taken for granted."[30] Already outsiders, prostitutes were not expected to protect their reputation, so they could freely engage in taboo activities like owning property, wearing makeup, drinking alcohol, and using birth control. In contrast, unmarried women often avoided or hid these activities and married women found themselves enslaved to the whims of husbands and the rules of society. As it had for millennia, the institution of marriage forced women to forfeit their rights or face domestic abuse and public ridicule. The only alternative, for some, was to sell sex. The question was whether prostitution should be considered merely a job that paid the rent or an identity that enveloped a woman's whole being.

Margy LaMont, a liberated woman who works as a prostitute, is the protagonist of the popular and scandalous 1926 Broadway play "SEX," written by and starring Mae West. A performer on the vaudeville stage at age six, West had not yet moved beyond dancing in burlesque shows at age twenty-six. During the early 1920s, she decided not to wait for others to give her a breakout role and wrote one for herself. West's plays, particularly "SEX" and "The Drag" (1927), disrupted the standards of propriety and decency on Broadway with subversive language and sexuality. The highbrow Broadway elite balked at West's overt sensuality and reviled her bawdy humor. Since sex and prostitution were featured in other Broadway plays, "something more complex than 'prudery' was at work here."[31] Respectable theater considered

sex a serious moral topic of high drama where the woman would be either reformed or punished by the last act. West, however, drew the ire of critics and city officials for making prudish decency the butt of her jokes and unapologetically portraying a successful, self-possessed woman who exuded raw, unromanticized eroticism, as she does in this portrait.

The police raided West's plays several times for supposedly corrupting public morals. In 1927, the State of New York charged her with obscenity, and her conviction resulted in a fine of $500 and a jail term of ten days.[32] West served eight days at the Welfare Island peniten-

Figure 2.2.　Mae West
Drawn by Emily Klein

tiary, released early for good behavior. She immediately penned "The Wicked Age" about a rebellious flapper that critiques beauty pageants for exploiting young women. She also described her prison experience for *Liberty* magazine, objecting to society's treatment of poor women of all races and asserting that many resorted to prostitution and other crimes out of economic necessity. West donated the $1,000 she was paid for the piece to the Welfare Island prison library, plus she provided several inmates she met financial assistance for nearly a decade after their release.

As West would later perfect in her film roles, her character in "SEX" broke the rule that a fallen woman needs to reform herself or succumb to ruin. The play challenged the conventions of society and the theater: "In the melodrama of vulgarity, Mae West changed the way the world saw women, and the way women saw themselves. She changed the way sex was treated on the stage."[33] Margy, to be clear, is not the proverbial prostitute-with-a-heart-of-gold. This self-possessed, empowered sex worker succeeds without renouncing her wild ways, regretting her moral choices, or transforming her personality. Prostitution is her job but not her identity. The play criticizes "decent folks" for lording their respectability over the so-called sinners without providing them the means for upliftment or a route to rehabilitate their reputations.[34] West played Margy as unabashedly sexual, as well as self-confident, independent, generous, ethical, and brutally honest, not someone who needs to be reformed or rehabilitated.

In the play's first act, Margy proudly asserts her autonomy and authority as a sex worker in Montreal's red-light district. She dominates her pimp and decides for herself which men to allow into her apartment and her bed. One of her favorites is the good-hearted Lt. Gregg, who she frequently engages in sexual word-play. After weeks at sea, Gregg demands and begs for her services, but she refuses, forcing him to treat her to dinner and dancing instead. Margy's friend Agnes is the typical fallen woman, an innocent and passive prostitute who obeys her pimp but wants to move back to her small hometown and rejoin her life as if she never left, similar to Bea's wishes in "The Dancing Girl."

The third female character, Clara, is married to a rich husband and goes to Margy's pimp for recreational sex. Like Diana's criticism of Ann, Margy sneers at Clara for being disingenuous and hypocritical, reacting strongly when asked to temper her criticism: "Rough on her? She ain't getting half of what she deserves. She's one of those respectable society dames who poses as decent, and is looking for the first chance to cheat without being found out."[35] Margy, on the other hand, considers herself socially upright and sexually honest. She rejects society's view that she does not count, taking pride in her identity and her professional approach to her job. When Margy saves Clara from an accidental drug overdose, the society woman accuses the prostitute of theft. Margy stands up to Clara, but a policeman threatens to imprison her if she does not leave Montreal. Margy leaves but vows she will get even with Clara.

In Act II, Margy follows the fleet to Trinidad. She becomes a singer in an unsavory nightclub where she meets Jimmy, a wealthy young man who falls in love with her without knowing that she is a prostitute. Margy sings and dances suggestively, but she retains her sexual and personal agency. Agnes shows up after being rejected by family, friends, and neighbors; she had failed in her attempt to go home to her small town and regain her pre-prostitute identity. She implores Margy to marry Jimmy, stating, "If he really loves you it won't matter to him what you've been."[36] Jimmy does propose marriage and Margy accepts, but Agnes, feeling unloved and despondent, commits suicide by jumping into the sea.

In Act III, Jimmy brings Margy to his home near New York City to meet his parents. His mother turns out to be Clara, who pleads with Margy to keep her secret and not marry her son. Margy criticizes her for being dishonest by marrying her husband for his money and then satisfying her sexual needs with young male prostitutes. Still wanting to marry Jimmy, Margy seduces him. The next morning Margy's pimp appears, seeking to blackmail Clara, but Margy chases him off. When a local police officer recognizes her as a prostitute, Margy tells her fiancé the truth and leaves for Australia with Lt. Gregg, the man who loves her for who she is.

West's "SEX" and Lovett's "The Dancing Girl" celebrate a woman's sexual self-expression as virtuous, rejecting the social convention that forces her to choose only one: virtue or sexuality. These works dig beneath the veneer of social respectability to expose its hypocrisy and denounce its domination of women. Lovett's popular and award-nominated film scenario portrays a socially and sexually assertive female hero, refuting a society that criticizes her as a whore and condemning those women who collaborate with the patriarchy and fake "true womanhood" just to get ahead. West's popular Broadway play goes a step further by making the hero a prostitute, subverting the traditional standards of behavior and altering what is considered proper sexual activity. In the play, the true "whore" is actually the married society woman who maintains a spotless public reputation while selling her sexuality and self-esteem. The audience is meant to deplore Clara for adopting a false image of social respectability and lording her power over Margy, a woman who proudly displays her authentic self.

THE FLAPPER COSTUME

Before unpacking specifics in the play and the film, I would like briefly to consider a few other cultural assumptions and limitations about a woman's body and her public image, which afforded men significant control over her life and sexuality. This control was based on prevailing stereotypes like a woman's supposed lack of reason, morality, and sexual restraint.[37] Framing the female body as inferior yet dangerous, men claimed it as their property. A commodity of male dominance, women were prohibited from expressing their own desire and social power. Furthermore, conformity was rewarded, causing women to internalize society's expectations of their behavior and appearance. The male gaze subjugated a woman by reducing her to a sex object instead of an autonomous subject and directing her to sacrifice individual will for the most superficial admiration and acceptance.[38]

One need look no further than Victorian fashion to understand why Jazz Age women wanted sexual freedom. The corset, which had been worn by the flappers' mothers, was not only confining to an unhealthy and disabling degree, but it also accentuated the bust, waist, and hips to restrict a person to a body type, an obsolete feminine ideal. The modern woman established a new look because "fashion and appearance became an important factor in the construction of the New Woman image and an integral part of feminist ideology in that period."[39] The goal was not to trade one confining image for another but to announce visually a free, confident femininity. Innovations in 1920s fashion reflected a liberated woman, clothing that reflected her desire to be more independent, active, flirtatious, and sexually self-possessed. The use of dropped waists and jersey fabric created a boyish appearance by deemphasizing the breasts, waist, and hips. The popular garcon silhouette, along with the introduction of trousers and the new bobbed hairstyle, aligned with women's desire for equality with their male counterparts and access to the public sphere.[40] "Many perceived a woman's increasing ability to move comfortably in her clothing to be both a product and a cause of her nascent political, and economic power."[41]

The flapper redefined what it meant to be a "good" or "bad" woman. The good women were self-reliant, honest, genuine, and "square" (as in treating someone fair-and-square). These women wished to be judged for their character and actions, like a man, not for their conformity to an outdated feminine image. To them, the bad women pretended to be dependent, demure, and obedient; they faked conformity to the Victorian image of womanhood to gain wealth, position, and admiration. The modern woman saw this falseness as corruptive to their moral character and self-respect. It was a confirmation of stereotypes that made it harder for attitudes to change and assertive women to succeed. Yet, they did overcome these attitudes, displaying their true selves and ignoring pressure to hide behind a mask of childlike innocence and submissiveness.

Trousers and shorter skirts also allowed women to engage in physical activities, that is sports and dancing, as well as show off their true bodies, not the false versions sculpted and confined. Women sought the freedoms already enjoyed by men, and the new style of clothing allowed them to embody roles that were more professional, sportier, and, if they wished, more authentically sexy. These clothes reflected a wider array of identities single and married women could portray, including sexual assertiveness. The shorter, thinner dresses enabled women to thumb their noses at convention, particularly when they did what upstanding ladies should not, such as go to nightclubs to drink, flirt, and dance.

When the Charleston swept the nation in the early 1920s, it captured the imagination of the modern woman. It wasn't just a dance; it exposed an integral part of one's inner self. Unlike the refined, stiff waltzes of the Victorian era, the Charleston celebrated the body and the propulsive energy of life, joy, and creativity. Moreover, this dance "gave expression to the unbuttoned sexuality of the period."[42] Coming out of the African style, the Charleston explodes from the hips and provides freer sexual self-expression. Its ties to the dynamic rhythms of jazz aroused criticism from conservatives as the type of music that invoked "savage instincts" and was "an influence for evil."[43] However, this sentiment was largely ignored and the Charleston became the most popular dance of the decade, beloved because it incited the utilization of powerful primal energy, a sexual vitality that need not be lurid or offensive.

This energy defines Diana Medford in "The Dancing Girl." In fact, the film's first shot is of Diana's feet as she dances the Charleston to lively jazz while putting on her flapper underwear and dress. The visual reflects a new image of glamour and leisure for women, which translates to increasing public expressions of sexuality. Later, Diana removes part of her skirt at a party to enable her dancing to be even more expressive. Other young people cheer her on and celebrate the joy and authenticity of her self-expression. It isn't until later, in retrospect, that her love interest Ben worries about her fitness as a proper wife, a concern that he will eventually realize is unfounded and irrelevant. In the play "SEX," the stage directions do not mention Margy's attire, but it is likely the prostitute would be scantily clad in her apartment, especially to contrast Clara, the society woman arrives at the apartment adorned in traditional propriety. West's second act nightclub costume also would have been skimpy to complement her singing "Shake That Thing" and performing the shimmy, another "dirty" dance.

Lovett and West recognized that what society called "decency" was a social construct. They criticized its use as a weapon to dominate and control a woman's body, her personal identity, and her public image. Lovett's film scenario and West's Broadway play confront this construct by dramatizing three responses women have to male control. First, the unrepentant rebel heroically rejects the restrictive misogynistic ideal by unleashing her sexuality. Second, the opportunistic conformist is a villainous collaborator who uses the image of propriety to hide her true self and manipulate the system. And third, the repentant conformist is a victim who accepts punishment for breaking society's rules but also betrays herself in a failed attempt to regain social acceptance and reclaim the oppressive image of traditional decency. These three responses come to life in "The Dancing Girl" and "SEX" to tell a contemporary story about the value of being true to oneself, challenging societal norms, and achieving sexual self-actualization.

UNREPENTANT REBELS

Taking a more detailed look at the main female characters, one can see that the works by Lovett and West mirror each other, dramatizing three specific ways women in the 1920s grappled with the tension between their true womanhood and society's expectations. The six characters all feel the weight of public opinion, coercing them to bow to outdated patriarchal mandates and display an image of propriety. While the conformists mask their sexuality behind a performance of conventional manners, the rebels express it openly and attempt to redefine what constitutes respectability.

Mae West, of course, proudly wore her "sinful" nature as a badge of honor, the foundation of a successful film career and a popular personal brand. Her ribald personality only enhanced the adoration her fans felt for the unabashed confidence and independence she expressed. West blatantly defied expectations by demonstrating in her films and with her personal image that female sexuality is not sinful, yet sexual hypocrisy, deceit, and self-denial are. She confronted conservative critics who attacked women like her and "Dangerous" Diana in Lovett's "The Dancing Girl" for expressing their sexuality openly. These characters blast an ideology that favors a false image over true virtue. The injustice is clear when the opportunistic conformists, Ann in "The Dancing Girl" and Clara in "SEX," rise to prominence by using a virtuous appearance to hide their true corruption, but the repentant conformists, Beatrice and Agnes, fall because moralists believe their sexual activity invalidates their virtuousness.

Unrepentant rebels Diana and Margy offer a more complicated and compelling character arc. They initially fall because they are branded as corrupt when, in fact, they are virtuous, similar to repentant conformists Bea and Agnes. However, the rebels refuse to obey traditional mores or grovel at the feet of social authorities. Instead, these women use their strength of character to maintain their self-respect and regain society's acceptance and admiration. Unlike opportunistic conformists Ann and Clara, rebels Diana and Margy will not pretend to conform to the ideals of "true womanhood" to get ahead. They stand strong in the face of critics who want to use their acts of rebellion against them. Thus, disillusionment accompanies the rebels' success, a rude awakening to the reality that society unfairly privileges women who merely perform decency (the conformists) over those who epitomize it (the rebels).

Evident in Lovett's film scenario and West's stage performance, the modern woman attempted to redefine gender boundaries and revise the accepted standards of decency. The prevailing attitudes empowered male bodies as strong and sexually self-actualized, while they diminished female bodies as weak, passive, unclean, and shameful. This sexual double standard identified women's bodies and their desires as wicked. Feminists opposed this connection of sexual agency with promiscuity and immorality. Therefore, even though Diana appears licentious and Margy is a prostitute, audiences are not meant to consider either character a whore. Distinguishing public image from personal identity, these women demonstrate dignified self-possession and the highest moral character while simultaneously expressing their sexuality.

Diana and Margy embody respectability, honesty, and forthrightness. The power of their sensuality matches and informs the strength of their personalities. Diana, unlike her friend Bea, is not self-conscious as she exhibits her sexuality in wild dancing and good-natured flirting. She is passionate and self-righteous, refusing to cede ownership of her sexuality to a man. Regardless of what others think or say, Diana does not consider her joyful public display of sexuality inappropriate, nor does she consider sexual activity improper. Margy also exhibits her sexuality and, unlike her friend Agnes, she is not self-conscious or ashamed. On the contrary, she is a proud sexual being, mainly because she maintains control over her sexuality and separates her desire from her sex work, feeling pride for both. Margy and Diana reject society's inhibitions and assert sexually responsible identities.

Recognizing one's sexual agency and finding a responsible manner to express it is part of being a self-actualized adult. The definition of "responsible" has long been the purview of men, allowing them to infantilize women, dominate their bodies, and confiscate their social and sexual power. The characters in the works by West and Lovett engage in the "missing discourse of [female] desire."[44] They debunk the belief that only men want and deserve sexual pleasure, choosing sexual subjectivity rather than suppress their passion. Diana and Margy clearly honor the voice of the body through their physical demonstrations of joy and vitality, as well as their sexual forwardness. They assert themselves, empowering their full personhood as they strive to break free of objectification by the male gaze. West famously reinforced her sexual agency in the 1932 film *Night after Night* when her character proudly explains the source of her material success, and presumably her personal happiness, "Goodness had nothing to do with it."[45]

In Lovett's film scenario, the description of Ben's fascination with Diana includes his amazement at how sexually free yet self-possessed she is. In the first scene, she is described as "gay, laughing, frank. There's something boyish about her lack of conceit and her open enjoyment of her own dazzling appearance."[46] Diana disarms Ben by adopting the masculine confidence to be forthright and uninhibited, causing him to wonder: "What *is* she?"[47] A few scenes later, Ben kisses her passionately and she "responds, instinctively—freely. It's not discretion nor fear that makes her withdraw from his arms—it's because this love is so perfect, so beautiful—she wants to realize it to the full."[48] Liberated in mind and body, Diana indicates her refusal to let old-fashioned social conventions stop her from getting the most out of life. She intends to experience and enjoy everything, not just what the systems of male power will allow. For instance, when Ben cautiously asks, "You want to taste all of life, don't you?"[49] Diana readily asserts, "All, all, every bit!"

This attitude plus her flirting and provocative dancing concern Ben because he assumes a proper woman should lack sexual agency and desire. It is clear Lovett rejected this assumption when Diana, attacked by Ann's unjust derision and moral superiority near the end of the story, publicly states that she loves Ann's husband Ben and will always love him, an honest admission clearly not meant to break up their marriage. Ann then demands the crowd scorn Diana as a shameless whore, but Ann's own shameful and deceitful acts cause everyone to turn their backs on her drunken tirade and appreciate Diana's genuine approach to life and love.

West's Margy is also independent and tough, not the helpless and defeated "fallen woman" Broadway audiences expected of a prostitute. She unapologetically asserts a significant amount of self-respect and bravado, laughing at the world and anyone who tries to tell her who she is or what she must do. Comfortable with herself, she refuses to be reduced to merely a docile body, expressing her sexuality through words, dress, dance, flirtation, and intercourse. "There was nothing posed about Margy's sexuality,"[50] and West "enacted Margy's sexiness straightforwardly." Equipped with the necessary self-awareness and self-confidence to exert ownership over her body, the character chooses when to put it to work and when to enjoy herself. She is a prostitute on her own terms, effectively self-employed. Her "no" is obeyed by her pimp and her male clients, but even if a john tries to be aggressive, he is immediately cowed by her no-nonsense demeanor and acid tongue just before she slams her door in his face.

Margy's sexual agency makes prostitution merely her source of income. She is an entrepreneur who considers prostitution a profession like any other:

MARGY: I understand that you got to get a grip on yourself or you'll never get anywhere.

AGNES: Anywhere in this life?

MARGY: Why not? There's a chance of rising to the top of every profession.

AGNES: Profession? You call this—Oh Gawd.

MARGY: Yes, I said rising to the top of my profession. Why not? Others do it, why can't I? Why can't you?[51]

Not defined by her sex work, Margy is a strong, brazen woman with a sharp wit, yet she is also a decent human being, caring about the feelings of her depressed friend, the reputation and happiness of her innocent fiancé, and even the health of a corrupt society woman.

Despite having pride in her personal identity and her professional prowess, Margy does want to marry a decent man who loves her for who she is, a love that goes beyond physical attraction and financial exchange. Margy's goals, far from a denouncement of her role as a prostitute, actually mirror the story of any young woman who seeks to be sexually self-actualized and socially empowered. West's popular play was culturally influential, forcing audiences to recalculate "the ethical arithmetic" so that "the wages of sin are reduced from mortal transgression to misdemeanor,"[52] or even normalized as they are for male sexuality.

Diana has many of the same attributes as Margy. Although she isn't a prostitute, Diana does express sexual freedom and rebels against the traditional social norms. Like her goddess namesake, Diana is a hunter and bacchant. Energetic and uninhibited, she ensnares the man of her desires with dancing eyes and feet. At their initial meeting, Ben has turned his male gaze on her active feet and legs, but Diana rebuffs his attempt at objectification and, as Lovett's scenario reveals, she gazes "directly at him"[53] with a "mischievous look" that demonstrates her independence and autonomy. Her look also gives her the moral and social upper hand. She leaves her dance partner, introduces herself, and drags Ben onto the dance floor. The rest of the evening involves Diana and Ann competing for Ben's attention, with Ann pretending to be demure and sober while Diana is true to herself—dancing, drinking, joking, and flirting until late into the night. Ben considers her an ethereal "fairy-like creature,"[54] but Diana defies this characterization, typifying a self-confident, down-to-earth human being who is comfortable with her sexuality and refuses to change, or even appear to change, for anyone.

Diana and Margy are beloved characters because they display personal authority and independence, saying no or yes to men as they choose. Because they refuse to live by the rules of a conservative, male-dominated society, they lack social power. Their defiance of social norms and their "dangerous" sexuality cause them to be ostracized, a taste of 1920s anti-feminist backlash that demonized women who trespassed into the public sphere and rejected sexist expectations of modesty.[55] The unrepentant rebels may be discredited by social authorities, but by staying true to themselves Diana and Margy gain the respect of those who know them and, perhaps more importantly, they do not compromise their self-respect.

The culture caters to men, paying women to wear revealing costumes and express their sexuality in public as long as the women and their sexuality remain under male control. For example, Mae West's plays were raided by New York City police, yet the popular burlesque shows like the famous Ziegfeld Follies were not. What the authorities considered indecent about "SEX" is that the protagonist refuses to be an object, dominated by men. Empowered, Margy owns her sexuality and rather than passively displaying her attractive body parts, she asserts her personhood and shamelessly commands an eroticism that disquiets and dominates the male gaze. Instead of mere titillation, West's performance was subversive to patriarchal conventions. She used strident sexuality and what was considered vulgar humor "to disrupt standards of propriety" and "sow the seeds of revolution."[56] She wasn't passive, and she didn't play nice. Margy boldly states at the beginning of "SEX" when warned that a policeman would cause trouble in order to control her body and the income it can produce for her: "Well, he can start it and I'll finish it."[57]

Among the men who fail to tame Diana and Margy are their love interests and would-be husbands. Ben and Jimmy are excited by the wild sexual energy the female rebels radiate, but they expect a wife to follow society's sexual norms, which they worry is impossible for Diana and Margy, due to their behavior and reputations. Ben rejects Diana because she displays sexual activity, which suggests corruption in her character. In addition, he expresses concern that her behavior will cause others to judge her and, more importantly, him in a negative light. Jimmy does not defend Margy and lets her walk out of his life for the same reasons, seemingly believing as Ben does that once a woman is judged to be a whore she is forever irredeemable. Certainly this fate befalls Bea and Agnes, but Diana and Margy are not defeated by this label. They epitomize genuine and positive sexual self-awareness, rising above the old social mores that shackle Ben and Jimmy. Because neither man can separate his sweetheart's virtue from the labels society places on her public behavior or her profession, Diana and Margy choose themselves over a marriage of confinement and self-denial.

Ben is conflicted because he enjoys many of Diana's qualities. Before fear overtakes his interest, he ignores her reputation as dangerous and initiates a secluded romantic tryst to the seashore to express his love for her. However, Ben has been indoctrinated into the patriarchal moral code and cannot approve of a girl who drinks, flirts, laughs, stays out late, and undresses in public. He visibly cringes when she removes her skirt so she can dance more wildly for an adoring crowd, cringing again when he replays the memory later. Ben loves Diana but cannot commit to her after he reconsiders her actions from the perspective of his friends and peers. She is maligned as too daring and free by the purveyors of morality in the story. It is gossip like, "No girl could be so free—and not *be* free,"[58] that Ann and others use against her. Ben is uncertain about which woman to choose, so Ann completes his change of heart by disparaging Diana and suggesting that her own obedience to social virtue will make Ann the more respectable wife.

Diana angrily but privately denounces Ann's hypocrisy. She is angry at the injustice of Ann's treachery and duplicity being rewarded while her own honesty and genuineness is punished. Nevertheless, Diana refuses to compromise her values or alter her behavior. When asked to make a toast, Diana pays tribute to herself, "I have to live with myself until I die—so may I always like—myself!"[59] Diana refuses to hate herself or her sexuality, as Bea does, nor will she pretend to be something she's not, as Ann does, just to conform to an outdated social standard. She sees that the need to conform troubles Ann and Bea to the point of misery and self-destruction. Despite what others say, Diana has a fine soul and a clean heart; she feels love and disappointment deeply and she approaches life with a fearlessness that others admire. Like Margy, Diana seeks a "normal" life, which includes marriage to a decent man who loves her for who she is. In the end, she chooses to leave the man she loves and the United States behind. After Ann dies and two years pass, Diana returns and marries the awakened and wiser Ben, who is finally able to look at Diana "seriously"[60] and "eye to eye," for he has learned to respect her, not her reputation.

Margy also likes and respects herself. When Margy first meets Jimmy, she broadcasts her sexuality but does not reveal that she is a prostitute. She is not ashamed of her profession, but she is concerned his family will not approve. When Jimmy brings Margy to meet his parents, Clara attempts to shame Margy, claiming the marriage will ruin her son. Margy stands tall and argues that Clara, who married for money and sought a male prostitute, is not morally superior, just someone who chose to submit to restrictive social norms. Conformity has led Clara to a sexually unsatisfying marriage, just as it leads Agnes in Act II to disappointment and suicide. Margy decides to seduce Jimmy not only to spite Clara, but also to model for him genuine and honest sexuality. In the end, she realizes the social stigma of her prostitution will harm Jimmy, so she, like Diana, chooses to leave her fiancé and American moral norms behind. She moves to Australia with Lt. Gregg, the former client who loves her for who she is.

The unrepentant rebel refuses to comply with patriarchal prejudices, choosing instead to be true to her own definition of virtue. She proudly displays sexual self-awareness and earns the respect of the audience. These roles became break-out performances for the stars, Joan Crawford in "Our Dancing Daughters" and Mae West in "SEX." Hollywood would offer the actors additional roles as confident, assertive, sexually transgressive women. Their films were box-office successes, and the public clamored for more. Crawford and West would become two of the most powerful women in Hollywood with large, loyal fan bases. Mae West, in particular, created an image that was "multivalent and powerful, consistent with the topos of female unruliness."[61] West's female fans respected her for honestly expressing the unruliness they privately thought and felt; they appreciated that she purposefully made a spectacle of herself to disrupt misogynistic norms and codes.

OPPORTUNISTIC CONFORMISTS

Margy and Diana, who are sexual in a genuine and self-expressive way, cry foul when Clara and Ann use their sexuality in a dishonest and retrogressive way to trick men into marrying them. Thus, the opportunistic conformists Clara and Ann are doubly villainous. First, they grant the restrictive, out-dated image of womanhood credibility by seeming to conform to patriarchal social expectations. Second, the respectability from their public masquerade provides cover for their secret extramarital liaisons. By publicly denying their sexual agency and marrying for wealth and position instead of love and sexual compatibility, Clara and Ann upset the rebels' sense of responsible sexual conduct and hinder feminist social reform. These opportunistic conformists are self-possessed, but, unlike the unrepentant rebels, their adoption of a corrupted image masks their fraudulent selfhood and affords them significant social power.

In "SEX," Clara looks down her nose at Margy but prostitutes herself by selling marital sex for wealth and social standing. Her true nature is revealed when she lies to her husband and secretly visits a male prostitute in Montreal's red-light district. The play portrays her as a cheat and a fraud for playing patriarchy's game and lording her false superiority over Margy instead of being her genuine self and fighting for social change. Clara represents one of the many women who were persuaded by anti-feminist backlash that called the rebels "perverts" and equated them with "being immoral, bad mothers and 'lesbians.'"[62] The propaganda warned that women who wanted to get ahead would destroy Western civilization, forcing ambitious women to be disingenuous and stab their rebel sisters in the back.

For the opportunistic conformist, playing the game may have been safer but it was only fulfilling on a superficial level. In her home life, Clara seems to have everything she wants, but she is neither happy nor satisfied. When she visits Montreal's red-light district and the male prostitute Rocky, she is

glad to be away from America's standards of respectability and her masquerade as a proper society wife, stating, "I'd like to stay here forever."[63] It
is "thrilling"[64] to experience life unimpeded by gendered conventions. Clara
enjoys being "daring" as the fling allows her temporarily to escape "the dull,
monotonous routine of my daily existence."[65] She admits that conforming to
the Victorian ideology nearly drives her insane, but she does not rebel in a
public way that would disrupt patriarchal norms. She describes the sacrifice
she makes as enduring a husband who supplies "everything that money can
buy, every luxury, but the one thing I need most of all—love."[66] Love is code
for sexual satisfaction, and her claim to need it "most of all" reveals to the
audience its value and calls into question Clara's personal choices, namely,
hiding her desires and confining herself to the role of proper wife and mother.

Margy calls Clara a hypocrite for profiting from a public image of decency
while straying from her marriage to satisfy her sexual needs. By seeking
both a traditional image and a libertine experience, Clara worries about being
caught, creating a scandal, and losing everything. As a husband's possession,
a wife's conduct and reputation directly impact his public standing, as well as
his pride and sense of self-worth. It is in Clara's self-interest to preserve the
status quo, which includes her passionless marriage and a repressive system
that rewards the women willing to sell out the feminist agenda and publicly
debase themselves. Moreover, the truth would reveal to her husband that
Clara has been presenting a fiction of herself to him throughout their relationship. Margy despises her, arguing that men and women must be honest with
each other to build healthy relationships and a better society.

Despite her precautions, Clara is discovered by the police in the red-light
district. She escapes punishment and exposure by trading on her social position and wealth. Clara reverts to her society-woman persona to lie about
Margy, accusing the prostitute of stealing her jewelry, which she has actually
given to Rocky for his sexual services. To finalize her safety and avoid the
publicity that would ruin her reputation, Clara pays off the policeman and
leaves Margy, who saved her life, to harassment and possible arrest. Thus,
the opportunistic conformist benefits from undermining the rebel's unconventional and transgressive identity. Clara counters the efforts of feminists
by upholding institutional standards of social normality, particularly with
regards to heterosexuality and marriage. It is no surprise that those who ben-
efited from a system based on female oppression, be they men or women, had
an interest in maintaining it.

In "The Dancing Girl," Ann also gets everything she wants by hiding her
true self and appearing to obey society's rules. She plays a role, pretending
to be an old-fashioned girl who is helpless, needy, pure, demure, and child-
like. Although Ben is fooled by her lies, her friends and the audience are not.

Just like our introduction to Diana, the film's first shot of Ann is of her bare legs as she prepares for a night out, which reveals her penchant for sexual and social freedom. Ann is just as much a jazz baby as Diana, but she, like Clara, conforms to a traditional public image to gain the privilege of private indulgence. Ann procures Ben's approval by claiming never to take more than an occasional sip of alcohol, but her boyfriend Freddy and the audience notice that her "sip" drains his previously full glass. She wants to have her cake and eat it too, but eventually discovers that duplicity and self-denial do not make her happy.

Unlike Diana, Ann does not love Ben, so her marriage is far from amicable. For her, Ben is a means to an end, not an equal partner she loves or respects. On their honeymoon, she makes fun of his desire for a deep emotional connection with her. Dissatisfied with her sexual obligation, Ann begins to buy an expensive bracelet for each month of "service"[67] to him and finds excuses to sneak out for drunken flings with Freddy. Ann's deception gives her a moral public image and financial wealth, but in actuality she is morally bankrupt and knows it. Her tantrums when Ben exposes her lies and her excessive drinking denote extreme unhappiness. She speaks to Freddy about her life and prospects with bitterness; plus, she refers to Ben and Diana with "vicious nastiness,"[68] finding relief in making them suffer.

Ann cloaks her inner corruption with an image of decency and respectability. This lie understandably upsets Diana, who snaps at her, "I wonder if there is a decent thought in your nasty little mind."[69] In a different way, the lying upsets Ann herself. She loves Freddy, but early in the film she must reject him after her mother shoots her a "cruelly hard" look and "yanks the girl's shoulder . . . then yanks the girl's head around so she is obliged to look at her."[70] Ann assures her mother that she will not marry Freddy, knowing he is not wealthy enough. The mother continually badgers Ann to maintain the "good girl" pretense, stating the only worthwhile goal is winning society's approval and marrying a rich, unsuspecting man. This mother-daughter relationship remains combative and abusive throughout the film. Diana's mother, on the other hand, is "thoroughly up-to-date."[71] She loves Diana for who she is and supports her rebellion from the traditional social norms. By the end, Ann despises her mother, her husband, and herself.

While Clara is never publicly exposed, Ann's drunken tirade at the end of the film makes her hypocrisy and corruption clear to all her friends. In addition to ridiculing Diana and Ben for being good people instead of just appearing to be good, Ann berates a trio of scrubwomen for not grooming their daughters as her mother did for the purpose of escaping their lowly station in life. Her self-hatred is at its peak as she ironically advises the scrubwomen to sanitize their daughters' reputations because "a rich man wants his money's worth!"[72] and as mothers they will want to sponge off the daughters' ill-gotten wealth. Despite her public success, Ann clearly hates the role she has adopted, and her drunken fall down the stairs symbolizing her fallen moral state. Her dead body lands at the feet of the scrubwomen who sadly comment that the jewels she's wearing will no longer do her any good. The implied message being that wealth and reputation are no substitute for quality character and free expression.

If they did not injure other women, Clara and Ann's ability to manipulate the system for their own gain might be laudable, similar to Anita Loos's conniving protagonist Lorelei Lee. However, their harmful performance causes Diana and Margy to denounce them in an effort to redefine what it means to be decent. It is problematic enough that the unrepentant conformists use the appearance of respectability to rise to social prominence, but the fact that this image hides their true moral corruption should prompt men to re-think their support for patriarchal assumptions, especially when the morally upright women are the ones being punished. Otherwise, the true victor is sin, that is to say the perversion of an individual's soul and the entire social body through the condemnation of a woman's sexual freedom and self-actualization.

REPENTANT CONFORMISTS

Considering the third version of female sexuality, West and Lovett showed that the traditional conception of decency does the most harm to the women who express their sexuality but believe the expression is sinful. The repentant conformists experience helpless resignation after their efforts to gain absolution for the so-called sin is confounded. Part of the reason the women repent their sexual awakening is that the conservative authorities deceptively promise forgiveness and re-acceptance into the repressive, soul-crushing role of traditional womanhood. Instead of forgiveness, they are attacked and told they deserve eternal scorn. These passive, self-pitying women are "effectively blamed for their own oppression. This tends to underestimate the significance of patriarchal backlash."[73] Seeing herself as a fallen woman means she can never escape the scarlet letter of misconduct. Forfeiting her social power and self-possession does not save the repentant conformist from permanent disgrace.

In "SEX" and "The Dancing Girl," Agnes and Bea accept society's verdict that their body, mind, and spirit are unclean. Unlike the unrepentant rebels, they regret their supposedly sinful position and cannot summon the strength or self-respect to fight for their sexual and social rights. Instead, they denounce their sexuality, conform to conventional expectations of decency, and hope to regain acceptance into society as a virtuous, subordinate, obedient woman. However, social rules, gossip, and the sexual double standard reduce them even further. They discover the "bad" woman in the virgin/whore social binary is marked forever as sexually and morally impure.[74] This figure is pilloried for failing to silence the voice of the body, publicly shamed for a lack of self-denial and sexual restraint that should not be expected of any human being. Agnes and Bea despair because they cannot be themselves nor can they revert to the conservative ideal. The result is a social rejection that destroys them.

In West's play, Agnes is Margy's sidekick, but she serves mainstream social values. While Margy is a rebel who champions a woman's sexual agency, Agnes is a stock character. She exemplifies the cautionary tale of a "good girl" who got a bad deal but must live with the consequences of her actions, the proverbial whore with a heart of gold. Unlike Margy, Agnes lacks control over her sexuality, doing what her pimp requests rather than what she wants, a victim of mainstream morality. Despite being a kind and decent person, she is forever branded as damaged, so no one will let her forget she is a prostitute even after she has given up that role. As a result of this rejection, she sees herself as a nothing and commits suicide. This upsets Margy, but her fiancé Jimmy shrugs it off with the comment, "Nothing to worry us, dear. Just one of those poor wretches that follow the fleet."[75] He does not see Agnes as a person, nor does he realize that his beloved Margy is also a poor wretch by his reckoning.

In Lovett's film scenario, Beatrice is Diana's sidekick. Like Agnes, Bea considers herself a fallen woman. After having a fling with a boy in their group, she becomes a prisoner to her sexual past. Even marriage cannot remove the stain of sexual impropriety, as Bea's husband initially says it doesn't matter but later forces them to have a private wedding and forbids her to see any male acquaintances. As a result, she must lie to hide casual encounters from her husband, something Diana would never do. Bea is decent and wants to reclaim her reputation, but her husband's mistrust and jealousy prevent him from accepting this image of her. Even though she bows to social pressure and gives up her sexual agency, her husband remains suspicious and, at times, treats her harshly. Bea is not suicidal, but she does cry in Diana's arms, feeling as much a "poor wretch" as Agnes.

While the heroes and villains in "The Dancing Girl" and "SEX" get the most attention for rebelling against "true womanhood" or exploiting it for personal gain, Bea and Agnes are important background characters who caution audiences against passively accepting unjust restrictions and punishments. Their economic need and sexual desire lead them to rebellious behavior, but they never rebel against established norms in their hearts. Where

Diana and Margy succeed, Bea and Agnes fail because they repent and want to re-acquire the status of chaste, submissive, pious, and domestic women. By not changing how society sees them, they allow themselves to be victims of society's judgment, in contrast to the rebels who prize independence and self-respect too much to surrender their selfhood in this way. In the end, audiences are meant to mourn Agnes and Bea's fate without deeming them role models.

THE CURTAIN FALLS

In conclusion, Josephine Lovett's film scenario "The Dancing Girl" and Mae West's play "SEX" contribute to a longer narrative of social change. They battled "deeply embedded contextual factors that legitimate the logic of misogyny"[76] and encourage its further normalization and institutionalization. During the 1920s, sexual norms were shaken but not shattered.[77] Flappers often entered traditional marriages of submission and domesticity. Women's fight against derision, abuse, and the sexual double standard faced strong opposition but these unrepentant rebels were only the first wave of change agents.

To future generations the flapper and the New Woman remained emblems of a new vision of femininity, the source of destabilizing patriarchal traditions and promoting female empowerment. "Dangerous" Diana and Margy, the proud prostitute, challenge the restrictions on a woman's social behavior by refusing to pretend to follow the traditional vision of what is proper. They choose to be true to themselves, modeling sexual self-awareness and opening deeper conversations among women, which is essential for the personal and social development of adolescent girls and young women: "By not talking about sexual desire with each other or with [older, sexually mature] women, a source for empowerment is lost."[78] Lovett's film and West's play helped young women understand and act on their own desire, which is important because "girls who trust their minds and bodies may experience a stronger sense of self, entitlement, and empowerment that could enhance their ability to make safe decisions."[79]

Diana and Margy succeed because they challenge repressive norms, form a new identity, and fight for sexual freedom. These unrepentant rebels demand society re-evaluate its traditional definition of respectability and end its criticisms of their values and their behavior. These characters maintain a truer virtuousness, forcing audiences to reconsider and revise what society considers bad behavior. Moreover, Diana and Margy argue that the gold-digging women, Ann and Clara, who masquerade as virtuous followers of traditional womanhood are, in actuality, corrupt, the ones who should be shunned. Unfortunately, Ann and Clara succeed because they conform to society's rules, attain unearned respectability, and use passive-aggressive manipulation to hide what they are and get what they want. The trick of using a spotless image that masks a corrupt character serves them until their own actions expose them as frauds.

Like Sara Smolinsky and Lorelei Lee in chapter 1, the protagonists of West's "SEX" and Lovett's "The Dancing Girl" argue that women deserve access to the same opportunities and rewards as men. For Diana and Margy, the rewards are sexual self-actualization and marriage to a partner that respects them as an equal. They lose the man they initially want but marry someone who understands them: Margy exchanges wide-eyed Jimmy for world-wise Lt. Gregg, and Diana sacrifices traditional Ben for awakened Ben. To build a healthy relationship, the men must accept and appreciate the women as intelligent, charismatic, sexual human beings. Thus, West and Lovett helped precipitate the creation of a new vision of womanhood, one that allowed women to be themselves and to like themselves. In other words, they followed a feminist version of morality that encouraged an honest, joyous presentation of a woman's sexual voice.

NOTES

1. Loos, *Gentlemen Prefer Blondes*, 106.

2. Jessica Gerard, "Lady Bountiful: Women of the Landed Classes and Rural Philanthropy," *Victorian Studies* 30, no. 2 (1987), 189.

3. Edith Wharton, *The House of Mirth* (Peterborough: Broadview, 2005), 103.

4. Mary Louise Roberts, "True Womanhood Revisited," *Journal of Woman's History* 14, no. 1 (2002), 151.

5. Judy Cornes, *Sex, Power and the Folly of Marriage in Women's Novels of the 1920s: A Critical Study of Seven American Writers* (Jefferson: McFarland & Company, 2015), 16.

6. Elsie Chenier, "Conjugal Misconduct: Defying Marriage Law in the Twentieth-Century United States by William Kuby (review)," *Journal of the History of Sexuality* 29, no. 1 (2020), 123.

7. Simmons, *Making Marriage Modern*, 179.

8. Simon Louvish, *Mae West: It Ain't No Sin* (New York: St. Martin's Press, 2005), 80.

9. Listerine advertisement, "The one true friend she has," *Delineator* 115, no. 1 (July 1929), 69.

10. Thorstein Veblen, *The Theory of the Leisure Class: An Economic Study of Institutions* (London: Macmillan, 1899), 53.

11. Neilsen, *Un-American Womanhood*, 9.

12. Ibid., 1.

13. Smith-Rosenberg, "The New Woman as Androgyne," 157.

14. Martha H. Patterson, Introduction to *The American New Woman Revisited: A Reader, 1894–1930*, ed. Martha H. Patterson (New Brunswick: Rutgers University Press, 2008), 16.

15. Robert M. Cover, *Auto Mania* (New Haven: Yale University Press, 2007), 30.

16. James Hinckley, Jim Hinckley, and Jon G. Robinson, *The Big Book of Car Culture* (St. Paul: Motorbooks, 2005), 8.

17. John Steinbeck, *Cannery Row* (New York: Penguin, 1994), 65.

18. Lynn Dumenil, *The Modern Temper: American Culture and Society in the 1920s* (New York: Hill and Wang, 1995), 135.

19. Dumenil, *Modern Temper*, 30.

20. Patterson, Introduction to *The American New Woman Revisited*, 15.

21. Ibid., 16.

22. Joshua Zeitz, *Flapper* (New York: Three Rivers Press, 2006), 100.

23. Zeitz, *Flapper*, 31.

24. Lucy Fischer, Introduction to *American Cinema of the 1920s: Themes and Variations* (New Brunswick: Rutgers University Press, 2009), 6.

25. Laura Mulvey, "Unmasking the Gaze: Some Thoughts on New Feminist Film Theory and History," in *Reclaiming the Archive: Feminism and Film History*, ed. Vicki Callahan (Detroit: Wayne State UP, 2010), 26.

26. Thomas Doherty, *Pre-Code Hollywood: Sex, Immorality, and Insurrection in American Cinema, 1930–1934* (New York: Columbia University Press, 1999), 2.

27. Charlotte N. Toledo, "She Would Not Be Silenced: Mae West's Struggle against Censorship," *The Downtown Review* 3, no. 2 (2016), 1.

28. Yezierska, *Bread Givers*, 21.

29. Cruea, "Changing Ideals of Womanhood during the Nineteenth-Century Woman Movement," 201.

30. Thaddeus Russell, *A Renegade History of the United States* (New York: Free Press, 2010), 101.

31. Marybeth Hamilton, "SEX, The Drag, and 1920s Broadway," *The Drama Review* 36, no 4 (1992), 86.

32. Lillian Schlissel, Introduction to *Three Plays by Mae West* (New York: Routledge, 1997), 16.

33. Schlissel, Introduction to *Three Plays by Mae West*, 28.

34. Hamilton, "SEX, The Drag, and 1920s Broadway," 88.

35. Mae West, *Three Plays by Mae West*, ed. Lillian Schlissel (New York: Routledge, 1997), 54.

36. West, *Three Plays by Mae West*, 66.

37. Rose Weitz, "A History of Women's Bodies," and Samantha Kwan, "Navigating Public Spaces: Gender, Race, and Body Privilege in Everyday Life," in *The Politics of Women's Bodies: Sexuality, Appearance, and Behavior*, ed. Rose Weitz (Oxford: Oxford University Press, 1998).

38. Maxine Sheets-Johnstone, *The Roots of Power: Animate Form and Gendered Bodies* (Chicago: Open Court, 1994).

39. Einav Rabinovitch-Fox, "[Re]Fashioning the New Woman: Women's Dress, the Oriental Style, and the Construction of American Feminist Imagery in the 1910s," *Journal of Women's History* 27, no. 2 (2015), 14.

40. Laura Doan, "Passing Fashions: Reading Female Masculinities in the 1920s," *Feminist Studies* 24, no. 3 (1998), 664.

41. Kendra Van Cleave, "Fashioning the College Woman: Dress, Gender, and Sexuality at Smith College in the 1920s," *The Journal of American Culture* 32, no. 1 (2009), 5.

42. Arnold Shaw, *The Jazz Age: Popular Music in the 1920s* (Oxford: Oxford University Press, 1987), 116.

43. Anne Shaw Faulkner, "Does Jazz Put the Sin in Syncopation?" *Ladies Home Journal* 38 (August 1921), 16.

44. Deborah L. Tolman, "Doing Desire: Adolescent Girls' Struggles for/with Sexuality," *Gender & Society* 8, no. 3 (1994), 325.

45. Schlissel, Introduction to *Three Plays by Mae West*, 24.

46. Josephine Lovett, "The Dancing Girl," original script, Binghamton University archives, 1928, 2.

47. Lovett, "The Dancing Girl," 42.

48. Ibid., 46–47.

49. Ibid., 46.

50. Marybeth Hamilton, *"When I'm Bad, I'm Better": Mae West, Sex, and American Entertainment* (Berkeley: University of California Press, 1997), 130.

51. West, *Three Plays by Mae West*, 40.

52. Schlissel, Introduction to *Three Plays by Mae West*, 10.

53. Lovett, "The Dancing Girl," 24.

54. Ibid., 28.

55. Susan K. Cahn, *Coming on Strong: Gender and Sexuality in Twentieth-century Women's Sport* (Cambridge: Harvard University Press, 1994).

56. Schlissel, Introduction to *Three Plays by Mae West*, 2.

57. West, *Three Plays by Mae West*, 36.

58. Lovett, "The Dancing Girl," 38.

59. Ibid., 5.

60. Ibid., 120–121.

61. Kathleen Rowe, *The Unruly Woman: Gender and the Genres of Laughter* (Austin: University of Texas Press, 1995), 122.

62. Cathia Jenainati, *Feminism: A Graphic Guide* (London: Icon, 2019), accessed December 17, 2021, https://books.google.com.

63. West, *Three Plays by Mae West*, 47.

64. Ibid., 48.

65. Ibid., 48–49.

66. Ibid., 49.

67. Lovett, "The Dancing Girl," 85.

68. Ibid., 113.

69. Ibid., 110.

70. Ibid., 113.

71. Ibid., 3.

72. Ibid., 118.

73. Sylvia Walby, "'Backlash' in Historical Context," in *Making Connections: Women's Studies, Women's Movements, Women's Lives*, eds. Mary Kennedy, Cathy Lubelska, and Val Walsh (New York: Taylor and Francis, 2005), 76.

74. Vivyan C. Adair, "Of Home-Makers and Home-Breakers: The Deserving and the Underserving Poor Mother in Depression Era Literature," in *The Literary Mother: Essays on Representations of Maternity and Child Care*, ed. Susan C. Staub (Jefferson: McFarland & Company, 2007).

75. West, *Three Plays by Mae West*, 70.

76. Sarah Banet-Weiser and Kate M. Miltner, "#MasculinitySoFragile: culture, structure, and networked misogyny," *Feminist Media Studies* 16, no. 1 (2015), 171.

77. Susan K. Freeman, *Sex Goes to School: Girls and Sex Education before the 1960s* (Champaign: University of Illinois Press, 2008).

78. Tolman, "Doing Desire," 339–340.

79. Ibid., 340.

Chapter Three

Racial Hybridity

Healing the Torn Self

Literary works from the 1920s that have gained the most attention for depicting female rebels were written by white authors about white social environments. These authors tackled serious injustices, but they were largely oblivious to the racial privilege that provided opportunities and a measure of respect denied their non-white contemporaries. Women of color had to confront racism in addition to sexism, which doubly restricted their access to professional employment, societal acceptance, creative expression, sexual freedom, and self-respect. Furthermore, these women commonly battled a misogynistic subculture that largely abided by the belief their self-sacrifice was necessary for men of color to succeed. Vilified and demeaned, women of color fought back. They asserted personal agency and demanded the mainstream recognize their humanity as they carved out fulfilling roles in public life.

This chapter examines self-aware and assertive women of color in two literary works, Nella Larsen's 1929 novel *Passing* and Mourning Dove's 1927 novel *Cogewea: The Half Blood*. The works disrupt intransigent attitudes on both sides of their respective color lines, white-black for Larsen and white-indigenous for Mourning Dove. Rebellious biracial characters, Larsen's Clare Kendry and Mourning Dove's Cogewea McDonald open doors to new identities and better interracial relationships because they "threaten the categories of a racially polarized society and remain caught at the fault line of a faulty ideology."[1] Undeterred by racist ideology, the characters do not limit themselves to either a white identity or a non-white identity; in fact, they reject the artificial and hierarchical binary of race altogether. Instead, Clare and Cogewea model a hybrid self-identity, connecting to two races without allowing themselves to be claimed and confined by either.

71

I will analyze how Larsen and Mourning Dove dramatized the confluence of racism and sexism in the 1920s. My focus will be the ways female characters in *Passing* and *Cogewea* modelled how women of color might navigate the treacherous cultural landscape to build empowered identities and forge equal, respectful relationships across and within racial groups. My goal is to give more careful consideration to the subversive strategy the biracial characters employ to create a single, unified consciousness. For them, passing as white is less a racial masquerade and more a social role, such as a trained lawyer or physician performing in that role before a client or a patient. Instead of being torn apart by the double consciousness of being American (having inalienable rights) and non-white (having those rights denied or questioned), the characters in these novels achieve the impossible of enjoying a non-white cultural identity without giving up, or even having to fight for, the legal rights and social privileges of a white person, which include being seen and valued as a human being. Before delving into the literature, though, I will provide a little historical context.

RACISM BEFORE AND DURING THE 1920s

Throughout the nation's history, women of color have borne the brunt of the white supremacy agenda, suffering denigration of their humanity and denial of their selfhood.[2] Enslaved African American women dealt with the same physical brutality and mental cruelty as their brothers, husbands, and sons, but they experienced the additional violation of rape, an act white men considered their unquestioned right. Because rape of slaves was legal, racially motivated sexual violence was widespread among slave owners. This abuse was "not merely a result of sexual desire and opportunity, or simply a form of punishment and racial domination, but instead encompassed all of these dimensions as part of the identity of white masculinity."[3] A degrading and disempowering act, rape was normalized as a "necessary" characteristic of the authority figures white men aspired to be. One consequence was that white women often excused their husbands' behavior, blaming and abusing the sexual victims in order to feel empowered.

As with female slaves, early encounters between white men and Native American women also resulted in domination, dehumanization, and sexual violence. Although women acted as the "first important mediators" between indigenous and European cultures, "Indian women were often raped by European men who forcibly entered their communities demanding goods, labor, or homage to particular leaders and religions."[4] There was a direct correlation between "the seizure of tribal lands and the seizure (rape) of Native women."[5]

Thus, "the use of rape and sexual assault as a weapon against indigenous peoples is deeply imbedded in the history of imperialism and domination,"[6] so much so that "the colonist mindset could not conceive of a legal wrong in raping a Native woman."[7] Even into the twentieth-century, sexual assault figures are "staggering,"[8] despite not counting the many violations that went unreported. As a tool of enslavement and colonization, rape has played a major role in shaping and defining white masculinity, itself a significant source of white male authority and supremacy in the United States.

The Jazz Age saw a renaissance of African American culture and creativity that did support some female authors and artists. Unfortunately, many women did not benefit from this cultural reawakening. "Black women faced greater economic discrimination and had fewer employment opportunities than did Black men"[9] or white women; plus, African American women faced "sexual exploitation from inside and outside of their families and from the rape and threat of rape by white as well as Black males."[10] Author Zora Neale Hurston dramatized the continued degradation of African American women in her 1937 novel *Their Eyes Were Watching God*. Protagonist Janie is told by her grandmother that the "white man is de ruler of everything."[11] Janie witnesses the abuses that accompany white power and privilege, but she also learns through her first two marriages, one during the 1920s, that African American men transfer their own feelings of resentment and impotence onto the women in their lives, sometimes violently. These women are abused and demeaned by everyone—men of both races and white women—because, as Janie's grandmother laments, "de nigger woman is de mule uh de world."

Hurston, though, did not believe it had to be this way. After years of self-sacrifice and obedience, her character Janie rejects the identity of an inferior being who must be subservient. Janie locates her own voice and demands an equal partnership with her third husband. This self-actualization, which inspired a generation of female readers, came straight from the lived experience of Hurston, "a woman bent on discovering and defining herself, a woman who spoke and wrote her own mind."[12] The author opposed the attitude of racial superiority that fed white privilege and justified, in the minds of society's decision-makers, racial segregation and gendered attacks against minority women.

Just as African American women were treated as the mules of the world, Native American women in the 1920s continued to endure exclusion from the mainstream and attacks on their identity. A large number of children, some estimate over 80 percent,[13] were forcibly removed from their tribal homes by the U.S. government and placed in boarding schools that stripped them of their cultural identity and acculturated the girls to the role of submissive wife and homemaker, "a government version of the ideal American woman."[14]

Without the same cultural renaissance as African Americans, Native Americans lacked the national platform to describe the physical and cultural cruelty they endured, a policy known as "Kill the Indian to save the man." The boarding schools brutalized many girls with impunity, including corporal punishment, starvation, medical neglect, and an "epidemic of sexual abuse"[15] that continued into the 1980s.

The indoctrination of European American values and beliefs imposed a pall of inferiority and invisibility upon Native American women. Courts upheld laws that "imposed a harsher penalty for the rape of a non-Indian woman than an Indian woman presumably because Congress viewed Native women as immoral and therefore unworthy of protection."[16] Restricting Native women's access to legal protection and civil rights, the white male authorities easily took advantage of their vulnerability. For example, coerced or forced sterilization gained legal authority in the 1920s, devastating a number of tribal communities.[17] "Virginia's Eugenical Sterilization Act of 1924 became the model for the nation after it survived constitutional review by the U.S. Supreme Court."[18] Even though the Nazis cited this court decision in their defense at Nuremberg in 1946, the Virginia law stayed in place until 1974. A disproportionate number of women sterilized against their will were Native American and African American, as the white male authorities believed these women "were not capable of being good parents and poverty should be managed with reproductive constraint."[19]

As I previously stated, rape of enslaved women was an integral component of white masculinity. But, what of the offspring? Those with dark skin were often sold for the slave owner's profit, while children with lighter skin could be legally and socially incorporated into white society, if the father wished. Mixed-race people were not warmly welcomed by society, but their light skin color and their white fathers' wealth and standing could shield them. By the early twentieth century, however, white men had become more concerned with the "purity" of their race, which resulted in attempts to exclude all multiracial individuals from their ranks.

This attitude was codified in laws like Virginia's Racial Integrity Act of 1924, which prohibited interracial marriage. At the time, consensual cross-racial relationships based on shared love and mutual respect were frowned upon by many on both sides of the color line. The anti-miscegenation law would not be overturned in Virginia until the *Loving v. Virginia* Supreme Court decision in 1967. In Alabama, the state constitution prohibited interracial marriage until 2000. The long life of laws protecting racist policies and practices were "the product of entrenched beliefs born of white supremacist notions."[20] White privilege and power depended on maintaining a racial hierarchy, thereby disrupting any cooperation or good will between the races.

Moreover, white male dominance thrived by separating, devaluing, and silencing women.

Laws like the Racial Integrity Act also mandated that people with merely "one-drop" of African American blood were legally "colored" and confined to second-class status, no matter their complexion.[21] Extreme segregation efforts disparaged the humanity of women of color and further diminished their economic prospects and sexual autonomy. In the Rhinelander court case of 1925, a rich white man publicly humiliated his biracial wife when he sued to annul their marriage because, he claimed, she tricked him into believing she was white. Native Americans were also segregated and dominated, though the Virginia law had a "Pocahontas Exception," allowing Native Americans to be classified as white if they could prove they had one-sixteenth or less Native American heritage and no other non-white blood.[22]

The one-drop restriction was reinforced by the 1920 census, which required "every American 'be one thing or the other,' black or white. Such moves made the job of policing 'the color line' both more urgent and more difficult."[23] In response to Jim Crow racism across the nation, some in the African American and Native American communities actively helped to enforce racial separation and created their own color hierarchy. Some with darker skin resented or envied the privileges granted those with lighter skin. Consequently, mixed-race individuals were caught in a no-man's land between cultures and, thus, between identities. The "half-blood" or "breed" was often treated as an unwanted outsider, someone the white community and the non-white community believed had suspect loyalties and diminished humanity. Therefore, being a mixed-race woman was perhaps the most complex and fraught identity of the 1920s, a selfhood that embodied the larger conflicts and compromises within a racist and sexist society.

PORTRAYING THE BIRACIAL EXPERIENCE

Larsen's *Passing* and Mourning Dove's *Cogewea* dramatize the personal and social challenges of being a biracial woman in the United States. Like their main characters, each author suffered the alienation and uncertainty of a mixed-race identity. Larsen (1891–1964) had a West Indian father and a Danish mother. Her upbringing in an interracial family was difficult, being a "colored" girl who was unwanted by some of her white family members. Larsen "no doubt felt like a shadow through much of her life"[24] because of ambivalence about her African American heritage, which created an "antagonistic relation to (black *and* white) American racial mores."[25] She associated herself with two racial identities but remained unattached to either racial community, inhabiting "the space between black and white, by necessity and by choice."[26]

Larsen's education and employment gave her extensive experience with both races. She studied at Fisk University, a historically Black institution, and the University of Copenhagen, living with white relatives. She spent 1915 as head nurse for the John Andrew Memorial Hospital and Nurse Training School at the Tuskegee Institute, a historically Black university in Alabama, followed by several years working with patients and colleagues of multiple races at the Lincoln Hospital and the Bureau of Public Health in New York City. In 1919, Larsen married Elmer Imes, the second African American to earn a doctorate in physics, and the couple moved to Harlem where they socialized with eminent African Americans like W.E.B. Du Bois and Langston Hughes, as well as white elites like Carl Van Vechten. During the first half of the 1920s, Larsen worked as a professional librarian for the New York Public Library, becoming the first African American woman to graduate from library school in 1923.[27] One can see her self-confidence and determination in this portrait.

As an artist, Larsen was hailed by prominent members of the Harlem Renaissance as one of the best African American novelists of that generation, yet she stopped writing in the 1930s and went back to nursing. Although mid-century literary critics would dismiss her work, it was rediscovered

Figure 3.1.   Nella Larsen
Drawn by Emily Klein, with permission from Box 52, Harmon Foundation, Inc, Records, Manuscript Division, Library of Congress, Washington, D.C.

at the end of the century. Today, Larsen is very highly regarded in literary circles as "one of the central figures of the African-American, modernist and feminist literary canons."[28]

Mourning Dove (1884–1936) was born into the Interior Salish tribe in the Pacific Northwest. She had three tribal grandparents and an Irish grandfather, which, according to her white editor/collaborator Lucullus McWhorter, "accounts for her deep sympathy so manifest throughout her book for the mixed-blood, the socially ostracized of two races."[29] The author's English name was Christine Quintasket and her Okanogan name was Hum-Is'hu-Ma, which translates as her pen name. Mourning Dove, like Larsen, selected an identity that draws on the beauty and power of multiple cultures without maligning any. Her self-possession and warm personality can be seen in this portrait.

Although she was not widely known in the 1920s, Mourning Dove played a key role in Native American literary history. It is believed she was "the first Indian woman to enter the realms of fiction"[30] and "the first to incorporate the oral traditions of her tribe into a literary work."[31] The author of "the first bicultural Indian/White novel,"[32] Mourning Dove was

Figure 3.2. Mourning Dove
Drawn by Emily Klein, with permission from L.V. Mc-Whorter Photograph Collection (PC 85), MASC, Washington State University Libraries

proud that *Cogewea* did the important cultural work of sharing an indigenous perspective with white America. In addition to telling a good story, the book communicates and preserves a set of values, beliefs, and traditions under attack from the hegemonic culture. Assimilationist policies at the time were "intended to suppress Indian cultures and promote the acceptance of white Christian Euro-American traditions."[33] However, Mourning Dove's progressive portrayal of a mixed-race woman "torn between two conflicting and mutually exclusive identities"[34] was a factor, along with the work of activists, in the U.S. government's shift from assimilationist policies to granting more tribes sovereignty, made law in the Indian Reorganization Act of 1934.

I have paired Larsen and Mourning Dove because they each struggled to find acceptance on both sides of the color line. Stymied at every turn, the authors composed strong, self-aware female characters whose biracial identities demonstrate how a person can handle external and internal racial disharmony. An important question they raise is whether a biracial woman can identify with her non-white community while claiming a complete set of human rights and unquestioned social acceptance, the exclusive domain of white America.

Larsen's main character Clare and Mourning Dove's protagonist Cogewea chafe at society's demand for biracial people to sacrifice one side of their identity. Neither is ignorant of the benefits that accompany the obvious choice of claiming white ancestry and attempting to live an entirely white existence. In the United States, whiteness has always meant freer self-expression and subjectivity; it has meant access to opportunities that should be available to all human beings. However, passing as white was extremely dangerous, evident in the Rhinelander divorce trial and explained by Du Bois in his glowing 1929 review of Larsen's novel: "in the minds of most white Americans, it is a matter of tremendous moral import."[35] Moreover, Du Bois asserted that passing as white damaged people of color irreparably because adopting an exclusively white identity drove them to internalize society's racist beliefs and deny the cultural enrichment and self-respect necessary for self-actualization.

The socially acceptable choice for a mixed-race person was to renounce her white ancestry and embrace a non-white identity. Unfortunately, moving to the "other" side of the color line usually reduced a person to a powerless object. Claiming a "colored" identity, the light-skinned woman was unfairly despised and abused by whites and non-whites alike. Plus, she was still burdened by the internal tension of "double consciousness," Du Bois's term for the pain of a divided identity that occurred when a non-white person attempted to reconcile being an American citizen yet having that selfhood delegitimized. This division created a "sense of always looking at one's self through the eyes of others, of measuring one's soul by the tape of a world that looks on in amused contempt and pity."[36] Mary Griffin commented in her 1929 review of *Passing* that a subordinated person of color could be consumed and destroyed by this heightened "consciousness of race that does not permeate those of us whose skins are white."[37] Larsen and Mourning Dove lived the "half-blood" experience of feeling rejected, dislocated, and isolated as they endured the pangs of double consciousness without a welcoming cultural refuge to turn to.

Passing and *Cogewea* show the emotional and spiritual toll of cultural self-denial, which leads a person to make bad decisions, alienate friends, and lose herself, at least temporarily. Using Du Bois's words, Clare and Cogewea feel their "two-ness . . . two souls, two thoughts, two unreconciled strivings; two warring ideals in one dark body, whose dogged strength alone keeps it from being torn asunder."[38] However, each character refuses to be irrevocably torn, marshaling her dogged strength to seek the unity of selfhood and follow Du

Bois's encouragement "to merge [her] double self into a better and truer self." The novels by Larsen and Mourning Dove highlight this need for biracial women to proudly embrace their white and non-white heritages as co-equal parts of a single, unified consciousness.

Advocates for social justice, Clare and Cogewea demand their rights as human beings to empower the non-white component of their cultural heritage and incorporate it into their personal identity. Major social change requires authority and status within the dominant culture, so the characters do not entirely divest themselves of their "whiteness," which elevates their public standing in mainstream society. To reconcile the warring halves of a dual self, they must apply the training they received from the dominant culture to claim the privileges reserved for whites without denying the cultural and interpersonal connections to their non-white communities.

This bi-cultural stance invites an onslaught of resistance and abuse from white and non-white camps. Clare's death, for example, is precipitated by her desire to keep a rich but racist white husband and maintain her respected public position in white society while reconnecting with the African American community and its cultural traditions. The refusal to choose one "side" upsets the stability of the color line and those who police it, namely, her white husband and her Black childhood friend, who are glad she falls (or is pushed) from a sixth-floor window to her death. Cogewea rebels against the "squaw" identity because she wants to take on the role of a white male ranch hand, yet she learns to respect and internalize the traditional, feminine wisdom of her Native American grandmother. The character strives to "find the middle road that will afford her the amenities of civilization without compromising her traditional beliefs."[39] Cogewea and Clare must withstand the battering of racism and disastrous relationships with white suitors if they are to succeed in a cruel world and ultimately locate their true selves.

WANTING WHITENESS

Langston Hughes's 1926 essay "The Negro Artist and the Racial Mountain" warns African Americans against the desire, "I would like to be white."[40] The piece honors the African American experience and directs artists and authors to faithfully express that experience. It is a reaction to generations of African Americans who attempted to write like white authors in the hope of gaining white society's respect, acceptance, and patronage. Hughes advised authors that running away from their racial heritage reduces the beauty and strength of their art, their culture, their community, and themselves. He believed the desire to be accepted as "white" by the dominant culture "is the mountain standing in the way of any true Negro art in America—this urge within the race toward whiteness, the desire to pour racial individuality into the mold of American standardization, and to be as little Negro and as much American as possible." In order to bring his community's artistic creativity and cultural experiences into the public consciousness, Hughes became a leading force of the Harlem Renaissance, a significant cultural and literary movement during the 1920s. Authors like Nella Larsen and Zora Neale Hurston answered his call, providing a female perspective on racial individuality and art that captured the true African American experience at a time when it was desperately needed.

What these authors faced was a society intent on dominating their bodies and silencing their voices. Racial turmoil was increasing and intensifying in the 1920s, as whites reacted strongly to the African Americans who proudly expressed their own cultural identities and defiantly refused to allow white aggression to continue unchallenged.[41] Anti-black race riots erupted across the country and the Ku Klux Klan rose to the peak of its influence, as "more lynchings were perpetrated in the Twenties than at any other time (51 in 1922 alone)."[42]

Larsen was well aware of the nation's racial sins, past and present. Her novel *Passing* provides several conversations between the African American character Irene Redfield and her husband Brian about "the race problem"[43] and how it would affect their sons. Irene wishes to avoid the subject and shelter her children, but when her son is called "a dirty nigger," Brian asserts, "they've got to know these things," to prepare them "for life and their future happiness."[44] Over Irene's objection, Brian directly answers his son's question about why white people were lynching African Americans: "Because they hate 'em, son. . . . Because they are afraid of them."[45] In addition to pointing out the painful impact of racism, Larsen's novel challenges the biological "truth" of race and demonstrates its social foundation, as Aubrey Bowser explained in her 1929 review of *Passing*, "Race is a matter of mind rather than body, of background rather than foreground. A white baby reared by a Negro family will grow up as much of a Negro as his dark foster-brothers and a black baby reared by white people will grow up hating Negroes."[46] This mindset of hating Black people and Blackness itself corrupts both communities, and, as a result, "society makes a fool of itself."

The painful foolishness of racism in the United States involved widespread indoctrination into an ideology of biological essentialism and the supremacy of white values. Elite white and Black people, such as W. E. B. Du Bois, supported eugenics efforts based on a belief of the superiority of certain bloodlines. In the 1920s, Du Bois called for leadership by the "Talented Tenth," his term for the "exceptional men" he considered the best representatives of his race. He and other African American intellectuals at the time believed men of "good breeding" (and only men) commanded the natural ability to be the leaders, artists, and scholars the race needed to claim equal standing.[47] The politics of color within the African American community ranked working-class and uneducated men below the well-bred, and placed women at the bottom. Mainstream society valued a different set of second-class citizens, white women, above Du Bois's "Talented Tenth."

In *Passing*, the death of Clare's father obliges her to live for years with two white aunts who forbid her from revealing she was branded by "the tar-brush"[48] and impel her to cut ties with her African American friends. Just like Anzia Yezierska's protagonist Sara in *Bread Givers*, young Clare is deter-mined "to be a person," which requires acceptance by the dominant society. While Sara leaves Jewish traditions and asserts herself into the mainstream, Clare refuses to be "a charity or a problem" and assimilates into white soci-ety. Poor and unwanted, she resolves to get wealth and self-respect, so she presents herself as white and marries a rich white man, John Bellew, without telling him the truth of her parentage. In other words, she embodies the traits and norms that the dominant society considered respectable, so she may claim her humanity.

In doing so, Clare deliberately oversteps the bounds set for Black women. Upset at her presumption, Irene criticizes Clare for possessing "a having way,"[49] but, as the previous chapters have discussed, the 1920s was not a time of self-denial. People not only wanted goods, but they also wanted self-ful-fillment, which required women break free of restrictive norms and empower themselves. Clare takes this rebellion a step further by establishing a selfhood outside of the binary mindset that formed white and non-white identities. This strong female character accepts herself and refuses to compromise her author-ity, ambition, or joy to fit within a racial category. A similar attitude is out-lined by Zora Neale Hurston in her 1928 essay "How It Feels to Be Colored Me," where she laughs in the face of "the sobbing school of Negrohood who hold that nature somehow has given them a lowdown dirty deal and whose feelings are all hurt about it."[50] Rather than bemoan her victimhood, Hurston states that she is "too busy sharpening [her] oyster knife" with plans to crack open the dominant culture and claim its opportunities for herself. As will be seen with Cogewea, Clare does not hate her whiteness, nor does she hate her non-whiteness. Instead of denying one, she chooses both; she loves and fights for her Black brethren while claiming personal authority and privilege in the white world as her due.

It was only three years earlier that Hughes's essay had advised African Americans not to adopt a white identity since it de-values their African American culture and selfhood. He asserted that passing may present greater opportunities for individual success, but it reinforces the false legitimacy of white supremacy that grants unearned privileges not available to all. However, Larsen's novel suggests that passing need not be an act of conformity and racial self-abnegation. It can be "a subversive form of counter-power, unseen and invisible. Through it blacks undermine white culture because they prevent it from achieving a complete understanding of their alterity. At the same time they participate in it, altering its traits and purity."[51] Recognizing Clare as "the character [Larsen] most admires,"[52] it seems clear that the novel prompts readers to consider Clare's mask of whiteness as an assertion of a non-racialized self and a subterfuge that hides her subversion of racial norms.

Once she has purged the racism she internalized as a child, Clare's self-aware passing may do more damage than if she played by society's rules, as her biracial friend Irene does. Unlike Irene, Clare does not whimper ineffectively into the void about her second-class status caused by the one-drop rule. Nor does she accept the role of whipping-girl many African American men expect her to play. Clare rejects voluntarily martyrdom to the racial binary, selecting self-actualization over the assumptions and limitations that attempt to check her on both sides of the color line.

Passing does not mean Clare wants to minimize her Blackness, as Hughes feared. On the contrary, she aspires to expand her racial self-understanding, which suggests she does not exploit her white appearance for mere convenience, like Irene occasionally does, or to conceal racial shame. Passing, for Clare, is an act of self-empowerment not self-hatred; plus, it camouflages a rebellious disregard for racial purity, demonstrating to fellow biracial characters and readers the absurdity of her husband's proud claim: "No niggers in my family. Never have been and never will be."[53] Thus, while the dominant society identifies people strictly by their racial appearance and background, Clare escapes the prison of the color line by acquiring "the power of the margins and disassembling the concept of racial identity."[54] Clare's approach is akin to songs sung by slaves that, on the surface, expressed religious devotion and congeniality, yet the underlying message, obvious to the slaves but not the slave owners, criticized racial injustice and outlined plans to escape physical, mental, and spiritual confinement.

Rebuffing enslavement within any racial or gendered category, Clare invalidates the very notion of white male supremacy or Black female victimhood. Passing asserts her humanity and repudiates the inherent superiority of whiteness. It enables her to act as a spy who can "jeer"[55] at Bellew for thinking he hates "niggers" when the love of his life is one, as is his beloved daughter. The irony is that when Clare's husband and other white people suddenly know the truth about her biracial background, they see her differently and treat her badly even though she herself has not changed. Thus, her act of passing demonstrates white hypocrisy to readers perhaps more sharply than light-skinned Irene's timid avowal of her non-white identity.

RACIAL SELF-DETERMINATION

The authorial dedication in *Cogewea* ends with the phrase, "her most unhappy race,"[56] which demonstrates Mourning Dove's sadness for the unjust treatment of her ancestors. The dedication begins by honoring the memory of her "great grandfather See-Whelh-Ken, venerated chief of the Schu-aylp[k]," whose good deeds cost his tribe dearly, as he "welcomed the coming of the pale face, only to witness the seeds of destruction scattered wide among his own once strong and contented people." Mourning Dove, like Larsen, aimed to help uplift her people by telling them the ugly truths related to race in the U.S. and giving them a path to self-actualization and socio-economic success.

By the end of the nineteenth century, the populations of many tribes had been decimated by the westward expansion of white settlements, weaponized disease, and a series of "Indian Wars." As to this last violation, army records show that there were at least 1,065 engagements between Native Americans and either the U.S. military or armed civilians in the years 1866–1891. The brutality of these campaigns on Native American men, women, and children across the West was more a form of murder than warfare. U.S. General Philip H. Sheridan led many of these campaigns, infamously stating, "The only good Indians I ever saw were dead."[57] Years later, Sheridan admitted, "We took away their country and their means of support, broke up their mode of living, their habits of life, introduced disease and decay among them and it was for this and against this they made war. Could anyone expect less?"[58]

As the U.S. military attacked Native Americans' bodies, the U.S. government attacked their body politic, revoking the tribal nations' sovereignty and displacing peoples from their ancestral lands. The battles waged against the tribes, particularly after the Civil War, were offensive, in both senses of the word. The army promoted "the advancing tide of civilization by nullifying the Indian's war power and forcing him to submit to Indian Bureau supervision on a reservation."[59] Even on reservations, Native Americans were not safe or happy, partly because of poor conditions and partly because of the new culture and identity thrust on them: "Once rulers of the plains, proud Indians were humbled, treated like beggars. . .[They] could not forage for food and had to have permission from the Indian agent to even leave the reservation."[60]

Not only did tribal members resent being removed from their ancestral lands and denied access to traditional hunting grounds, but also many were not interested in being "civilized" and assimilated. Mourning Dove, during her early education at the Goodwin Catholic Mission, "shared the common Native American experience of being punished for speaking 'Indian' instead of English."[61] Her goal in writing a novel was to share the history, values, and voice of her people, forcing the public to acknowledge them and learn what was being done to them.

Mourning Dove explicates the "Indian problem"[62] through the musings of her protagonist. Cogewea abhors the violent conquest and domination of the tribes by the U.S. military, "But bloody though the subjugation, it did not compare with the deadly effects of the *benevolent* manner in which her race had been ruled since the enactment of the various treaties."[63] The character bitterly describes the government's dictatorial Indian Bureau as an octopus and a vampire that legalized injustice and, thereby, normalized brutal domination of the tribes. Cogewea also complains that government policies and their underlying beliefs violate the democratic and Christian values that the smug white majority claimed as its guiding light. In reality, white people acted like thieves and murderers who, "skilled in the art of white washing," claimed intellectual, biological, and moral superiority for their race and their ideology.

Just as Clare is forced to leave the African American community and live with her white aunts, Cogewea is forced to leave her tribe as a child and attend the Carlisle Indian Industrial School in central Pennsylvania.[64] Like many Native Americans at the time, the young girl receives a "white" education, which likely included cruel physical and psychological tactics to remove all remnants of her tribal culture and language. As it happens, she graduates with high honors before returning to the location of her ancestral homeland near the border of Washington state and Canada. As an adult, Cogewea respects her sister Mary for living a more traditional life with their grandmother, but Cogewea locates herself within the dominant culture like her sister Julia, who marries a white man and helps him run a cattle ranch.

The novel demonstrates the uncertain identity of a "half-breed," swinging from pride and independence to self-loathing and isolation. Cogewea attempts to assimilate by speaking English, wearing European clothing, and seeking a white husband. She hopes to "equip herself for a useful career, but seemingly there was but one trail for her—that of mediocrity and obscurity. Regarded with suspicion by the Indian; shunned by the Caucasian; where was there any place for the despised breed!"[65] She is part of a generation of mixed-race Native Americans who struggled to find a place for themselves "within a discourse of Indianness that denies their realities."[66] Just across the border, Canadian Native American women were being forcibly removed from their tribes because they married non-Native men and lost their tribal status.[67] The result of similar policies in the U.S. was that individuals who aligned with a single racial identity "reported significantly higher levels of depression and trait anxiety symptoms"[68] compared to those who experienced "a validated Biracial identity."

In response to mainstream society's attacks on and exclusion of biracial people, including negative labels like "half-breed," Mourning Dove created a strong, self-aware character who speaks up for herself. Cogewea evokes a spirit power that draws on her experience in the white and the indigenous worlds. For example, she manifests a hybrid identity when confronting a rattlesnake. In addition to abasing the serpent for being a descendant of the Garden of Eden troublemaker, she recognizes the evil that serpent-power has long perpetrated against her tribal ancestors. She admits that because of its powerful medicine her grandmother would not kill the snake, but not being a full-blooded Native American means she does not fear its magic. Pulling a pistol from a holster on her belt, Cogewea shoots the snake several times, exhibiting a fearlessness and steadfastness ascribed to male ranch hands. Following the indigenous tradition, she understands and respects its magic, but following the white tradition, she conquers it.

Cogewea breaks from the expectations of Native American women by boldly asserting the right to live and work and love as she desires, regardless of what her white fiancé or her indigenous grandmother wishes. Experience in the white world and her own character traits drive her to stand confidently in her personhood and command respect, which she receives as a result of talent and attitude. Cogewea easily works alongside white male ranch hands, having earned their admiration and trust; in fact, "they worshiped this free, wild girl of the range,"[69] more for her abilities than her beauty. Several of the men state that they would marry her, but they feel intimidated and unworthy because she can hold her own and routinely bests them in riding and roping. Her presence confutes the white men who overvalue their masculinity and their whiteness, forcing them to see her as a peer, if not their superior.

Utilizing elements of her whiteness and her indigenousness, Cogewea establishes a hybrid identity. Frequently, she and biracial friend Jim lament feeling trapped between opposed cultures, simultaneously confined and excluded. To address this unjust condition, Cogewea exposes wrong-headed assumptions and defends generative attitudes and relationships. Throughout the novel, she attempts to justify her multicultural perspective to her jaded grandmother Stemteemä and her ignorant fiancé Densmore. Cogewea often acts as a cultural translator, explaining and defending aspects of white culture to Stemteemä and indigenous culture to Densmore, who has trouble even pronouncing her name. Moreover, Cogewea's ability to speak two languages, English and Okanogan, connects her to the world of her grandmother's stories and allows her to explain that culture to her white fiancé in an attempt to bring them closer. Her efforts do not achieve the result she desires, for Densmore abuses her trust to steal from her and attempts to murder her. Nevertheless, her intensions are honorable, and she does create goodwill with the people, white and Native, that genuinely love and respect her.

Mourning Dove attempted to overcome some language and cultural barriers by using Okanogan words in her writing, as well as sharing traditional customs and stories. Although the context helps the white reader understand, McWhorter added ethnographic footnotes during his editing of the manuscript. Some critics consider the writing an uneven mix of romance and social criticism, different voices competing in the same textual space, but others contend that the novel's "multiple voices illustrate Cogewea's refusal to be solely Anglo *or* Native and develop the mixed blood-dilemma theme."[70] In addition, author and editor model a successful biracial collaboration, as "both Mourning Dove and McWhorter were complex cultural subjects who occupied various overlapping positions and spoke from those various positions."[71] The result is a work that seeks to bridge the indigenous-white divide, a "complex, ambivalent, and polyvocal" text that "relentlessly and courageously" crosses and collapses boundaries.

Therefore, Cogewea's hybrid identity, similar to Clare's in *Passing*, undermines the color line. For example, she rejects white men who dare to diminish her humanity by calling her "squaw," and she demands her Okanogan compadre not use the epithet either, even as a joke.[72] Although she prefers living in mainstream society with the respect and opportunities given to white men over an impoverished life on the reservation, she prizes her indigenous heritage and forcefully repudiates the dominant society's dishonest and oppressive treatment of Native Americans. When pressed, she claims her indigenousness as the highest honor over her whiteness, a reversal of the national mythology disseminated by the white propaganda machine.

She consciously defies the color line during a Fourth of July celebration by entering the "squaw" horse race and the "ladies" horse race. Cogewea ignores all attempts to exclude her, a clear metaphor for her identity battles throughout the novel. During the "ladies" race, the favored white woman, upset at Cogewea's presumption, begins to strike her violently with a quirt. Cogewea snatches the riding whip and wins the race. She also wins the race dedicated to Native American women. When the white judges discover she is not fully white, she is disqualified from the "ladies" race and cheated out of the prize money. After losing the argument against the white authorities, she refuses to accept money for her victory in the "squaw" race, denouncing it as polluted by racist attitudes that do not reflect the American ideals of merit, fairness, or basic human rights. Cogewea drives this point home by identifying herself as both Caucasian and American, suggesting that she, not the white judges, are living up to America's highest ideals.

What bolstered the color line in the 1920s was "a society deeply invested in the connection between white superiority and American national identity."[73] Thus, policing the color line corresponded with the "ongoing racial war between civilization and savagery," a war that positioned non-white races as less than fully human and lacking "a claim to the rights spelled out in the founding documents of the United States." It was bad enough that personal attacks against individual Native Americans were excused, but major military and institutional atrocities were justified, if not applauded, as necessary and proper. White people have had difficulty seeing any connection between themselves and indigenous peoples, equating Native Americans with a mythological Wild West. Considerable damage has been done by the perception that "Indigenous culture is static and must exist in some past state to be authentic."[74] A refusal to see Native Americans as anything but primitive and helpless reduced someone like Cogewea to an aberration, alien and unacceptable within the racist national identity.

The character undercuts the white national identity by indicating that only indigenous people are true Americans. Mourning Dove made this point again in her autobiography, "There are two things I am most grateful for in my life. The first is that I was born a descendant of the genuine Americans, the Indians; the second, that my birth happened in the year 1888. . . . I was born long enough ago to have known people who lived in the ancient way before everything started to change."[75] This change, the result of acculturation and genocide, was not the goal of the hybridity Cogewea strives to embody.

RACE WOMAN

Despite the deadly risks, men and women of color in the 1920s stood up to bigotry and fended off attacks on their personhood, a shining example for others.

> The term "race man" has been used historically to characterize high achieving Black men who devote themselves to the betterment of Black people, and live counter to stereotypes about the inferiority of Black people. They believe in the pursuit of race consciousness, race pride, and race solidarity. So every Black man is not a race man.[76]

In addition, African American women were also fearlessly outspoken about their community and its future. Larsen knew race men and race women were not merely exceptional contributors to mainstream U.S. culture; they proudly owned their heritage and sought racial uplift for every one of their people. Thus, while Irene wants to believe she is a race woman as she climbs the social ladder, it is Clare who does the important work of sabotaging the racial hierarchy and connecting with the common folk in the Black community.

Throughout *Passing*, Irene criticizes Clare for convincing white society that she is one of them. However, it is Irene who adopts the binary mindset propagated by white supremacy and Black victimhood, causing her to accept a disempowered African American self. Irene wears a mask of racial pride, but she often feels slighted and dismissed without standing up for herself or her community. She remembers when Clare, as a child, fought other children for taunting her working-class Black father, yet Irene remains mute in the face of vicious racism. In fact, she requests her friends and her own husband not talk about racism with her. "The stakes are too high for Irene to admit to herself that Clare, not she, is the real 'race woman,' with genuine racial affection and loyalty."[77] Irene lacks this affection, passing herself off as a race woman without adopting the role's values or fully appreciating its responsibilities.

Rather than love her race and her people as Clare does, Irene desires and performs a fixed racial identity. She refuses to "separate individuals from the race"[78] because she believes the rise of the African American bourgeoisie may be halted if she attacks and destabilizes existing racist attitudes and structures. Irene has already found a way to work within the white system, causing her to accept a safe, second-class position without disrupting the status quo.

Irene is mystified by Clare's deviant attitude and risky behavior as a "principled passer."[79] By espousing a white perspective, Irene cannot read Clare's "Negro eyes! mysterious and concealing."[80] Upon their first meeting after many years, Irene fails to understand Clare's strong individuality. However, no amount of study will help Irene gain the first clue about Clare, her racial subjectivity or her feminist consciousness because "Irene consistently aligns herself with conservative and bourgeois elements in [white] American society."[81] Nevertheless, Irene is troubled by the seductive quality of her rival's voice and smile, which make her begin to question the subordinate role she has taken. The allure is Clare's assertiveness and self-assuredness that allows her to ignore the opinions of others. Comfortable in her own skin, Clare damns being safe, which makes her "capable of heights and depths of feeling that she, Irene Redfield, had never known."[82] Irene may not pass on a regular basis, yet she succumbs to "the desire to pour racial individuality into the mold of American standardization," which Hughes condemned.[83]

The nickname 'Rene makes plain that Irene lacks an "I," a true selfhood. Instead, she conforms to what she believes is the proper African American identity, forever under the thumb of whites and their stereotypes. For all of Irene's claims to wear her Blackness proudly, she maintains a white mindset and often distances herself from other African Americans. As stated earlier in this chapter, Irene may recognize the racial problems in the U.S., but to her dark-skinned husband's frustration she refuses to confront them. Like white tourists who visit Harlem, she can participate in the African American experience and then escape to her light-skinned, upper-class position, discarding her Blackness when it hampers her. She justifies passing as a convenience, enjoying a white's only restaurant where she reunites with Clare after years of separation. The difference between them is that Irene's passing is not subversive. She self-consciously worries others will recognize that she does not belong, that she is unworthy of white privileges like self-assuredness, respect, and comfort in this upscale public place. It infuriates Irene that Clare effortlessly owns her humanity and claims the privileges of racelessness.

Larsen underscores the insidious influence of whiteness by having Irene denounce her own white skin but adopt a mindset that betrays a "white-approximate self-image."[84] As a member of what Hughes termed "the Nordicized Negro intelligentsia,"[85] Irene benefits from being "respectable," so she does not shatter the whites' illusions about racial stereotypes or their assumptions that African Americans desperately aspire to whiteness. The security of wealth and social position leads Irene to be repressed and obliged to maintain the color line. On the other hand, these opportunities direct Clare to be more independent and less confined or obligated to race. During one conversation, Clare challenges the notion of not rocking the boat, which completely unsettles Irene's trust in the stability of her role in the racial status quo: "I'm beginning to believe. . .that no one is ever completely happy, or free, or safe."[86]

Irene resists any change to her racial ideology. She continues to court white intellectuals like Hugh Wentworth who was modeled on Carl Van Vechten, the famous white intellectual and author of the 1926 novel *Nigger Heaven*, as well as Larsen's close friend. Irene seeks white approval for her noble sacrifice, her acceptance of what others consider is an "inferior" African American identity when she could have passed as white, an equal. Although she is seen as a step below the white elite, her obedience to the role they have given her provides its own privileges. No rebel, Irene follows the example of the rich white liberals and becomes a patron of African American causes. She serves on boards and holds fundraisers with sympathetic white friends, all the time keeping her distance from the ugliness of racial conflict and disparity. Accepting the color line as a necessary evil, she flits safely within her refined circle, a class line that causes her to avoid fraternizing with her own African American servants. At one point, Irene even sympathizes with Clare's racist husband, feeling a strange kinship with his understanding of the importance of protecting the color line.

Lacking the courage of her supposed convictions, Irene claims Blackness more out of martyrdom than true race pride. A "colored" identity for 'Rene requires self-denial, shame, humiliation, and compliance. It also means assuming a superior attitude to the Black underclass. "Irene has internalized both colorism and a social code that tells her not to love anyone with less access to a white-approximating middle-class Blackness than herself and ultimately is not satisfied with herself or her life."[87] She safeguards the color line, placing herself on the "other" side because she does not believe she deserves more. Irene also chides her husband in front of her son "for ever wanting something that he couldn't have."[88]

Moreover, Irene resents Clare's racial flexibility. When Bellew discovers Clare is, in his words, "a damned dirty nigger,"[89] Irene seems less upset at his insult than with Clare's smile, unwilling to accept that Clare might free herself from the confines of race. Irene, worried that Brian will leave her for Clare, redoubles her efforts to police the color line, hoping to maintain the "outer shell of her marriage, to keep her life fixed, certain."[90] This shell and her fixed life replaces the hard work of facing problems and initiating change, keeping Irene trapped within "the walled prison of [her own] thoughts."[91]

Unlike Irene, Clare's identity is founded on equality and an authentic racial affection. She is not dishonest about her whiteness or, arguably, about her Blackness, owning both without repressing either, even when she passes. Recognizing the strength and importance of her whiteness and her Blackness, Clare makes them equal partners, or perhaps a better way to say it is that she rejects race-"ness" by choosing to be herself and loving members of both races without fear, doubt, or self-immolation. Irene might argue that the racial "sides" of Clare's identity remain separate but equal parts of her public persona, and by passing she chooses whiteness over Blackness. This impression, though, is a consequence of white prejudice and not Black shame. It is not Clare's fault that her white husband and Black friend buy into the binary racial mindset, giving them only a superficial understanding of her and her racial hybridity.

Clare refuses to feel guilt over passing as white or fear at being found out. Irene bristles at the recklessness of "stepping always on the edge of danger. Always aware, but not drawing back or turning aside."[92] However, Clare scorns playing it safe or "feeling the outrage on the part of others." Her independence and defiant refusal to back down exhibit a confidence and boldness alien to Irene. Having a hybrid identity gives Clare strength and imagination, necessary components for combatting racism and dismantling the color line. "She appropriates white power and uses it to her advantage."[93] Clare is no more self-conscious when she demands service in a whites-only restaurant than when she jokes and gossips with Irene's African American servants. Freed from the limitations of racial self-congratulation or self-sacrifice, Clare brushes off the criticism from Irene or others who police the color line. She will not allow disciples of the white mindset to taint her awareness and assuredness as she communes with her African American brothers and sisters while standing apart from a self-destructive sense of race.

CULTURAL SELF-DISCOVERY

Clare and Cogewea promote a biracial (or, perhaps, a race-free) mindset that does not value white superiority or non-white victimhood. To construct a hybrid identity that delegitimizes the color line, they devote more attention to non-white cultures, as the dominant culture is already widely understood and validated. The characters feel an impulse that contains more than a desire for justice and equality in the white world; they also need to soothe a cultural ache and satisfy a racial longing. They live and work in mainstream society, but, feeling an unexplained restlessness, they gravitate toward non-white people, values, and cultural practices. The connection is apolitical, as the hybrid characters do not take a militant position as activists or martyrs. They want acceptance in the dominant culture as human beings, but they need that culture to value them as women and racial "others."

Clare and Cogewea find that owning their whiteness allows them to live an equal life among whites, but it can be an emotionally and spiritually empty life. To find true freedom and fulfillment, they must embrace their "color" as Hurston advocates in "How It Feels to be Colored Me." Her essay's speaker describes being transported by jazz to her African roots, amazed that her white companion has only a lukewarm reaction to the music. She pities his lack of insight into the beauty and energy of the African American experience: "The great blobs of purple and red emotion have not touched him. He has only heard what I felt. He is far away and I see him but dimly across the ocean and the continent that have fallen between us. He is so pale with his whiteness then and I am so colored."[94] Here, whiteness is a deficiency, pathetic and lifeless compared to the colorful vitality of African American culture and the spirit it inspires.

In *Passing*, Clare holds on to her rich, white, racist husband, but this choice does not stop her from reconnecting with African Americans and her own Blackness. Irene attempts to bar Clare from her community, but Clare will no longer accept isolation from her roots, which inspires her to echo Hurston's sentiment by stating, "in this pale life of mine I am all the time seeing the bright pictures of that other that I once thought I was glad to be free of."[95] At first, Irene is merely unsettled by what she considers Clare's duplicitous intrusion into her elite social circle, but she later becomes downright appalled by Clare's rebellious break with class protocol when she jokes and gossips with Irene's African American servants.

Irene strongly believes that upholding the lines of race and class separation is the best strategy for uplifting the race and giving her and other women autonomy and social authority. This attitude makes her and Clare "strangers in their desires and ambitions. Strangers even in their racial consciousness."[96] Irene considers herself on higher moral and cultural footing, but the reader recognizes that she has fallen in line with racist ideology. As a woman, Irene feels added pressure to present a successful and spotless image. By submitting to society's rules, she ascends to the highest levels as a wife and society woman. However, Irene soon feels "bound and suffocated" by the role of a respectable woman and "the burden of race."[97] Far from improving her life, Irene's conformity has caused estrangement from her race, her husband, and herself. The expectations and self-sacrifice are overwhelming, causing her to devalue her femininity and wish "she had not been born a Negro."

Clare, on the other hand, is unbound and unburdened as she gladly chooses friendship over a faulty conception of race or gender. She, like Hurston, bears no obligation to the "sobbing school of Negrohood" or womanhood, knowing that the world is gained by courage, action, and a strong sense of identity. Glad she was born "a Negro" and a woman, Clare unites her privileged life with her cultural needs and disregards all social barriers, stating, "I want to see Negroes, to be with them again, to talk with them, to hear them laugh."[98] A strong woman with a biracial identity, Clare avoids the burdens Irene carries. Clare expresses a self-confidence and joy that attracts everyone to her, including Irene's husband. Contrary to most stories of someone returning to the race after passing as white, Clare experiences no crisis of conscience; she just wants the freedom to live, love, and laugh without being trapped into racial or gender stereotypes. She expresses an empowered femininity, feeling sexually and socially free, which threatens Irene because it allows Clare to retain "the ability and desire to connect with Black people across lines of class and color."[99] Irene notices that this desire makes Clare's femininity "luminous" and "radiant,"[100] aglow with self-love and insubordination as she crosses all borders.

This freedom destabilizes Irene's racial and sexual identity. She notices that Brian, who is already restless, admires Clare for breaking free of the repressive color line. Irene asks Clare to "be reasonable"[101] and adopt a cold, rigid façade, but she refuses and agrees to pay the price for "gettin' darker and darker,"[102] which Brian finds appealing. Irene feels genuine concern about Bellew's caustic warning, "if she don't look out, she'll wake up one of these days and find she's turned into a nigger." In fact, Clare does look out. She analyzes the white world through "Negro eyes" that are secretive, arresting, seductive, and reproving. Also, her reconnection with Blackness makes her even more self-possessed, and unself-conscious with a "dim suggestion of polite insolence"[103] that others find attractive. At her core, Irene is threatened by Clare's hybridity, a woman comfortable being a "creature utterly strange and apart"[104] from standard conventions. The destabilization of Irene's fixed racial and gender identity provokes the thought, "She couldn't have [Clare] free,"[105] and compels her to wish for and help cause Clare's death.

Mourning Dove also aimed to destabilize the racial and sexual identity assigned to Native American women. She relates in her autobiography that although it was necessary for her to adopt some white practices to function in mainstream society, "I speak the Indian language of my own tribe better than I do the adopted lingo of the English-Americans. I had the opportunity to learn the legends, religion, customs, and theories of my people thoroughly."[106] The author considered herself fortunate to spend time "living the real Indian life" and "learning the ancient Indian teachings passed on to children, which the present generation of Indians has largely had the misfortune to regard as only historical customs rather than current beliefs." She also valued the example set by female elders, such as her grandmother, of a woman's power and pride.

Like Clare, Cogewea "burned with an undefinable restlessness"[107] and feels "longings" for a connection with non-whites, in her case the Okanogan people and culture. She has chosen to live in modern white society, to the chagrin of her grandmother, but she is also a "free girl of the outdoors"[108] who responds when "the wild blood of a wilder ancestry was calling." Cogewea exhibits racial and feminine power and pride when she balks at her white fiancé's assertion of his moral and cultural superiority. She declares, "The true American courses my veins and *never* will I cast aside my ancestral traditions."[109] She considers indigenous people as the only true Americans and rejects the white male notion that a Native woman must be a possession or disappear into the landscape.

She chooses to work on the ranch owned by the white man married to her sister because it is surrounded by rugged countryside. This location of her ancestral lands retains "a lingering semblance of the wild."[110] Cogewea is an educated, modern American woman, yet "the wild appealed to her,"[111] as it represented personal freedom as much as cultural tradition. Mourning Dove's childhood involved listening to the animals' songs and feeling gratitude for nature: "It was wonderful to be alive and inhale the clear spring air."[112] However, this kindred with wildness was not romantic. Mourning Dove respected her people's relationship with nature, a respect for the importance of medicinal and spiritual knowledge that prompted a deeper engagement at odds with the savage-civilized hierarchical binary. In the novel, Cogewea turns the dominant worldview upside down and berates the whites' "alien, rum-flavored civilization"[113] for dehumanizing Native American women as a mere feature of the natural world, objects to be essentialized, dominated, and polluted.

Cogewea connects with her tribal traditions through her grandmother Stemteemä. In his introduction to the novel, McWhorter compares this relationship with Mourning Dove's love for her maternal grandmother, Soma-how-atqu. Both the real and the fictional elders teach their acculturated granddaughters "the principles of ancestral philosophy"[114] and traditional feminine skills like preparing edible roots and berries, weaving baskets from local materials, learning ancient stories and songs, and understanding spiritual energy like the "sacred power of the sweat-house."[115] Multiple chapters include long oral stories Cogewea translates for the reader, where Stemteemä provides tribal history and womanly advice. These stories express the pain and misery young women endure when white men, the Sho-yah-pee, abuse and deceive them. Unfortunately, Cogewea must learn this lesson through personal experience.

Mourning Dove's novel is more overtly critical of the white race and its mindset of superiority than Larsen's, yet Cogewea initially rejects the biracial Jim as a suitor. There is no full-blooded Okanogan man in the story, indicating that her romantic relationships must occur in the white world. Refusing to see Jim as a viable mate suggests that she has embarked on the path to establishing an exclusively white identity. Soon, though, her white fiancé reveals his true intentions: he steals her money, ties her up, and leaves her for dead. It is a sober reminder of the physical, psychological, emotional, and spiritual toll on Native women who completely align themselves with the white male mentality. Cogewea survives and after a year begins dating Jim. Her story shows female readers the importance of confidence, self-reliance, and resilience, as well as avoiding unhealthy relationships without giving up on love. She ascertains that a hybrid identity can only succeed if she can engage her feminine and masculine characteristics, as well as find a partner who values indigenousness yet lives in the modern world.

Similar to Clare and Brian, Cogewea and Jim share a restlessness and a need to establish an identity that transcends the color line. The pair relies on each other for emotional support because, as Cogewea muses, "We are maligned and traduced as no one but we of the despised 'breeds' can know."[116] She trusts Jim's judgment as they battle a common enemy, not the white man himself but the mindset of arrogance and superiority white men broadcast to justify individual and institutional crimes against Native Americans. Cogewea and Jim continue to live and work in the white world, but they also eagerly learn from the wisdom of their elders.

Cogewea's (mis)adventures provide her a newfound respect for traditional knowledge. Near the end of the novel, a voice speaking from a buffalo skull aligns with her own realization that Jim's honorable love should be returned with more than "insipid friendship."[117] McWhorter provides a note about the tradition of the speaking skull: "To hear voices from inanimate objects as intermediary to the Great Spirit or Great Maker, is not uncommon in Indian philosophy."[118] Cogewea is not going to put on beaded moccasins, affect "Indian coyness and modesty of manner,"[119] or move into her grandmother's tepee, but Stemteemä's traditional stories and Cogewea's own experiences teach her to incorporate elements of Native American philosophy into her worldview. Cogewea's hybridity requires her to utilize her training from Okanogan and white cultures, as she frees herself from the prejudices and obligations of either.

TOGETHER BUT UNEQUAL

During the 1920s, professional and personal relationships across the color line were rarely equal because whites had more power over what was valued and who benefitted. For instance, many whites embraced jazz, a hybrid musical form developed by African Americans melding African polyrhythms and improvisation with European harmonies and instrumentation. Ted Gioia calls it a "dynamic interaction, the clash and fusion—of African and European, composition and improvisation, spontaneity and deliberation, the popular and the serious, high and low."[120] However, as much as "race music" captivated whites, it

> did not lead to any substantial crossing of racial barriers in the music's performance and consumption. When whites began performing the music, they did not include any Black artists in their bands, and when whites went to hear Black artists perform as they did at numerous clubs in Harlem, they insisted that no Blacks be allowed in the audience.[121]

In addition, white producers largely controlled the record industry, refusing to record some artists and limiting what was recorded by others. When the music's popularity exploded, it was whites more than African Americans who profited.

Of course, a considerable portion of the white population criticized "race music" as corruptive, evidence of the supposed dangers African Americans posed to white society. In 1921, the head of the music department for the General Federation of Women's Clubs, Anne Shaw Faulkner, wrote the widely read essay "Does Jazz Put the Sin in Syncopation?" for *The Ladies Home Journal*. She claimed jazz invokes "savage instincts" and corrupts the morals of young people, associating it with "the voodoo dancer."[122] Faulkner contended that jazz's sordidness springs from its use of syncopation, which was "the natural expression of the American Negroes and was used by them as the accompaniment for their bizarre dances and cakewalks."

Although a "jazz-as-black view" dominated the era, there was also an interest in a "jazz-as-multicultural perspective."[123] The musical form not only represented "American democracy and nationalism,"[124] but it also reflected the complicated multi-racial nature of the United States. By the 1920s, mixed-race people were central to the American national identity, yet their very existence was upsetting the white establishment. As has been discussed, there was an outcry against miscegenation as a corruption of white bloodlines and culture. Knowing this, Larsen and Mourning Dove showed that the biracial woman walks on a knife's edge, especially if she attempts simultaneously to claim privileges hoarded by whites and to flaunt her non-white cultural heritage. Such a combination was risky and dangerous. Clare and Cogewea nonetheless brush aside the warnings of their biracial friends, opting to press their hybrid identities and face the inevitable disaster that accompanies the trailblazer.

In *Passing*, Irene warns Clare that she must choose a side, either identify with the white public persona and leave behind any connection to her Blackness or perform as a person of color and accept second-class status and public debasement. If the color line did not exist, a person would be able to commune with all aspects of her heritage without losing any of the rights and esteem due every human. Of course, the color line did exist, perpetuating injustice. Studies done on income, health and life expectancy, education, and other quality of life metrics have shown that conditions on the non-white side of the color line were markedly worse. In fact, "utilizing observations and data from the 1920s and 1930s, several writers suggest that the living conditions of blacks in these decades were no better than they had been during the era of slavery."[125]

The color line "traumatized"[126] Nella Larsen, and white society did everything possible to silence people like her. In the years after writing two well-received novels, she disappeared from the public eye and many friends' lives. "Larsen did not cut off her friends because of a warped value system and internalized racism, as previously believed; she cut them off because she feared that, white or black, they would leave her."[127] *Passing* is directly concerned with people's connection to and disconnection from each other. Initially, Clare disconnects from her race to find financial success and make herself into a person. Once she has attained the privileges of the dominant society, she desperately seeks to reconnect with her childhood friends and her racial roots. When these worlds collide, she drops from a sixth-floor window, destroyed for not permanently disconnecting from one group or the other.

Larsen's fears of abandonment and isolation are realized in Clare's demise, a consequence of being rejected by her white husband and her Black childhood friend. At first, Bellew dismisses the idea of her existence as a proud mixed-race person without realizing it. He jokes about his racist nickname for her, "Nig," to the horror of Irene.[128] The slur, however, does not upset Clare, as it does not compromise her view of herself. She stays with Bellew, in part, because her smile has the power to "transform him, to soften and mellow him, as the rays of the sun does a fruit."[129] Through him, she maintains a connection to the white world, which Irene interprets as a self-serving slap in the face to her own racial martyrdom. However, Clare considers it an opportunity to change the white supremacist mindset from the inside, if not for Bellew then perhaps for the reader. For example, when Bellew rejects Clare many readers see him as an ignorant bigot since Clare and her friends do not fit the "damned dirty nigger" image he ascribes to them. The reader sees him as a hypocrite in the vitriol he shouts at his wife in the last scene since she has not changed, only his perception of her has. His statement actually supports the idea that race is a social construct that cannot adequately define or contain a whole person.

Throughout the novel, Irene also rejects Clare and the idea of race as social construction because it disturbs her secure, privileged life. She disconnects from Clare by tearing up her letter, but Clare and her mindset further invade Irene's world. Although Irene avoids discussing the color line, particularly with her husband and children, its existence is central to her choices and her identity. She stands firmly on one side and polices the line. The few times she herself crosses into white territory, Irene is either fearful of being discovered or resentful for feeling obliged to protect Clare from discovery. From either side of the color line, Clare's identity is viciously attacked, her hope and her life destroyed by those who cling to the necessity of race and cannot conceive of an alternative to their assigned roles in the contentious racial drama. It is unclear who causes Clare's death, but the beliefs and actions of Irene and Bellew initiate her disappearance out of the window and out of herself. This ending demonstrates why Larsen would sever ties with friends and become invisible, doing so before others can erase her.

In *Cogewea*, Jim is not tied to the color line like Irene, but he does warn the protagonist that marrying a white man is risky, believing she would be better off with someone who understands her biracial experience. White tenderfoot Densmore pursues Cogewea for her money, having no intention to elevate her into his white family or lower himself to become part of her Okanogan community. He considers himself of a "higher cast"[130] and looks down on Cogewea as a "breed" and a "squaw." At one point, he refers to all Native Americans as "slaves"[131] who must learn their place beneath their white "masters." Nevertheless, he is charming and persistent, eventually convincing Cogewea to marry him. Lost in love, she will not associate the stories of white abuse and abandonment told by her grandmother to her own relationship. Although her motives are not as mercenary as Clare's, Cogewea does expect her marriage to Densmore will legitimize her connection to the white world. Clare's anti-racist efforts are more subtle, a warm smile to ripen Bellew's tolerance; whereas, Cogewea's efforts are more direct, a firm public repudiation of Densmore's notion that she is inferior.

Unfortunately for Cogewea, Densmore only pretends he loves her and wants to learn about her culture. Like Bellew with Clare, Densmore rejects the idea of Cogewea. Throughout the novel, he finds Native Americans and the spaces they inhabit bewildering and uncomfortable. Rather than humble himself before Cogewea's grandmother and learn about her culture, Densmore remains defiantly superior. He believes that the dominant point of view represents universal truth by "assuming the Euro-American colonial narrative to be identical to a divinely ordained narrative of Human History."[132] He can only see the primacy of his own narrative. As a white man, he will not tolerate an American story that does not center on him: "For Densmore, representative of a malign white culture, Native history and Native reality remain non-narratable and no middle ground seems possible on which a narrative could be constructed that might accommodate or reconcile these apparently incommensurable points of view."[133]

Cogewea's blindness to Densmore's scheme demonstrates her optimism, the belief in a new story that will heal the racial wounds. Her resilience further highlights that she is an independent, capable woman who is not defeated by the oppressive and destructive white male mindset. Despite Cogewea's failed relationship with Densmore, the novel ends with her younger sister, the one devoted to their traditional grandmother, embarking on a honeymoon to Europe with her new husband, a wealthy Frenchman. This narrative shows that much like Mourning Dove's own collaboration with McWhorter, people from different backgrounds can locate a middle ground and build meaningful relationships across cultures and points of view.

LOOKING TO THE FUTURE

Institutionalized racial segregation and violence created intense animus across the color line in the 1920s, yet consensual sexual relationships between whites and non-whites contributed to a substantial and growing biracial population in the nation. Undeterred by the centuries-long horror of unchecked physical, sexual, emotional, and cultural abuse by white men, people of color built supportive, compassionate, respectful cross-racial relationships and interracial communities. For instance, the Peace Mission Movement of African American evangelist and civil rights activist George Baker, Jr., better known as "Father Divine," championed desegregation and racial equality.[134] With an estimated global following in the millions, Divine's national network of "kingdoms" provided interracial communal living. Divine himself engaged in social agitation, marrying a white woman and lobbying for federal anti-lynching legislation.

The novels *Passing* and *Cogewea: The Half-Blood* dramatize the challenges biracial women face when attempting to validate their humanity and unite the races. Defying racial definition and confinement, Clare and Cogewea model enlightened attitudes and positive interracial (and intraracial) relationships. However, aggressive attacks on their idealistic hybridity and their womanhood shine a spotlight on racial divisiveness and sexist domination in the Roaring Twenties, emphasizing the destructiveness of mistrust and aggression from the entrenched attitudes on both sides of the color line. Novels like these are "a revelatory catalyst for anyone who tries to pin these [biracial] women down into an identity,"[135] as the stories expose society's faulty assumptions and unjust prejudices. Larsen and Mourning Dove intended their works to encourage readers to examine their own racial attitudes and decide whether they wish to invest the effort needed to resolve deep-seeded social problems.

The authors believed a biracial female experience can act as a bridge to social inclusivity and respect. Their novels offer a hybrid identity, a meaningful connection between white privilege and non-white cultural perspectives. Refusing to remain at the bottom of the social hierarchy, Clare and Cogewea free themselves from a racist and sexist ideological framework that even some non-white activists accept and maintain. The characters demonstrate the difference between idolizing whiteness and merely performing it as a means to exist outside of inequity and abuse. Moreover, they relate to a non-white community and embrace its values without assuming the full weight of double consciousness.

Although the biracial woman must navigate a divided society, her own identity can remain whole. Nella Larsen and Mourning Dove indicated that breaking down the hierarchical binary of the color line is necessary for every woman to have the opportunity to live her best self, as Zora Neale Hurston proposes in "How It Feels to Be Colored Me": "At certain times I have no race, I am me. . . . I belong to no race nor time. I am the eternal feminine with its string of beads. I have no separate feeling about being an American citizen and colored. I am merely a fragment of the Great Soul that surges within the boundaries. My country, right or wrong."[136]

NOTES

1. Rafael Walker, "Nella Larsen Reconsidered: The Trouble with Desire in 'Quicksand' and 'Passing,'" *MELUS* 41, no. 1 (2016), 166.

2. Jason Reynolds and Ibram X. Kendi, *Stamped: Racism, Antiracism, and You* (New York: Little, Brown and Company 2020).

3. Rachel A. Feinstein, *When Rape Was Legal: The Untold History of Sexual Violence during Slavery* (New York: Routledge, 2018), accessed December 17, 2021, https://books.google.com.

4. Gwenn A. Miller, "Contact and Conquest in Colonial North America," in *A Companion to American Women's History*, ed. Nancy A. Hewitt (Hoboken: John Wiley & Sons, 2005), 36.

5. Sarah Deer, "Toward an Indigenous Jurisprudence of Rape," *Kansas Journal of Law & Public Policy* 14 (2004–2005), 131.

6. Deer, "Toward an Indigenous Jurisprudence of Rape," 129.

7. Ibid., 125.

8. Ibid., 123.

9. Darlene Clark Hine, "Rape and the Inner Lives of Black Women in the Middle West," *Signs* 14, no. 4 (1989), 913.

10. Hine, "Rape and the Inner Lives of Black Women in the Middle West," 914.

11. Zora Neale Hurston, *Their Eyes Were Watching God* (Champaign: University of Illinois Press, 1978), 29.

12. Sherley Anne Williams, Foreword to *Their Eyes Were Watching God* (Champaign: University of Illinois Press, 1978), x.

13. Andrea Smith, "American Indian Boarding Schools," in *Encyclopedia of Women and Religion in North America*, eds. Rosemary Skinner Keller, Rosemary Radford Ruether, and Marie Cantlon (Bloomington: Indiana University Press, 2006), 98.

14. Robert A. Trennert, "Educating Indian Girls at Nonreservation Boarding Schools, 1878–1920," *Western Historical Quarterly* 13, no. 3 (1982), 271.

15. Smith, "American Indian Boarding Schools," 100.

16. Deer, "Toward an Indigenous Jurisprudence of Rape," 125.

17. Jane Lawrence, "The Indian Health Service and the Sterilization of Native American Women," *American Indian Quarterly* 24, no. 3 (2000), 410.

18. Elizabeth Wong, "A Shameful History: Eugenics in Virginia," *ACLU Virginia*, January 11, 2013, accessed Dec. 17, 2021, https://acluva.org/en/news/shameful-history-Eugenics-virginia.

19. Alexandra Minna Stern, "Forced Sterilization Policies in the US Targeted Minorities and Those with Disabilities—and Lasted into the 21st Century," *The Conversation*, August 26, 2020, accessed December 17, 2021, https://theconversation.com/forced-sterilization-policies-in-the-us-targeted-minorities-and-those-with-disabilities-and-lasted-into-the-21st-century-143144.

20. Ashok Bhusal, "The Rhetorical of Racism and Anti-Miscegenation Laws in the United States," *IAFOR Journal of Arts & Humanities* 4, no. 2 (2017), 83.

21. Lisa Lindquist Dorr, "Arm in Arm: Gender, Eugenics, and Virginia's Racial Integrity Acts of the 1920s," *Journal of Women's History* 11, no. 1 (1999), 143.

22. Kevin N. Maillard, "The Pocahontas Exception: The Exemption of American Indian Ancestry from Racial Purity Law," *Michigan Journal of Race & Law* 12 (2007), 351.

23. Carla Kaplan, "Introduction: Nella Larsen's Erotics of Race," in *Passing*, ed. Carla Kaplan (New York: Norton, 2007), xvi.

24. George Hutchinson, *In Search of Nella Larsen: A Biography of the Color Line* (Cambridge: Harvard University Press, 2006), 1.

25. George Hutchinson, "Nella Larsen and the Veil of Race," *American Literary History* 9, no. 2 (1997), 330.

26. Hutchinson, *In Search of Nella Larsen*, 9.

27. Ibid., 8.

28. Kaplan, "Introduction: Nella Larsen's Erotics of Race," ix.

29. Lucullus McWhorter, "To the Reader," in *Cogewea: The Half-Blood* (Lincoln: University of Nebraska Press, 1981), 9.

30. McWhorter, "To the Reader," 9.

31. Dexter Fisher, Introduction to *Cogewea: The Half-Blood* (Lincoln: University of Nebraska Press, 1981), xiii.

32. Ann McCarthy, "Inside Stories: Stemteema's Histories of Early Contact in Mourning Dove's 'Cogewea: The Half-Blood,'" *Australasian Journal of American Studies* 25, no. 1 (2006), 32.

33. Alicia Kent, "Mourning Dove's Cogewea: Writing Her Way into Modernity," *MELUS* 24, no. 3 (1999), 42.

34. Susan Castillo, "Narratives of Blood," *Early American Literature* 41, no. 2 (2006), 345.

35. W.E.B. Du Bois, "Passing." *The Crisis* 36 (1929), 234.

36. W.E.B. Du Bois, *The Souls of Black Folk* (New York: Norton, 1999), 11.

37. Mary Griffin, "Novel of Race Consciousness," *The Detroit Free Press,* June 23, 1929, 58.

38. Du Bois, *The Souls of Black Folk*, 11.

39. Fisher, Introduction to *Cogewea*, xix.

40. Langston Hughes, "The Negro Artist and the Racial Mountain," in *Within the Circle: An Anthology of African American Literary Criticism from the Harlem Renaissance to the Present*, ed. Angelyn Mitchell (Durham: Duke University Press, 1994), 55.

41. U.S. National Archives and Records Administration, "Photographs of the 369th Infantry and African Americans during World War I," *National Archives Educator Resources*, 2016, accessed Dec. 17, 2021, https://www.archives.gov/education/lessons/369th-infantry.

42. Kaplan, "Introduction: Nella Larsen's Erotics of Race," xv.

43. Nella Larsen, *Passing* (New York: Norton, 2007), 73.

44. Larsen, *Passing*, 74.

45. Ibid., 73.

46. Aubrey Bowser, "The Cat Came Back," *The New York Amsterdam News*, June 5, 1929, 20.

47. Daylanne K. English, *Unnatural Selections* (Chapel Hill: The University of North Carolina Press, 2004), 42.

48. Larsen, *Passing*, 19.

49. Ibid., 14.

50. Zora Neale Hurston, "How It Feels to Be Colored Me," *The World Tomorrow*, May 1928, 215.

51. Anna Camaiti Hostert, *Passing: A Strategy to Dissolve Identities and Remap Differences*, trans. Christine Marciasini (Plainsboro: Associated University Press, 2007), 87.

52. Hutchinson, *In Search of Nella Larsen*, 294.

53. Larsen, *Passing*, 29.

54. Hostert, *Passing*, 88.

55. Larsen, *Passing*, 28.

56. Mourning Dove, *Cogewea: The Half-Blood* (Lincoln: University of Nebraska Press, 1981), 5.

57. Thomas C. Leonard, "The Reluctant Conquerors: How the Generals Viewed the Indians," *American Heritage* 27, no. 5 (1976), accessed Dec. 17, 2021, https://www.americanheritage.com/reluctant-conquerors#1.

58. Oliver Knight, *Following the Indian Wars: The Story of the Newspaper Correspondents Among the Indian Campaigners* (Norman: University of Oklahoma Press, 1993), 6.

59. Ibid., 13.

60. Donald L. Fixico, *Bureau of Indian Affairs* (Santa Barbara: ABC-CLIO, 2012), 60.

61. Louis Owens, *Other Destinies: Understanding the American Indian Novel* (Norman: University of Oklahoma Press, 1994), 41.

62. Mourning Dove, *Cogewea*, 146.

63. Ibid., 140.

64. Ibid., 16.

65. Ibid., 17.

66. Bonita Lawrence, "Gender, Race, and the Regulation of Native Identity in Canada and the United States: An Overview," *Hypatia* 18, no. 2 (2003), 6.

67. Bonita Lawrence, "Legislating Identity: Colonialism, Land and Indigenous Legacies," in *The SAGE Handbook of Identities*, eds. Margaret Wetherell and Chandra Talpade Mohanty (Thousand Oaks: Sage, 2010), 516.

68. Victoria H. Coleman and M. M. Carter, "Biracial Self-Identification: Impact on Trait Anxiety, Social Anxiety, and Depression," *Identity: An International Journal of Theory and Research* 7, no. 2 (2007), 1.

69. Mourning Dove, *Cogewea*, 279.

70. Beverly G. Six, "Mourning Dove (Hum-Ishu-Ma) [Christine Quintasket] (1882?-1936)," in *American Woman Writers, 1900–1945: A Bio-bibliographical Critical Sourcebook*, ed. Laurie Champion (Westport: Greenwood, 2000), 255.

71. Linda K. Karell, *Writing Together, Writing Apart: Collaboration in Western American Literature* (Lincoln: University of Nebraska Press, 2002), 79.

72. Mourning Dove, *Cogewea*, 29.

73. Patrick B. Sharp, *Savage Perils: Racial Frontiers and Nuclear Apocalypse in American Culture* (Norman: University of Oklahoma Press, 2007), 4.

74. Gregory Younging, *Elements of Indigenous Style: A Guide for Writing by and about Indigenous Peoples* (Edmonton: Brush, 2018), 18.

75. Mourning Dove, *Mourning Dove: A Salishan Autobiography*, ed. Jay Miller (Lincoln: University of Nebraska Press, 1990), 3.

76. Adrien Katherine Wing, "Henry J. Richardson III: A Critical Race Man," *Temple International & Comparative Law Journal* 31, no. 1 (2017), 380.

77. Kaplan, "Introduction: Nella Larsen's Erotics of Race," xx.

78. Larsen, *Passing*, 71.

79. Jennifer Devere Brody, "Clare Kendry's 'True' Colors: Race and Class Conflict in Nella Larsen's Passing," *Callaloo* 15, no. 4 (1992), 1058.

80. Larsen, *Passing*, 21.

81. Brody, "Clare Kendry's 'True' Colors," 1055.

82. Larsen, *Passing*, 47.

83. Hughes, "The Negro Artist and the Racial Mountain," 55.

84. Milo Obourn, "Disabling Racial Economies: Albeism and the Reproduction of Racial Difference in Nella Larsen's *Passing* and Toni Morrison's 'Recitatif,'" in *Reading Contemporary Black British and African American Women Writers: Race, Ethics, Narrative Form*, eds. Jean Wyatt and Sheldon George (New York: Routledge, 2020), accessed Dec. 17, 2021, https://books.google.com.

85. Hughes, "The Negro Artist and the Racial Mountain," 55.

86. Larsen, *Passing*, 48.

87. Obourn, "Disabling Racial Economies."

88. Larsen, *Passing*, 9.

89. Ibid., 73.

90. Ibid., 77.

91. Ibid., 68.

92. Ibid., 5.

93. Brody, "Clare Kendry's 'True' Colors," 1056.

94. Hurston, "How It Feels to be Colored Me," 216.

95. Larsen, *Passing*, 7.

96. Ibid., 44.

97. Ibid., 69.

98. Ibid., 51.

99. Obourn, "Disabling Racial Economies."

100. Larsen, *Passing*, 15, 74.

101. Ibid., 51.

102. Ibid., 29.

103. Ibid., 21.

104. Ibid., 29.

105. Ibid., 79.

106. Mourning Dove, *Mourning Dove: A Salishan Autobiography*, 12.

107. Mourning Dove, *Cogewea*, 22.

108. Ibid., 139.

109. Ibid., 160.

110. Ibid., 148.

111. Ibid., 17.

112. Mourning Dove, *Mourning Dove: A Salishan Autobiography*, 14.

113. Mourning Dove, *Cogewea*, 98.

114. McWhorter, "To the Reader," 10.

115. Ibid., 11.

116. Mourning Dove, *Cogewea*, 41.

117. Ibid., 282.

118. Ibid., 302.

119. Ibid., 43.

120. Ted Gioia, *The History of Jazz* (Oxford: Oxford University Press, 2011), 25.

121. Mark Naison, "Appropriating Black Music while Segregating Black People: The Paradox of 1920's American Culture," DigitalResearch@Fordham, Bronx African American History Project, 2020, accessed December 17, 2021, https://fordham .bepress.com/cgi/viewcontent.cgi?article=1009&context=baahp_essays.

122. Faulkner, "Does Jazz Put the Sin in Syncopation?" 16.

123. Nicholas M. Evans, *Writing Jazz: Race, Nationalism, and Modern Culture in the 1920s* (New York: Routledge, 2016), 2.

124. Evans, *Writing Jazz*, 14.

125. Reynolds Farley and Walter R. Allen, *The Color Line and the Quality of Life in America* (New York: Russell Sage Foundation, 1987), 29.

126. Hutchinson, *In Search of Nella Larsen*, 10.

127. Ibid., 11.

128. Larsen, *Passing*, 28.

129. Ibid., 30.

130. Mourning Dove, *Cogewea*, 82.

131. Ibid., 249.

132. Robert Holton, "The Politics of Point of View: Representing History in Mourning Dove's Cogewea and D'Arcy McNickle's The Surrounded," *Studies in American Indian Literatures* 9, no. 2 (1997), 72.

133. Holton, "The Politics of Point of View," 74.

134. R. Marie Griffith, "Body Salvation: New Thoughts, Father Divine, and the Feast of Material Pleasures," *Religion and American Culture: A Journal of Interpretation* 11, no. 2 (2001), 120.

135. Jeff Shoemaker, "Nella Larsen's Passing and Color Theory: Beyond Black & White" (Honors Thesis, Portland State University, 2014), 5.

136. Hurston, "How It Feels to Be Colored Me," 216.

Chapter Four

Lesbian Pride

Decoding the Erotic Self

In their effort to acquire equality in the public sphere, women of the 1920s became the subjects of their own lives rather than mere accessories or servants to men. Sexuality was an important aspect of this subjectivity, for Jazz Age women "accepted themselves as sexual creatures for the first time in modern history."[1] The flapper and the New Woman consciously rebelled against the demure, submissive model of femininity by sporting less restrictive clothing, dancing the Charleston, drinking in nightclubs, and initiating sexual liaisons. Unwilling to be the passive object of male attention, the confident and self-possessed modern woman made active choices in her life and commanded her own desire.

The less prudish moguls of mass media capitalized on women's emerging eroticism. Recognizing the profit to be made by joining this shift in social norms, they gave female sexuality a public airing. Record producers marketed suggestive jazz rhythms and blues lyrics by singing stars like Bessie Smith, Hollywood films featured sexually aggressive and confident "It" girls like Clara Bow, and dance halls across the country endorsed sexy moves like The Shimmy and The Black Bottom. Singer, actor, and flapper icon Helen Kane elucidated this attitude in the saucy 1929 song "I Want To Be Bad," in which the speaker confesses she prefers to be bad since it is considered "naughty to rouge your lips, / Shake your shoulders and shake your hips."

Although media contributed to the momentous change in U.S. culture, it did not challenge all of the underlying prejudices. Notably, female sensuality and sexual subjectivity still conformed to a heterosexual ideal. Sexual freedom had been commandeered by white middle-class straight women, who pioneered a new culture of pleasure that viewed "with suspicion those who resisted it or did not fit. Homosexuality, especially, became a threat to be contained and suppressed."[2] Moreover, conservatives characterized heterosexual marriage as an essential element of "patriotic Americanism."[3] They indicated that sexuality, like other aspects of a woman's identity, exists to serve male needs and expectations. Thus, if female sexuality could not be contained, everything would be done to control it, including punishing those who seized sexual agency in defiance of the "white male sexual prerogative."[4]

During the Jazz Age, a number of popular and respected female artists used poetic language and blues rhythms to perform their non-binary sexuality proudly, normalizing it for the queer community and helping it become "a public discourse"[5] in the heterosexual mainstream. Among these voices were singer-songwriters like Bessie Smith, Gertrude "Ma" Rainey, Billie Holiday, Gladys Bentley, Lucille Bogan, Ethel Waters, and Alberta Hunter, as well as poets like Amy Lowell, Gertrude Stein, Djuna Barnes, Edna St. Vincent Millay, Nathalie Barney, Mercedes de Acosta, and H.D. (Hilda Doolittle). This chapter will focus on the homosexual, homosocial, and activist perspectives presented in the blues lyrics written and/or sung by Bessie Smith (1894–1937) and the poetic lyrics written by Amy Lowell (1874–1925), Gertrude Stein (1874–1946), and Djuna Barnes (1892–1982).

Of course, sexual orientation is only one component of these women's complex identities. Not all of their works deal with same-sex relationships, and Bessie Smith faced additional prejudice as an African American coming from a poor background. I do not intend to reduce the authors or their art-creation to a single characteristic, but I will examine how some of their poems and blues lyrics publicly expressed an empowered lesbianism that disrupted the larger culture's restrictions on gender identity-formation. After giving a little social and literary context, I will discuss the authors' presentation of a lesbian sensibility that celebrated collective sisterhood, erotic desire, devoted companionship, and social activism.

HETERONORMATIVITY AND HOMOPHOBIA

One result of modern women gaining a greater public presence was increasingly unwarranted and vicious attacks on intimate female relationships. Previous generations were sexually repressive, but they did favor "wholesome" intimacies between women in the domestic sphere. Pairs of women could openly engage in "Boston marriages" or "romantic friendships." These homosocial partnerships were "actually encouraged from the pulpit, in etiquette books, and in medical tracts. . . In a world where women and men were expected to occupy separate spheres, it was acceptable and even preferable that unmarried women should enjoy close bonds. It was expected that they would kiss, hug, and even sleep together in the same bed."[6] Late-nineteenth-century

U.S. society promoted these close relationships of love and support where two women lived together without a man's presence or financial assistance.

Of course, the Boston marriage was expected to have non-erotic emotional and physical intimacy, a love that was sweet and charming but platonic. Condemned as sinful, homosexuality was largely believed to be a male deviance, considered completely foreign to women of "polite society." Since men arrogantly assumed that female sexuality did not exist separate from them, lesbian was not even a distinct identity category until the end of the nineteenth century.[7] Some Victorians did use terms like Boston marriage as code for lesbianism, sniggering at the homoerotic behavior happening behind closed doors, but it was not until the twentieth century that sexual intimacy between women was widely denounced as taboo.

By the 1920s, lesbianism was gaining acknowledgment and tolerance among the younger generation of women who broke norms and forced their way into public life. Once they secured a career and a private residence, these women stood up for a wider range of sexual identities: "It was among the new professional women of the 1920s that the articulation of any sort of publicly recognizable lesbian identity became possible for the first time."[8] Greater acceptance led to the development of visible and vibrant lesbian subcultures in several major cities. By asserting ownership over their sexuality and exhibiting it openly, women-loving women contested and destabilized what had long been considered respectable behavior.

However, straight white men resisted what they viewed as a brazen disregard of their authority, and soon "lesbian relationships were considered a major problem within many heterosexual circles. In fact, lesbianism was seen as a threat to heterosexual marriage as well as to maintaining feminine roles for women within society."[9] Conservative social leaders did their best to reestablish conventional gender identities and sex roles. They redirected all female desire toward heterosexual dating and marriage in an attempt to reassert male supremacy and demonize homosexuality: "The newly heterosexualized woman made possible her opposite, a menacing female monster, 'the lesbian.'"[10] The "new pleasure woman" had emerged, but she must only desire the "new pleasure man."

Popular media sowed the seeds of heterosexual allure and competition into young women's friend circles, weakening the intimate bonds that women had cultivated and relied upon for generations. Songs and films hyped heterosexual coupling, prodding women to join men in behavior meant to lower inhibitions, such as secretive automobile excursions and wild nightclub drinking and dancing. Print advertisements marketed products to women like makeup and weight-loss equipment, pushing them to enhance their sex appeal and compete with other women to attract male admiration. At a time when

economic and social constraints on women were weakening, heteronormativity and homophobia gained strength, culminating in the more repressive
1930s that saw censorship of lesbian plays and films, plus restrictions on
hiring and service in restaurants and stores.

Lesbians faced greater challenges than gay men, who were able to develop
"a more extensive and visible subculture."[11] Gay men had access to better
wages, time away from family life, and public meeting spaces. Of course,
lesbians could choose to pass as heterosexual and benefit from the privileges
of the dominant group. However, like light-skinned African Americans who
passed as white, lesbians experienced their own form of double consciousness, an internal conflict born from denying an important part of who they
were and presenting a false self in public to "fit in." Fitting in was safe, but
the 1920s was not a time to play it safe. Many lesbians recognized that this
era of female advancement in politics, commerce, and culture offered opportunities to change public attitudes about sexual identity.

The first step was to shed feelings of shame or denial and own her love and
sexual desire for another woman. The next step was to share that identity with
the world, setting an example for others. For a lesbian, living one's authentic
self and conveying it publicly was an act of defiance against stereotypes and
a validation of her humanity and unique womanhood. Several prominent
1920s authors opened doors for lesbians across the nation by bravely choosing to make their lesbian identity and lifestyle visible through the public act
of creative self-expression.

A lesbian sensibility had begun to appear in U.S. literature in the late nineteenth century through the pioneering work of writers like Sarah Orne Jewett,
Kate Chopin, and Mary Eleanor Wilkins Freeman. Fiction provided a relatively safe medium for silenced voices to share unpopular beliefs and ignored
experiences, but not all lesbians were comfortable exposing themselves to
public scrutiny and attack. For example, the homosexual openness of Jewett
contrasted an adherence to heterosexual norms by Willa Cather, who was not
publicly known as queer until the 1980s.[12] Cather may have been ashamed
of her homosexuality or she may have hidden her personal sexual orientation
out of a practical fear that books by lesbian authors would not sell to a mass
audience. Regardless, Cather's concerns were legitimate during an era "in
which love between women was labeled as deviant and pathological and in
which lesbians could be subjected to discrimination and brutal repression."[13]

The Broadway stage was another avenue for gay and lesbian self-expression. For example, Mae West's plays "The Drag" (1927) and "The Pleasure
Man" (1928) countered homophobia by starring gay men and featuring
elaborate drag balls. The police raided the performances, arresting West and
her cast for indecency. Edouard Bourdet's play *The Captive* (1926), which

spotlights a lesbian relationship, also scandalized New York City at the time. The review of a 2015 revival of the play begins, "*The Captive* was written in 1926 when homosexuality was considered to be 'the love that dare not speak its name.' Its Broadway run was halted by censors and the cast members were arrested. This revival proves that the play was a mature treatment of the subject, far ahead of its time."[14]

Censors in the 1920s were concerned about the infiltration of lesbians into the ranks of "normal" women, afraid they would unsettle straight women's obedience to heteronormativity and corrupt them. The portrayal of a lesbian as feminine "was far more disturbing"[15] to the censors than the "easily recognizable Other (i.e., the mannish lesbian)." Like *The Captive*, the poetry and song lyrics in this chapter confound the stereotypes of lesbians as inhuman, grotesque, and repulsive. Instead, the works depict lesbians as attractive, seductive, and feminine, alongside their ability to be as tough, intelligent, and self-assertive as any man.

The cinema largely avoided "the lesbian chic era of the 1920s,"[16] a reference to a homosexual character in Djuna Barnes's 1928 novel *Ladies Almanack* who states, "In my day I was a Pioneer and a Menace. It was not then, as it is now, *chic*."[17] Attempting to appeal to a wide audience, many film producers followed the culture's heterosexual norms. Censors were already complaining that women in 1920s films were too sexually active, playing the role of a sexual aggressor or femme fatale, a "vamp." As a result, lesbian characters were largely absent from the silver screen. Notably, the 1929 film *Pandora's Box* "featured what is probably the first explicitly drawn lesbian character on film,"[18] though the character "largely represses her love"[19] for the female lead. In 1930, Marlene Dietrich cross-dressing and mischievously pretending to seduce another woman in the film *Morocco* was immediately deemed transgressive for openly expressing "lesbian desire and sensual androgyny."[20]

Women-loving women subversively disrupted male control of their bodies, identities, and voices. Asserting their subjectivity, these women not only realized their own sexual selfhood, but they also became more self-aware and self-actualized than was previously expected or allowed. An individual woman's choice to define herself as lesbian was not strictly limited to sexual orientation, as some heterosexual women identified as lesbian because they wanted to join others who opposed "the institution of heterosexuality,"[21] and some bisexual women identified as lesbian even though they considered their homosexual interest "nothing more than a part of a larger sexual repertoire." Thus, the new lesbian sensibility of the 1920s was multi-dimensional, promoting sisterhood networks, erotic lovemaking between women, life-long loving relationships for female couples, and feminist activism.

Socialized to repress their impulses and emotions, lesbians in all parts of the U.S. had been denying their true sexual orientation. The blues and poetry discussed in this chapter demonstrate female artists who publicly lauded lesbian desires, a rejection of the contemporary notions that homosexuals were biologically unnatural, medically sick, morally corrupt, or socially abnormal. I should note that some texts mentioned here were published in the 1910s or 1930s, but they all relate to the authors' 1920s oeuvre. These works by Djuna Barnes, Amy Lowell, Bessie Smith, and Gertrude Stein encouraged women across the country to build strong lesbian networks where they could empower themselves and each other.

LESBIAN SISTERHOOD

Amy Lowell writes in "The Sisters" (1925): "Taking us by and large, we're a queer lot / We women who write poetry. And when you think / How few of us there've been, it's queerer still."[22] Alerting her readers to the rarity of famous and respected female poets, Lowell's poem emphasizes the important role a strong network of women can play in the literary world and the larger society. During the nineteenth century, women's clubs and associations thrived, teaching new skills, engaging in community improvement, participating in civic affairs, and helping members "develop a group consciousness as women."[23] Local club activity was coordinated by national organizations like the General Federation of Women's Clubs and the National Association of Colored Women's Clubs, "the largest and most enduring protest organization in the history of Afro-Americans."[24] These organizations brought women together, gave them a public voice, and coordinated social reform on the local and national level, such as the passage of constitutional amendments for women's suffrage and alcohol prohibition.

However, the white club movement had significantly diminished by the 1920s, once these women had gained greater individual access to public life. They earned college degrees, joined the professional workforce, and voted, all without being members of larger organizations. The capitalist ethos prized individualism and competition, particularly among women fighting for scarce opportunities within male-dominated arenas, which disrupted supportive female networks. Professional women also ran up against the "old boys club"— networks of men who resisted allowing women entry into their ranks. Years of living on their own and fighting for recognition in professions filled with men caused many women to feel alone and discouraged.

As women stepped into the public eye, lesbians were especially isolated and vulnerable. Nevertheless, some formed communities that united and empowered their members. Strong homosexual subcultures flourished in several large cities during the 1920s. At a time when lesbian identities faced public opposition, the "Paris-Lesbos" community met at salons hosted by well-respected women like American expatriates Gertrude Stein and Natalie Clifford Barney, whose gatherings were frequented by famous artists and authors. A site of cultural development and social power, the salon straddled private and public worlds, nurturing women emotionally while connecting them with important ideas and famous people from mainstream society. Of course, the members were the artistic and social elite, those who had the means to live in Paris and the intellect to be welcomed into the salons' high-minded discussions and witty repartee.

The United States offered a more working-class version of the Paris-Lesbos scene in Harlem. Rather than conform to a racist cultural tradition and a repressive moral tradition, African American authors, artists, and musicians of the Harlem Renaissance expressed the raw, and sometimes raunchy, lived experience of a new generation, including the hardships and pleasures of women who love women. Harlem "provided a safe space for a black lesbian subculture to materialize" and "black lesbian identities to flourish."[25] Unlike the Parisian salons, African Americans outside of the social and artistic elite could enjoy lesbian interactions at rent parties and jazz clubs. "Harlem represented the potential dissolution of a strictly regulated ideal of chaste black bourgeois female sexuality, imported from the South, to working-class lesbians."[26] African Americans moved to Harlem to escape the religious and conservative ideologies of parents and neighbors. Black lesbians were accepted and supported by all levels of the community, from everyday folk to acclaimed blues singers Bessie Smith and Ma Rainey.

It should be noted that white men and women also took advantage of the permissive sexual environment that Harlem offered. They acted as voyeuristic tourists, "slumming" in an exotic and erotic subculture. Stricter policing of sexuality in other parts of the city made Harlem a "safer alternative"[27] for same-sex encounters of all races, protecting lesbians from homophobic attitudes in "upstanding" white and African American communities. Homosexuality was discouraged on all sides of the political spectrum; both conservative religious devotion and progressive social uplift conflated heterosexuality and respectability. Some African Americans saw homosexuality as ungodly, while others believed it compromised efforts to gain acceptance and respect from white society. The pressure on Black lesbians was immense, since the "sin" of reclaiming their sexuality supposedly embarrassed the whole race and held back its possible advancement. It was a conflict between who they were and what society wanted them to be.

Of course, most lesbians in the United States, white or Black, did not have the opportunity to attend jazz clubs in Harlem or salons in Paris. Those living towns that lacked these safe spaces found it difficult to locate other lesbians, which increased their self-doubt and loneliness. Thus, a wider sisterhood had to be created through different means. The poetry and blues lyrics discussed in this chapter spoke to lesbians all over the country, validating their desires and affirming their selfhoods. In fact, one specific reason Djuna Barnes used the roman à clef approach in her 1928 novel *Ladies Almanack* was "to estab-

lish an 'imagined community' of lesbian practices and identities into which others can be recruited."[28] Barnes herself embodied a lesbian identity that was open and fashionable, as indicated by this portrait.

In addition to her novels, Barnes wrote poetry to speak to the challenge of otherness, addressing her peers' struggle to survive social rejection and exclusion. For example, "Lullaby" (1923) relates the loneliness of being a girl in U.S. society. The speaker fondly remembers her carefree days as a young tomboy, but when forced to adopt a traditional "girl" role, she mourns no longer being allowed to play with the boys or share her bed with the dog.[29] Feeling disempowered and alone, the girl must be quiet and inactive to gain social

Figure 4.1.   Djuna Barnes
Drawn by Emily Klein, with permission from Djuna Barnes papers, Special Collections and University Archives, University of Maryland Libraries

acceptability, forced to tame her exuberance and forget her ambitions. She despises the requirement to behave as if she is weak and helpless, eyeing a pistol as she recognizes an endless series of empty, pointless tomorrows. The poem does not suggest same-sex desire, but it does express a broader lesbian sensibility of being isolated and feeling out of step with the societal expectations for women.

Several poems by Barnes do explore the frustration of having to hide one's same-sex love and lesbian identity. The narrator in "The Rose" (1923) dreams of passionate reciprocation from a close female friend. The rose represents a love that is taboo, as the narrator broods about the woman who "walked my dreams, forbidden, lost to me."[30] In Barnes's "Love Song in Autumn" (1923), the love between two women is reciprocated but risks public condemnation. The poem contrasts the joy at finding someone to love with the fright that social whispers might destroy them and their love. The speaker worries, "Where warm birds slumber, pressing wing to wing, / All pulsing faintly, like a muted string / Above us, where we weary of our vows."[31] Although the women are united, society's rules mute their passion, limiting it to a faint pulse. Even more distressing, their vows become less consequential without the support of a lesbian community that would pressure society to accept their passion and their marriage bond as legitimate.

In her novel *Ladies Almanack*, same-sex passion and lesbian identities are supported by a strong subculture. Barnes herself had a sexual affair with salon host Natalie Clifford Barney, who is the model for the promiscuous main character Evangeline Musset. Dame Musset aggressively challenges the heteronormative and prudish attitudes she encounters. Throughout the novel, Dame Musset ignores society's prejudices and happily seduces different types of women, which helps to build a lesbian community they all enjoy. As in heterosexual relationships, the novel asserts that same-sex couples feel love, desire, jealousy, and rejection. Not the monsters of homophobic rants, lesbians have the same normal, natural impulses and interactions as their heterosexual brethren.

Amy Lowell employed a less satirical manner to promote meaningful connections among women. "The Sisters" appeared in the collection *What's O'Clock* (1925), which was awarded the Pulitzer Prize for poetry in 1926. The poem places Lowell among three esteemed "sister" poets—Sappho, Elizabeth Barrett Browning, and Emily Dickinson. Lowell's poetic persona has no wish to try to copy or best these poets; she merely wants to applaud their work and model how to build "spiritual relations"[32] between female authors and readers in the present and the future. Lowell's poetic intensity and focus are reflected in the portrait on the next page.

As I stated earlier, "The Sisters" begins by noting the "queerness" of publicly acknowledging female poetic genius, deemed unworthy of recognition by the male literary elite. Not only were women discouraged from establishing a strong lesbian subculture, but it was not easy to form female networks in the literary world. Lowell had individual poet friends like fellow imagist H.D.; however, "The Sisters" notes the disconnection she felt from the many ignored and silenced female authors. Lowell had to conjure their physical and emotional existence through her imagination, framed as the narrator's dream of a new poetic sisterhood. The issue certainly is not the female poets' ability. Lowell and her gifted, "man-wise"[33] peers were certainly capable, but they were excluded from the male literary circles. "The Sisters" argues that female poets are due the same respect as male poets, which includes the composition of in-depth biographies and the support to become serious artists. Starting with Sappho, Browning, Dickinson, and herself, Lowell wished to build a network that bolstered new female authors to help them find their own voices, so future poets, especially the most disaffected women, would be able to speak more directly and personally with each other and their readers.

The poem complains that forming networks is impossible when women's personal lives and creative output are excised

Figure 4.2.   Amy Lowell
Drawn by Emily Klein

from history, suppressed by marriage, or confined to "cold, white paper"[34] by misogynistic biographers or critics. Rather than deify the greats of the past, Lowell considered them sisters, equals who aid fellow female authors in developing unique identities and poetic styles. She heard each poet's "speaking soul"[35] and used her words to establish a dialogue, the first step in building her own lesbian poetic network. Another member of this network was Italian stage actor Eleonora Duse, "Lady, to whose enchantment I took shape / So long ago."[36] As Lowell explained in "Eleonora Duse" (1925), she began writing poetry after witnessing Duse evoke strong emotions from an adoring audience in 1902. The performance initiated Lowell's professional creative output and shaped her personal sense of womanhood.

Like Sappho, Browning, and Dickinson, Duse was a pioneer that gave so much of herself to feed the souls of women like Lowell, "who bless [Duse] in their prayers even before their mothers."[37] Lowell proclaimed in the poem "To Eleonora Duse in Answer to a Letter" (1923) that her idol's brilliance as a performer and a person embodied a higher level of artistic self-assertiveness and generosity. Lowell recognized the actor's tremendous influence over her, claiming a deeper attachment to Duse than a mere adoring fan. Lowell's appreciation of her idol caused her to commit to encouraging and supporting other creative women. For her, sisterhood was about paying forward the inspirational brilliance supplied by a mentor, evident in Lowell's promise to Duse, "What you gave I give back again."[38]

The challenges of forming a lesbian sisterhood are expressed in Lowell's "On Looking at a Copy of Alice Meynell's Poems, Given Me, Years Ago, By a Friend" (1927). Initially, the poem warns readers to remember the past, as in "The Sisters," but it concludes with Lowell realizing she must "shut the door" on Meynell's ladylike Victorian verses because "the living have so much to do."[39] The "past" in the poem is a budding love affair and a book of poetry. While pursuing the woman of her desire, the speaker feels confident in her own lesbian identity, vowing to remember who she is and what she wants. Unfortunately, her love interest rejects her, conforming to a culture that devalued female poets and shamed lesbians. In the end, the speaker must move on from the blindness of others, and forge personal relationships with women who reciprocate her love. A casualty of this self-fulfillment was Meynell's well-made lyrics, which gather dust on a forgotten shelf. No admirer of the old-fashioned poems that tout sexual self-denial, the lesbian poet must assert her own voice, separate from musty predecessors. As indicated by "The Sisters," a lesbian sensibility needs to be included in the literary canon. Its job is to honor female excellence and disrupt outdated literary biases and cultural exclusion.

While Lowell created an imagined sisterhood, the Paris salons were concrete locations where supportive groups of women and artists could develop. Natalie Clifford Barney's salon catered to the elite and famously held weekly Sapphic parties. Conversely, Gertrude Stein's salon focused on a more middle-class and heterosexual community, catering to male artistic and literary luminaries like Picasso, Matisse, Ernest Hemingway, F. Scott Fitzgerald, and Ezra Pound. Nevertheless, Stein was "seen as a feminist and a lesbian icon,"[40] so well-respected lesbians made appearances at her salon. Moreover, Stein's poems and her book *The Autobiography of Alice B. Toklas* (1933) normalized lesbian identities. One literary critic called Stein's works, "a gift to future lesbians who will see ourselves in the writing and will kiss Stein for the empowering celebration of our sexuality which she has given us."[41] The writing envisions a space where lesbians can enjoy their love and their passion openly, though Stein herself faced hostility and prejudice. One can see her world-weariness in this portrait.

Stein's poem "Lifting Belly" (1917) acknowledges the obstacles and links empowerment to cooperation among women.[42] The phrase "lifting belly" has erotic implications, but it also suggests lifting oneself and one's sisters out of domestic dependency and misogynistic oppression. The poem defends quarrels with objectionable men and excluding them from a woman's life. The poem frequently uses the first-person plural, which indicates the power and pride of working within a lesbian network. Imperative verbs encourage women to find their individual voices and sing their truths. Second-person pronouns direct the reader to develop individual authority. The lesbian network is collaborative but exclusive. As Amy Lowell indicated, only women open to changing the social system and their place within it can form a supportive lesbian cohort and participate in feminist upliftment.

Figure 4.3. Gertrude Stein
Drawn by Emily Klein

The poem "Before the Flowers of Friendship Faded Friendship Faded" (1930) by Stein also alludes to unity among women. A sisterhood emerges with the speaker vowing to courageously join others like her. The poem professes that cooperation and solidarity help lesbians freely express their selfhood, a freedom of not needing to hide and instead finding "there is a well inside / In hands untied."[43] Depth of feeling and mental toughness will lead to success for the individual and the community. Stein challenged all women to unite in breaking open the doors closed to them and enter the public sphere without apology or reparation.

Solidarity among women is also presented in Bessie Smith's blues lyrics that aimed to empower each listener to be more independent and self-confident. One can see the regal, dignified, uncompromising, self-assured nature of the "Empress of the Blues" in the portrait on the next page.

Smith was one of the highest paid, most recorded, and best known African American women of the Jazz Age. She raised the blues "to an art form that was to be the hallmark for every woman blues singer who recorded during the 1920s."[44] Smith and other singers ushered "black culture into the American mainstream due to the emergence of the recording industry."[45] Marketed to African Americans, "race records" did a booming business, and Smith herself made over 150 recordings between 1923 and 1933.[46] White "jazz babies" and "flaming youth" of the time also bought "race records," which "enriched the cultural mix and encouraged the cultural rebellion of disaffected segments of the white population"[47] but also led to cultural appropriation and a "condescending dilution of the original art forms." A true original herself, Smith avoided generic love tunes, writing and singing lyrics that "redefined women's place and reaffirmed the identity of African-American women."[48]

Figure 4.4. Bessie Smith
Drawn by Emily Klein, with permission from Dr. Edward M. Burns, Successor Trustee, The Carl Van Vechten Trust

In addition to an ingrained homophobia, African American lesbians had to overcome bad publicity as newspapers, even in the Black community, sensationalized the rare cases of domestic violence among lesbians. Several newspaper accounts during the mid-1920s "served to conflate the emerging concept of 'lesbianism' with violence, aggression, vice, and pathological behavior. The newspaper accounts not only informed northern urban readers about the networks of women in their midst who loved women, but also depicted them as 'unnatural' and immoral."[49] By employing "moralistic language," these newspapers warned their readership of "the dangers that could befall African American women who made a home and a life together" and consciously contributed to "the ongoing attempts to regulate the sexual comportment of African American women through this discourse."[50]

Smith's songs offered an alternative discourse, legitimizing same-sex desire and subverting the standard blues tropes of women competing for men and being devastated and alone after losing the men they love. Her "I Used to

Be Your Sweet Mama" (1928) features a scorned woman who refuses to give her man a second chance. She reaches out to the sisterhood, "all you women understand," and then screams to the world, "No man can treat me mean / And expect my love all the time."[51] The lyrics to "Pinchbacks—Take 'Em Away" (1924), co-written by Bessie Smith, advise female listeners to pick a lover that respects them and treats them properly.[52] In "Preachin' the Blues" (1927), lyrics by Smith, the speaker promises her female network that she will "learn you something." Confident and experienced, she bonds with her audience and commands, "Let me tell you, girls, that your man ain't treating you right."[53] Members of a sisterhood look out for one another and refuse to permit any form of abuse.

The song "I've Got What It Takes" (1929) asserts a sense of self-respect Smith wanted all women to feel. The speaker advises female listeners to protect their bodies, their hearts, and their incomes. She warns aggressive suitors, "You can look at my bank book / But I will never let you feel my purse."[54] The speakers in "Down Hearted Blues" (1923) and "Sam Jones Blues" (1923) demand respect and refuse to allow abusive men back into their lives. "Hard Time Blues" (1927) and "Lost Your Head Blues" (1926) declare that good women must develop enough self-esteem to leave the wrong men without even a goodbye. If peaceful means fail, women may resort to threats and engage in violence to fend off physical and emotional attack, as sanctioned in "Sing Sing Prison Blues" (1924) and "Aggravatin' Papa" (1923).

Other blues women championed an African American lesbian sisterhood. The revered Ma Rainey wrote and sang "Prove It on Me Blues" (1928) to express "contempt for a society that rejected lesbians"[55] and proudly validated her same-sex partners: "They must've been women, 'cause I don't like no men."[56] The song follows the traditional blues trope of the loss of a lover, but instead of a man leaving her, it is a "gal" she's lost. Nevertheless, she wants "the whole world to know" that she has not given up on love. Lucille Bogan sang "B.D. Woman's Blues" (1935), which asserts the pride and authority of the "bull dagger," a slang term for butch lesbians.[57] The song reverses society's moral assumptions about lesbians being sinners: "the way they treat us is a lowdown dirty sin." These women are so self-sufficient and strong that they "ain't going to need no men," which echoes the title of Bogan's 1927 song "Women Don't Need No Men." Alberta Hunter sang "Someone Will Take Your Place" (1923), which begins with the conventional, "Pretty baby left me, but soon someone else will take your place," but then upends the listener's expectation: "So if you didn't want me, tell me to my face / 'Cause five or six women going to take your place."[58] Ethel Waters croons to a female lover in "Dinah" (1925) that no one is finer than the woman into whose eyes she loves to gaze.[59]

These songs and the poems mentioned earlier recognize and elevate the lesbian subculture as a source of support and solidarity. They also describe lesbian passion and pleasure, giving the sisterhood permission to cherish and enjoy the female body.

LESBIAN EROTICS

Although female heterosexual agency was boosted by 1920s popular culture, a woman's expression of love for another woman remained taboo. Poets and blues performers countered this attitude by validating lesbian subjectivity and normalizing same-sex pleasure. In their lyrics, the homoerotic did not mirror the masculine heterosexual model. It displaced the dominating and possessive male gaze in favor of a cooperative and empowering female gaze, whereby the viewer was aroused by a woman's body and spirit without feeling the need to objectify and control her.

Amy Lowell writes in "Fool o' the Moon" (1925) about "gazing" at the "amazing" sight of a woman's bare breast, noting that her "carnation" nipple is "urgent for a lover's lip."[60] The female speaker's gaze eroticizes the woman's "wheat-white thighs," yet the woman remains the subject of her own sexuality. When the woman boldly tosses aside her garments during a wanton dance, the speaker notes that the dancer's actions are cold and self-possessed, more self-assertion than display for others' approval or gratification. It is the dancer, not the spectator, who acts on her own behalf, empowered to select a lover. The female gaze in the poem expresses the spectator's legitimate lesbian desires, but this gaze does not control the dancer. Observing the dancer ably withhold her attentions from a group of admiring men, the poem's speaker hopes she will be the one out of a hundred that the dancer chooses. The speaker respectfully relates this powerful, sensual, independent woman to the celestial feminine. She ends the poem aspiring to "have lain with Mistress Moon,"[61] a sexual satisfaction that is natural and transcendent.

Lowell's lesbian love poems express an unapologetic desire for the lively and sensual female body. "In Excelsis" (1925) expresses sexual consumption, "I drink your lips, / I eat the whiteness of your hands and feet,"[62] as well as sexual availability and satisfaction, "As a new jar I am empty and open. / Like white water are you who fill the cup of my mouth." The poem "A Bather" (1919) begins with a description of a woman's "bright, naked body"[63] as she confidently strides through a forest. Evocatively lush scents, textures, tastes, sights, and sounds of nature accompany this perfect figure. The lesbian erotic sensibility produces a rich description: "Triumphant in smooth, supple roundness, edged sharp as white ivory, / Cool, perfect, with rose rarely tinting your lips and your breasts, / Swelling out from the green in the opulent curves of ripe fruit." The poem relies on second-person pronouns, inviting female readers to experience being desired in a feminine way that activates their sexual subjectivity.

Gentle and tender touching is central to Lowell's lesbian eroticism. "The On-Looker" (1925) and "A Rainy Night" (1915) portray women in bed together, reclining naked and waiting expectantly for sexual contact. In "Vespers" (1925), the speaker muses that she would like to lift her lover up to a greenhouse roof to duplicate with touch the sensual "burning"[64] appearance of foxgloves at sunset. The short poem "Aubade" (1914) demonstrates Lowell's groundbreaking imagist style with its concrete description of lovemaking. The speaker strips the outer green husk of her beloved's white almond and then "finger[s] the smooth and polished kernel"[65] until pleasure makes it a glittering gem. Another short poem, "A Shower" (1919), uses seemingly innocuous touching to suggest sexual contact. During a rainstorm, the speaker revels in "the touch of you upon my arm / As you press against me that my umbrella / May cover you."[66]

Aware that male poets have long delighted in using flowers to objectify female beauty and fetishize female genitalia, Lowell reclaimed this association to empower women and their sexuality. "Thorn Piece" (1927) compares her lover's physical beauty to a flower. "Merely Statement" (1925) uses the passion-flower to signify her craving for a new sexual partner.[67] "Planning the Garden" (1919) entices a woman with the sensuality of closely packed flowers, which rub each other and "thrust"[68] against swaying, "sticky leaves." The poem ends with the line, "Let us go to bed and dream of flowers." The first lines of "The Weather-Cock Points South" (1919) also uses flowers to describe the female body and suggest sexual contact:

I put your leaves aside,
One by one:
The stiff, broad outer leaves;
The smaller ones,
Pleasant to touch, veined with purple;
The glazed inner leaves.
One by one
I parted you from your leaves,
Until you stood up like a white flower
Swaying slightly in the evening wind.[69]

Nature "imagery, crucially, enabled Lowell to write about lesbian lovemaking without attracting censorship—something she experienced indirectly through her friend D.H. Lawrence, whose novel *The Rainbow* was banned in 1915, in part due to a lesbian love scene."[70]

Gertrude Stein also uses flower imagery to describe and defend lesbian sexuality. Her 1926 poem "Preciosilla" indicates arousal and interest with flower and water imagery: "Lily wet lily wet while. This is so pink so pink in stammer."[71] The repetition of words and sounds establishes an erotic rhythm that could accompany intercourse: "Please be please be get, please get wet, wet naturally . . . go go go go go go, go. Go go."[72] The poem directly denotes the sexual act and finishes by associating desire and affection for a woman named Susie with ice cream, a tasty and pleasurable treat one consumes with the tongue. The line also references Stein's 1913 poem "Susie Asado," a tribute to Spanish flamenco dancer Antonia Marce, or "La Argentina," that Stein and her life-partner Alice B. Toklas admired in Spain. The dancer, "one erotically pulsing woman,"[73] represents sexual agency and female capability. Playful and energetic, the poem repeats a link between Susie Asado and "Sweet sweet sweet sweet sweet tea."[74] Its flamenco rhythm is tied to homoerotic enticement and physical pleasure.

In Stein's 1926 poem "As a Wife Has a Cow: A Love Story," the cow is considered by scholars as a synonym for female orgasm.[75] The poem's repetitious rhythms and sounds, the warmth of long o's and a's and e's, creates a hypnotic sensual energy. In addition, Stein's writing expresses eroticism through "circularity"[76] and "continuous action"; thus, "the text itself is a form of sexual pleasure and fulfillment." This connotation is strong from the beginning: "There is a key to a closet that opens the drawer."[77] Once that drawer is open, the female couple can "do they as they do so. And do they do so."[78] As in much of Stein's poetry, sexuality is presented in terms of repetitive musical tones and seductive dance rhythms.

The lengthy "Lifting Belly" (1917) encourages lesbian readers to see themselves and their desire in sensual language and erotic rhythms: "Kiss my lips over and over and over again she did."[79] Stein used poetic style to "bring her silenced sexuality into language"[80] and arouse female readers.[81] Rather than explicit descriptions of body parts or sex acts, Stein relied on innuendo and readers' imagination. For example, the repeated use of Caesar suggests seizure, or the tremor during orgasm. Certainly the repetition of "lifting belly" suggests lovemaking, representing the joy the speaker experiences with other women and the joy of the speaker achieving her own sexual self-discovery, easily giving pleasure to others and herself. This eroticism is frequently portrayed as natural, normalizing it for uncertain readers.

In addition, Stein's "Pink Melon Joy" (1914) explores the challenges and enjoyment of same-sex intimacy. The poem's "stanzas are meditations on the body, desire, lesbian sex, and love."[82] At one point, the speaker wrestles with her desire by first repeating the word "willing" four times, and then admitting, "I am not more pleased. I am so repressed and I can state it. I can say. It was bitter."[83] Later, she notes several other things that are not pleasing to her, but eventually affirms, "Pink melon and enjoy. / Pink melon by joy."[84] It is clear that "Stein's melon is a woman's sexual pleasure zone, of which Stein is absolutely fascinated with making, witnessing, and describing how they are made pink. To be made pink, they must be touched, pleased, and brought into a state of in-joy."

Unlike Stein and Lowell, Djuna Barnes was conflicted about her own homosexuality, shielding that part of her personal biography from public view. Nevertheless, a number of her poems and novels explore the erotics and emotions of lesbianism without fear or shame. In fact, her work was so influential to twentieth-century lesbian authors that she unintentionally started her own tradition: "As text written by others about women's affective and sexual exchanges, fictions in the Barnes tradition lure and inform."[85] For example, "Six Songs of Khalidine: To the Memory of Mary Pyne" (1923) memorializes a female *New York Press* reporter with whom Barnes had a brief romantic relationship. In the poem, the speaker describes watching her lover sleep, praising the beauty of her body as it repels society's gloominess. Mortality makes their passion stronger yet more tragic, for "It is not gentleness but mad despair"[86] that initiates their kissing. This love is both carnal and transcendent: "Your mouth and mine, and one sweet mouth unseen / We call our soul." After lovemaking, the speaker perceives the specter of death. The poem ends with a hearty farewell from a breathless voice, perhaps made so by another type of death: *la petite mort.*

Barnes's subversive poems from *The Book of Repulsive Women* (1915) disrupt restrictions on female sensuality and champion a lesbian sensibility. The first poem, "From Fifth Avenue Up," glories in a woman's physicality as the speaker and the readers "strain to touch those lang'rous / Length of thighs, / And hear your short sharp modern / Babylonic cries."[87] The speaker asks society to hear the "bitter secret" this woman holds so that "we'll know you for the woman / That you are." The speaker describes her "naked—female" body, enjoying her erotic "pulsing" as "the dappled damp from some vague / Under lip, / Your soft saliva, loosed / With orgy, drip." With this, Barnes attempted to break the binary of patriarchal discourse and carve out "a new space for feminine discourse"[88] that does not consider the female body grotesque or lesbian erotics repulsive.

The poem "From Third Avenue On" plays on society's view that a woman is soiled and immoral, as she "rolls beneath a dirty sheet"[89] and "does not kneel low to confess, / A little conscience, no distress." The tone is sarcastic, lamenting that if she settles down in the way society desires, "her powers slip away" and she loses her direction: "she draws back day by day / From good or bad." She also loses her voice and her vitality: "Sits mouthing meekly in a chair. . . . A vacant space is in her face." Instead of staring into the heavens with ambition and joy, the women become the "living dead." The woman's attempt to avoid being seen as repulsive has made her become repulsive, a state Barnes does not wish upon herself or any other woman. Female sexual otherness is also made visible in "Seen from the 'L,'" which begins with the sight of a nude woman through her apartment window. Wrongly assumed to be repulsive, she is in the glorious prime of youth. Not caring for society's virtues, she is "ravelling grandly into vice."[90]

Barnes's novel *Ladies Almanack* is bawdy and playful as it satirizes social norms and humorously extolls lesbian pleasure. The first paragraph introduces Evangeline Musset who gladly serves as "the Relief and the Distraction of such Girls as in their Hinder Parts, and their Fore Parts, and in whatsoever Parts did suffer them most."[91] She teaches her young protégés that "nothing so solaces it as other Parts as inflamed, or with the Consolation every Woman has at her Finger Tips, or at the very hang of her Tongue." Musset spends the novel introducing women to sexual pleasure, yet she is beholden to no one since she ignores the expectations of her father and the larger society by being active in business and refusing to marry. Barnes's book rejected "compulsory heterosexuality in which women are funneled into traditional marriage, at those marriages which leave women unsatisfied emotionally and/or sexually."[92] As Dame Musset satisfies herself and the members of her Paris salon, Barnes seduces readers to a lesbian eroticism through her explicit descriptions and sharp wit.

A real-life Dame Musset, Bessie Smith was a wildly popular cultural icon, in part, because she was known to be rough, vulgar, and lascivious. Her drunken bawdiness was legendary, as was her resistance to social conventions and restraints.[93] Her lovers included female dancers that toured with her, as well as Ruby Walker, niece of her second husband Jack Gee. The songs Smith chose to sing claimed a sexual freedom that belied the economic and social restrictions on African American women at the time. Her voice is "harsh and coarse, [which] implied she was not trying to please anyone,"[94] except herself. Smith did sing the standard blues tropes of a woman suffering pain and disillusionment at the hands of a man, yet more often than not the women in her songs were confident and triumphant. In "They'll Be a Hot Time in the Old Town Tonight" (1927), she sang her appreciation that "there'll be girls for ev'ry body,"[95] including herself. After a tryst with a like-minded woman, the speaker brags, "I just hugged her and I kissed her." This woman expresses sexual agency, unafraid of desiring another woman or acting to fulfill that desire.

The title of a song Smith performed, "It's Dirty But Good" (1928), indicates the tension of same-sex passion in a sexually repressed society. Early in the song, the speaker tasks the listener with guessing what is "dirty but good" because she is not going to tell. However, the song later reveals, "I know women that don't like men / The way they do is a crying sin." This moral critique against lesbian desire is immediately dismissed in the chorus: "It's dirty but good, oh yes, / It's dirty but good" followed by "There ain't no difference, / It's just dirty but good."[96] The implication is that prudish U.S. society considers all sexual intercourse dirty, so one might as well enjoy it. Moreover, the lyric undermines the negative connotation of "dirty," suggesting that both sexualities should be seen as morally good.

Other songs seem to express a woman's arousal and pleasure from a heterosexual perspective. However, Smith started her career as a male impersonator, and her performances sometimes included gender role reversal, playing the man as she expressed sexual desire for other women.[97] In addition, the nature of the blues defies a "straight" reading of songs about men and women. Not only did Smith refer to female lovers as "my man" and "daddy," but she also altered pronouns in her song lyrics during live performances.[98] For example, she occasionally reversed the gender of her lover while singing "Empty Bed Blues" (1928), proclaiming, "I want a deep-sea diving woman that got a stroke that can't go wrong. / Yeah, touch that bottom, gal, hold it all night long."[99] Thus, she intended blues audiences to consider women in the male roles of seducer and lover.

Songs like "Empty Bed Blues" are filled with sexual imagery and innuendo. In addition to deep-sea diving, the lover grinds the speaker's coffee and thrills her by giving pleasure that "make me wring my hands and cry."[100] The speaker in "I Need a Little Sugar in My Bowl" (1931) desires "a little steam-heat on my floor."[101] She wants the object of her affection to "move your finger, drop something in my bowl." The song ends with reference to oral sex: "Get off your knees, I can't see what you're driving at / It's dark down there looks like a snake." The snake, an ancient reference to women's knowledge of sexuality, joins the more contemporary phrase "jelly roll," mentioned in several songs, as well as Gertrude Stein's poem "Lifting Belly": "Did she say jelly. / Jelly my jelly."[102]

Not ashamed of her sexual interest, Bessie Smith co-wrote the song "Baby Doll" (1926), which boldly asserts a woman's sexual need: "I mean to get my loving all the time."[103] The speaker wants a partner who "can eagle rock and ball the jack," two types of dances that suggest wild physical exertion. Smith wrote the lyrics to "Young Woman's Blues" (1926), which defends a woman's interest in sexual intercourse, "I'm a young woman and ain't done runnin' round."[104] Smith's songs aim to "explode the bourgeois decorum . . .

and negotiate new frontiers for female sensuality."[105] Just as Dame Musset's tongue outlived her, Smith's sexual and musical influence, saved onto records, delighted and inspired listeners long after her death.

LESBIAN LOVE AND FAMILY

Victorian society, comfortable with homosocial love and companionship among women, approved of the "Boston marriage" largely because it was not associated with lesbian eroticism. As the last section discusses, rebellious poets and songwriters of the 1920s intentionally upset this assumption by detailing lesbian desire and physical pleasure. The sexual encounters could be enjoyed as temporary and unemotional liaisons, which some of the songs and poems imply; however, most lyrics frame same-sex passion as important within a committed relationship. Acknowledging lesbian sexuality's existence and characterizing it as positive, these authors helped legitimize and normalize it in the public's eyes. Part of this process was to shift the presentation of erotic desire and pleasure from a titillating performance for the male gaze to one of many important components in a lesbian's personal identity and the serious relationships she pursued. It was not uncommon for the poem or song to place eroticism within an emotionally supportive, intellectually challenging, and spiritually harmonious coupling of women.

Gertrude Stein often wrote about her devotion to Alice B. Toklas, commonly referring to her as "wife." In "Love Song of Alice B" (1921), Stein lauded Alice's kisses and fidelity, especially since "she had everything to choose and she chose me."[106] The poem celebrates their physical passion and links it to their daily lives together. For example, the speaker fondly ruminates on all the things they have done together, like travel abroad and eat specific foods. As she recounts all that they do with and for each other, the speaker admits that they do not often need these foods or trips, but she definitively avows, "How often do we need a kiss. Very often." Additional poems, like "As a Wife Has a Cow: A Love Story," align physical affection and passion with the emotional depth and daily support required for a healthy marriage, a mutual dedication the couple enjoyed from 1907 until Stein's death in 1946.

Stein's "Bundles for Them" (1923) also expresses a sweet devotion and a tender sharing of her life with another. The speaker acknowledges the importance of sacrifice in her relationship and recognizes the difference between love and lust: "If you hear her snore / It is not before you love her."[107] The same quality of deeper affection emerges in "Lifting Belly" when the speaker reports being delighted by her lover's snoring[108] because "I want you to mean a great deal to me."[109] These poems confirm that a lifetime commitment

between women requires physical attraction, deep feelings, and appreciation for daily routine. This commitment also includes a direct understanding and respect for one another. Continuing a relationship with eyes open,
the speaker is not merely in-love with the physical pleasure or an abstract
romantic dream; she is in-love with a specific person and appreciates all her
quirks. "Bundles for Them" expresses admiration Stein had for every quality
Toklas exhibits, calling her "my tender sweet."[110] The speaker is overjoyed
to be near her partner, signaling a sense of consensual co-ownership of each
other's bodies and hearts.

The twenty-ninth section of Stein's "Before the Flowers of Friendship
Faded Friendship Faded" announces her adoration for Toklas and her commitment to same-sex intimacy. Loving another forces the speaker to love herself, resulting in her elevating their relationship to an exalted and regal status.
She calls them king and queen, a socially and divinely sanctioned union in
which they rule themselves and their community. The poem culminates in a
series of lines listing the reasons why same-sex love is beautiful, concluding
with a marital expression of respect and desire, calling the woman her bride.
The speaker emphasizes their mutual support by thanking her lover for being in her life, plus she admits that no one else cares for her as deeply. Stein
declared that without Toklas's enduring love she could only weep.

This partnership enhanced Stein's literary success. Toklas "published
Stein's early works, served as agent and publicist, and nurtured Stein as an
artist. She—and sometimes she alone—was the generous and affirming audience that encouraged Stein in her literary experiments. Toklas offered the
'yes' that Stein claimed every writer needed."[111] It was the valuable yes of
a lover, yes of a "wife," yes of a literary broker and Paris salon host. Their
attachment was so important that Stein wrote *The Autobiography of Alice B.
Toklas* about their life together, a book that has been "canonized as perhaps
the most significant woman-authored autobiography of the twentieth century."[112] As Toklas was a writer who published her own articles and books,
Stein seems to have written *The Autobiography* to honor Toklas and their
marriage rather than appropriate her voice and perspective. Countering the
resentment and disgust expressed by family and admirers, Stein signified the
endless love and respect she shared with her partner.

Amy Lowell also wrote romantic poems to express her devotion to a long-
time partner. Lowell and stage actor Ada Dwyer Russell lived together from
1912 until Lowell's death in 1925.[113] In her work, the poet evoked Russell's
presence with affectionate terms like "dear" and "beloved," reflecting the
deeply personal and emotional foundation for her passionate desire. In "Exer-
cise in Logic" (1925), the "dazzle"[114] of the woman she calls, "my Dear," lin-
gers for years, signaling a life-long bond so intense that it causes the pigments

on a painting to slowly fade. "White Currants" (1925) suggests the offer of sensual, erotic gifts belies a deeper emotional need in the couple's relationship: "You may find them tart, or sweet, or merely agreeable in colour, / So long as you accept them. / And me."[115] The emotional implications of these love poems demonstrate her deep connection with Russell.

Lowell's erotic lyrics highlight the power and joy of sensual touching, the physical contact that intensifies the couple's emotional ties. Her poem "The Anniversary" (1925) explores a tactile exchange between women that engages their emotions, "Touch me with your love."[116] While flowers in other poems represents the female body and lesbian sexuality, the speaker in "The Anniversary" claims she has roses to offer even when flowers are not in bloom, implying a deeper emotional commitment. She gives humor and praise to her life-partner, requesting mercy and forgiveness when her words or actions wound her beloved. The true expression of her love does not come from her words but straight from her heart, including the revelation that one death will kill them both because "your veins hold my sap."[117] The poem ends with the expectation of longevity for their love and their relationship, "With morning we start again. / Another ten years."[118] The same sentiment appears in "A Decade" (1919), in which her initial sensation of sensual hunger, "you were like red wine and honey," develops over the years into emotional nourishment, "Now you are like morning bread, / Smooth and pleasant."[119]

The poetic persona sings to "the lady of my choice"[120] in Lowell's "Song for a Viola d'Amore" (1925). This lady, Ada Russell, is "perfectness complete"[121] because of her lovely presence and voice, as well as her sweet body. In addition to feeding herself on the lady's sensuality, the speaker internalizes what she feels and engages what she thinks. Just as Lowell's eroticism is more about women being sexual subjects than sexual objects, the relational and familial aspects of her poetry encourage her partner to "Speak, speak, Beloved,"[122] in "Prime" (1925). By speaking what she feels, Russell will "say little things" that run to the heart of the poet, deepening their bond. This connection can also be expressed through silence, as the poem "April" (1919) implies that a lover need not speak because merely sharing the same space with her life-partner will make everything in that space more beautiful and precious.[123]

As in Stein's poems, these works by Lowell demonstrate an appreciation for the little things her lover does. The focus of her admiration in "A Sprig of Rosemary" (1919) shifts from the woman's face (i.e., superficial beauty) to her hands (i.e., actions that unite the couple and build them a better future). Watching her sew or hold a book reveals "the soft brightness which is your soul,"[124] creating a bond that defies time and death. "Penumbra" (1919) is set after Lowell's death, a forecast of Russell's life without her. Lowell comforts

Ada by stating she will not feel lonely while looking at the furniture in the house they shared, "For these things are a part of me. / And my love will go on speaking to you / Through the chairs, and the tables, and the pictures."[125] They love with their bodies, but their love transcends the physical. "Madonna of the Evening Flowers" (1919) projects a spiritual tone, in which the speaker, mirroring the sacred union of a traditional marriage, kneels in religious devotion to the woman she loves.[126]

The composition by Lowell most reminiscent of marriage is probably "On Christmas Eve" (1927). In it, the speaker makes what she believes is a futile attempt to explain the depth and importance of her love. She rejoices that her life with Russell has made her whole, given her purpose, and forced her to build toward the future. She praises their relationship for making Lowell a better person and a better author, one with greater purpose and foresight. Russell does a "hundred kindly daily things" [127] to dispel Lowell's self-doubt and spark her creativity. She rejoices at feeling the peace and joy her dearest leaves like a scent in each room of their house. Lowell concludes that her lover's existence is vital to their happiness, that life is pointless without her partner's physical, intellectual, emotional, and spiritual presence.

Similar to Stein with Toklas and Lowell with Russell, Djuna Barnes writes about her long-time partner Thelma Wood. The poem "Six Songs of Khalidine" refers to their deeply felt love and the novel *Nightwood* (1936) shares the betrayal she felt after their relationship ended. The profits from her novel *Ladies Almanack* were used "to help pay for her companion Thelma Wood's appendectomy."[128] Barnes denied her lesbian identity for practical reasons, as she worried the publicity would suppress book sales. Nevertheless, her writing shares the physical sensations and emotional depths of being a lesbian and finding, or losing, a life partner.

The theme of unrequited love appears in a number of Barnes's poems, particularly the ones that explored lesbian chivalry. The medieval courtly love tradition had been revived by the Victorians, scenarios in which a man expresses his admiration and affection to a woman who is outside his social circle and he cannot marry. At a time when lesbians could not legally marry, a number of female poets adopted a chivalrous dynamic to present lesbian desire on the same level as the purest, more honorable vision of heterosexuality. For example, Barnes's "To One in Favour" (1919) and Lowell's "In a Castle" (1914) used "traditional Gothic elements such as knights, castles and manor houses . . . to emphasize the romantic and affective elements of lesbian desire."[129] Lowell's poem confronts masculine possessiveness and heteronormativity: "Is it guilt to free a lady from her palsied lord, absent and fighting, terribly abhorred?"[130] Barnes's poem contests society's erasure of homosexuality by asking a queen, after the death of the king, to "raise up"[131] and find true contentment with the woman she kissed "wilder, madder" than her husband. The poems honor true love and suggest that lesbians should be allowed to marry.

Bessie Smith wrote and sang songs that salute lesbian eroticism and champion a sisterhood among women. However, it does not appear she sang about lesbian life partners. Blues lyrics do not typically hale healthy and harmonious heterosexual relationships either, focusing on how distraught a woman feels when a spouse or lover cheats on her and leaves her for someone else. For instance, the speaker in "Lady Luck Blues" (1923) bemoans her loneliness after her best friend ran off with her man.[132] Another example is the bitter competition between two women for the same man in "My Man Blues" (1925), co-written by Smith.[133]

In the blues, a woman believes a new love-interest is on the horizon. Unfortunately, there is no reason to trust the new love affair will last longer or be any happier than the failed one. In "It Won't Be You" (1928), written by Smith, the speaker confidently asserts that she will easily replace the person who left her.[134] However, she admits that she is willing to accept anyone, including someone that would abuse her, just to spite her former lover. Smith's songs may not offer a route to long-term romantic bliss, but many of them do defend unconventional female identities and exhort social activism.

FIGHT FOR SOCIAL CHANGE

Mainstream culture of the 1920s resisted seeing lesbianism as anything but a sinful perversion of nature, attacking anyone associated with it in order to eradicate it, or at least confine it to the silent, dark corners of society. Lowell, Barnes, and Stein composed poetic lyrics and Smith wrote and performed blues lyrics that counteracted the restrictive patriarchal and heteronormative discourses shaping women's identities and regulating their behavior. They brought a lesbian sensibility to the public's attention and championed the sisterhood, the eroticism, and the long-term companionship that they shared with the women in their lives.

Blues women like Bessie Smith wrote and performed songs that raised awareness about deeply held racist, misogynistic, and homophobic attitudes. The speaker in Smith's song "'Tain't Nobody's Business" (1923) ignores the criticism of her lifestyle, proclaiming that she does what she wants without asking anyone's permission.[135] It is one of several songs Smith performed that emphasize why a lesbian African American woman needs to remain defiant about her self-worth and autonomy. Smith knew the blues artist's biggest impact was on her own community, as her work "speaks directly of and to the

folks who have suffered pain and assures them that they are not alone; someone understands."[136] Smith and other blues women were advocates for the
underrepresented and ignored, speaking out against "the intense repression of
the black female and lesbian voice."[137] A strong feminist figure of her time,
Smith wrote and performed songs that laid important groundwork for larger
social and political movements. What would later become important "activist
stances are inconceivable without the consciousness such songs suggest."[138]

Smith's songs defended female sexuality, as she commanded the ability to
act in her own self-interest and not remain dependent on a man. Her persona
in these songs actively battled male disrespect and domestic violence, asserting her quality as a human being and a woman. Smith demonstrated the
ability to speak on her own behalf just by performing in nightclubs and performance halls, which portrayed her as a vocal self-advocate and a teacher-
mentor for other women who had not yet learned these skills.

Liberated and independent, Smith modeled strength and confidence. Just
as "she wore her blackness with pride,"[139] I would argue that she also wore
her sexual orientation with pride. Her libidinous and rebellious blues persona
reflected an ardent reclamation of her body and validation of a healthy but
unconventional sexuality. Smith voiced her opposition to injustice with songs
that demanded freedom, respect, and equality for women. She and other
"blues women had no qualms about announcing female desire. . . . Such af-
firmations of sexual autonomy and open expressions of female sexual desire
give historical voice to possibilities of equality not articulated elsewhere."[140]
Smith's medium, music, was perhaps the most communal and democratic
form of self-expression at the time, as her voice was heard by a wide swath
of the nation and her subversive messages influenced blues singers, poets,
and the general public.

Like Bessie Smith, Amy Lowell used her voice to communicate a feminist
message of social change. In her article "Poetry as a Spoken Art," Lowell
implies that poetry can be a way to claim one's humanity: "Words are the
birthright of humanity. To be dumb is to be deformed."[141] Her poetry readings
and public lectures were a "battlefield"[142] where Lowell created controversy
and invited debate. In addition to promoting the work of female poets, she
scandalized conservative audiences by speaking frankly about female sexuality and displacing traditional poetics in favor of the radical "New Poetry."[143]
She justified the new poetic style of imagism, liberated from tired Old World
conventions, and lampooned sexist critiques of women's writing.

Her long satirical poem *A Critical Fable* (1922) bluntly outlines the typical male critic's opinion that he "hardly can bear to allow that a woman / Is
ever quite equal to man in the arts; / The two sexes cannot be ranked counterparts."[144] Arguing with Lowell like audience members at many of her lectures,

the male critic in the poem expresses outrage at one woman's literary success and declares, "Man will always love woman and always pull down / What she does."[145] He feels it is his duty to combat her attempt to gain recognition and authority, crashing her dreams like so many fancy lady's dishes. Lowell rebuffed such patriarchal nonsense with the contention that women can and do succeed as poets because they have something worthwhile to say to an audience eager to hear it. The truth of this claim is substantiated by successful literary careers like hers and popular literary magazines founded and run by women, such as *Poetry: A Magazine of Verse* (1912–), *Egoist* (1914–1919), and *The Little Review* (1914–1929).

Lowell further challenged the male gaze with "To a Gentleman Who Wanted to See the First Drafts of My Poems in the Interest of Psychological Research into the Workings of the Creative Mind" (1927). The poem's speaker resents the double standard male critics teach readers to use with a woman's creative output, and she criticizes the expectation that she may write only what will please them. The male critic, hoping to expose her work as a fraud, accepts payment to "dissect"[146] the female poet and judge her work via abstract calculations and equations. He entirely misses the subtlety behind her imagery and words, namely her lived experience that exists "'twixt an ecstasy and heartbreak."

Finding the scholarly gentlemen unqualified to judge or even fully understand her work, Lowell resists his aggressive and sexual attacks on her poetry, criticizing his prying hands because they "wrench me flesh from bone."[147] Upset he has not asked permission to penetrate the secrets of her writing, she considers the male critic blind, foolish, and insulting. She refuses to consent to his vivisection of her poems with a commanding, "I tell you 'No!'" The poem intimates that female poets, critics, and readers must choose to take a different approach than this gentleman. Her poems purposely lie to this critic and other male readers, but she knows women will read between the lines to find the true power and beauty of a lesbian sensibility, causing them to join her in telling the patriarchal establishment, "No!"

Lowell also takes the establishment to task in "East, West, North, and South of a Man" (1925), referring to "the absurd lie"[148] that makes men assume they possess "vast importance." This attitude causes "his women to weep and regret"[149] because they are not permitted scholarly, creative, economic, or leadership opportunities. In the poem, famous female storyteller Scheherazade dismisses this common criticism of talented women: "who are you to aspire."[150] Instead, she spins her tales for the purpose of enchanting her audience and saving her life. By the third section, the male character's superior self-image and absolute social control fades and vanishes, causing him to become old, blind, and inactive. The poem concludes with Lowell asking female readers to "Draw the curtains. . . . Since neither the old gentleman nor Minerva will speak to us, / I think we had best ignore them and go on as we are."[151] Thus, the final curtain comes down on the stage production of male superiority and misogyny once women dare to ignore male self-importance and aspire to greatness on their own.

Djuna Barnes started performing her public opposition to social norms years before beginning her literary career. Taking a job at twenty-one as a freelance reporter for the *Brooklyn Daily Eagle* in 1913, Barnes wrote sensationalist articles that combined "performative journalism and feminist activism."[152] For example, she underwent being force-fed to write "How It Feels to Be Forcibly Fed," an exposé about the cruelty being imposed on British suffragists in 1914. She sacrificed her body to get the story and protest an unjust government policy. However, after eight years of faithful work, she was fired for not publishing an interview with a woman who was raped six times. Barnes herself was raped as a young child, which she later retold in the novels *Ryder* (1928) and *The Antiphon* (1958). Her compassion for this victim, like her outrage at the treatment of the British suffragists, caused Barnes to make a principled stand for a woman's right to dignity and basic humanity. Barnes's stunt reporting did spotlight important social issues U.S. society grappled with, particularly "the ways people look at bodies . . . especially the female body as a spectacle."[153] Consequently, Barnes's poetry and novels appropriated the male gaze, as she invited readers to witness and appreciate non-standard bodies and sexualities.

Wanting to sell her poetry and fiction to a wide audience caused Barnes to be ambivalent about using her own sexual orientation to make a political statement. She famously answered a question about her relationship with Thelma Wood by stating, "I'm not a lesbian, I just loved Thelma."[154] Barnes did not want to make her homosexuality public after having critics and readers turn her work *The Book of Repulsive Women* against her, using it as a tract to endorse misogyny and homophobia.[155] She intended the poems to undermine patriarchal heteronormativity, but that was clear only if the readers decoded the verses' true message. Most readers misunderstood the satire and applauded the poems' superficial repulsion of sexually active women and the supposed grotesquery of the lesbian body. Barnes's poems about "repulsive" women attempted to elevate readers above a binary view of sexuality, presenting women who thrive outside the realm of acceptable femininity and represent "a form of radical alterity."[156] The poet was disappointed that heterosexual readers did not make this connection, but she did not abandon her quarrel with compulsory heterosexuality.

Barnes's *Ladies Almanack*, published a decade after *The Book of Repulsive Women*, is a satire much more explicit in its rebuke of homophobic social codes. The novel makes a case against heterosexual conformity and traditional marriage, which prove unsatisfactory for many women. The book's lesbian characters speak frankly about the pleasures of their sexuality and the merits of same-sex marriage. Dame Musset tells the younger generation that a woman is wise when she realizes she can have a meaningful identity without being a conventional wife and mother. Her use of wit and wisdom make traditional views look ridiculously rigid and old fashioned. Barnes, through her characters, intended to convert women to a lesbian sensibility.[157] In particular, Dame Musset's erotic seduction aligns with a broader feminism, advocating women's resistance to patriarchal regulation of their bodies and sexual identities, as well as the freedom to love and support other women in personal and professional situations.

It is noteworthy that Barnes drew her own illustrations for her newspaper articles and books, including *Ladies Almanack* and *The Book of Repulsive Women*. Her images add to the transgressive nature of her writing, with numerous images representing sexual pleasure and depicting women urinating.[158] Her work challenged the status quo by humanizing lesbian identities and by gesturing "toward a queer futurity."[159]

In her Paris salon, Gertrude Stein also employed poetry to raise the visibility of lesbianism and undercut gender and sexual binaries. Stein and Barnes "embrace aspects of traditional feminine identities that had become denigrated or marginalized . . . but at the same time they challenge and reinvent representations of women."[160] Stein's texts deconstruct representational politics and destabilize "what is already massively stabilized through institutions, laws, entrenched practices, and habits of mind."[161] These works resist patriarchal control and validate alternative identities, directing readers to open their minds and hearts to unconventional ideas. For example, "Lifting Belly" refers to open expression of female sensuality and pride for one's lesbian identity, but it also refers to changing how society views lesbian self-representation, that being proud and vocal changed other women's minds and brought them together. Stein demonstrates in poems like "Love Song of Alice B" that women have a choice of who to love and, luckily, her beloved Alice B. Toklas chose her.

Stein aimed to inspire lesbian readers, encouraging them to see themselves in her writing and to speak their minds in public. Her "Before the Flowers of Friendship Faded Friendship" seeks to unshackle women who want to express their passion for other women and for their own identity. In "Lifting Belly," "there is no subordinate position, only association"[162] as Stein's writing empowers, enriches, and encourages all women, but especially lesbians. The poem asks women to throw off the weight of male-dominated society by rising above its expectations and restrictions. This act of personal capability unites women, who together can disrupt patriarchal discourse. "Lifting belly is a language,"[163] a feminine discourse of passion, protest, and self-assertion that enables each woman to communicate her splendid physical, intellectual, emotional, creative, and spiritual selfhood.

In conclusion, the 1920s was certainly a decade of heterosexual revolution, where "Victorian values were challenged, sex was celebrated as an icon of freedom, and women asserted themselves as sexual agents."[164] It was also a time of aggressive repression and policing of gay and lesbian sex, yet "Local gay and lesbian communities formed, grew, and diversified across the United States" as those "interested in same-sex sex, love, and intimacy developed support networks, social bonds, and cultures of resistance." Unfortunately, the homosexual community faced too many obstacles to mount a full-fledged revolution at that time. Such efforts would have to wait a few more decades. Nevertheless, authors and blues singers of the Roaring Twenties gave lesbianism a public voice that helped women love themselves and each other.

NOTES

1. Lillian Faderman, "Lesbian Chic in the '20s," UCLA Film and Television Archive, 1990, accessed Dec. 17, 2021, https://www.cinema.ucla.edu/sites/default/files/Lesbian%20Chic%20Lillian%20Faderman%201990.pdf.

2. Francis, *The Secret Treachery of Words*, xvii.

3. Neilsen, *Un-American Womanhood*, 18.

4. Kevin Mumford, *Interzones* (New York: Columbia University Press, 1997), 4.

5. Thomas Fahy, "Unsilencing Lesbianism in the Early Fiction of Gayl Jones," in *After the Pain: Critical Essays on Gayl Jones*, eds. Fiona Mills and Keith B. Mitchell (New York: Peter Lang, 2006), 216.

6. Zeitz, *Flapper*, 119.

7. Raymond A. Smith and Donald P. Haider-Markel, *Gay and Lesbian Americans and Political Participation: A Reference Handbook* (Santa Barbara: ABC-CLIO, 2002), 5; and Jonathan Ned Katz, *The Invention of Heterosexuality* (Chicago: University of Chicago Press, 2007), 43.

8. Jeffrey Weeks, *Sex, Politics and Society: The Regulation of Sexuality since 1800*, 4th ed., (New York: Taylor and Francis, 2017), 146.

9. Audrey Hampshire, "The Lavender Lens: Lesbianism in the United States 1870–1969," *Nonviolent Social Change: the Bulletin of the Manchester College Peace Studies Institute* 35 (2008), accessed December 17, 2021, http://ww2.manchester.edu/peacestudies/bulletin/2008/documents/Hampshire.pdf.

10. Katz, *The Invention of Heterosexuality*, 90.

11. George Chauncey, *Gay New York: Gender, Urban Culture, and the Making of the Gay Male World 1890–1940* (New York: Basic Books, 1994), accessed Dec. 17, 2021, https://books.google.com.

12. Hermione Lee, *Willa Cather: Double Lives* (New York: Vintage, 2017), xiv.

13. Melissa J. Homestead, "Willa Cather, Sarah Orne Jewett, and the Historiography of Lesbian Sexuality," in *Willa Cather and the Nineteenth Century. Cather Studies 10*, eds. Richard Millington and Anne Kaufman (Lincoln: University of Nebraska Press, 2015), 27.

14. Steve Cohen, "The Captive, a pioneering play about a lesbian," *The Cultural Critic*, accessed April 2, 2021, https://theculturalcritic.com/the-captive-a-pioneering-play-about-a-lesbian.

15. Sherrie A. Inness, "Who's Afraid of Stephen Gordon?: The Lesbian in the United States Popular Imagination of the 1920s," *NWSA Journal* 4, no. 3 (1992), 303–304.

16. Lillian Faderman, *Odd Girls and Twilight Lovers: A History of Lesbian Life in Twentieth-Century America* (New York: Columbia University Press, 2012), 309.

17. Djuna Barnes, *Ladies Almanack* (New York: New York University Press, 1992), 34.

18. Vito Russo, *The Celloid Closet: Homosexuality in the Movies* (New York: HarperCollins, 1987), 24.

19. Pamela Hutchinson, *Pandora's Box* (London: The British Film Institute, 2018), 18.

20. Laura Horak, *Girls Will Be Boys: Cross-Dressed Women, Lesbians, and American Cinema, 1908–1934* (New Brunswick: Rutgers University Press, 2016), 1.

21. Faderman, *Odd Girls and Twilight Lovers*, 5.

22. Amy Lowell, *What's O'Clock* (New York: Houghton Mifflin, 1925), 127.

23. Christine Woyshner, "Teaching the Women's Club Movement in United States History," *The Social Studies* 93, no. 1 (2002), 12.

24. Hine, "Rape and the Inner Lives of Black Women in the Middle West," 917.

25. Emily Milton, "Triangular Identities and Flourishing Sexualities: 1920s-'30s Harlem as a Positive Queer Space for the Formation of a Black Lesbian Identity," *Hard Wire: The Undergraduate Journal of Sexual Diversity Studies* (2013), 16.

26. Sally Munt, *Heroic Desire: Lesbian Identity and Cultural Space* (New York: New York University Press, 1998), 40.

27. A.B. Christa Schwarz, *Gay Voices of the Harlem Renaissance* (Bloomington: Indiana University Press, 2003), 9.

28. Kathryn R. Kent, "'Lullaby for a Lady's Lady': Lesbian Identity in Ladies Almanack," *Review of Contemporary Fiction* 13, no. 3 (1993), 90.

29. Barnes, *Collected Poems* (Madison: University of Wisconsin Press, 2005), 89.

30. Ibid., 99.

31. Ibid., 88.

32. Lowell, *What's O'Clock,* 133.

33. Ibid., 127.

34. Ibid., 135.

35. Ibid., 132.

36. Ibid., 237.

37. Ibid., 238.

38. Lowell, *The Complete Poetical Works of Amy Lowell* (New York: Houghton Mifflin, 1955), 551.

39. Ibid., 537.

40. Lucy Daniel, *Gertrude Stein* (London: Reaktion, 2009), 7.

41. Rebecca Mark, Introduction to *Lifting Belly* (Tallahassee: The Naiad Press, 1995), xxxii.

42. Gertrude Stein, *Lifting Belly* (Tallahassee: The Naiad Press, 1995), 4.

43. Gertrude Stein, "Before the Flowers of Friendship Faded," *Poetry Nook*, accessed April 2, 2021, https://www.poetrynook.com/poem/flowers-friendship-faded-friendship-faded.

44. Daphne Duval Harrison, *Black Pearls: Blues Queens of the 1920s* (New Brunswick: Rutgers University Press, 2000), 52.

45. Marta Miquel-Baldellou, "The Beloved Purple of Their Eyes: Inheriting Bessie Smith's Politics of Sexuality," *Miscelanea: a Journal of English and American Studies* 36 (2007), 71.

46. Aaron Bachhofer, "Smith, Bessie" in *LGBTQ Americans in the U.S. Political System*, ed. Jason Pierceson (Santa Barbara: ABC-CLIO, 2019), 385.

47. William Barlow, "Black Music on the Radio during the Jazz Age," *African American Review* 29, no. 2 (1995), 325.

48. Miquel-Baldellou, "The Beloved Purple of Their Eyes," 73.

49. Cookie Woolner, "'Woman Slain in Queer Love Brawl': African American Women, Same-Sex Desire, and Violence in the Urban North, 1920–1929," *The Journal of African American History* 100, no. 3 (2015), 406.

50. Woolner, "'Woman Slain in Queer Love Brawl,'" 409.

51. Song Lyrics, "I Used to Be Your Sweet Mama," accessed April 2, 2021, http://www.songlyrics.com/bessie-smith/i-used-to-be-your-sweet-mama-lyrics.

52. Song Lyrics, "Pinchbacks—Take 'Em Away," accessed April 2, 2021, http://www.songlyrics.com/bessie-smith/pinchbacks-take-em-away-lyrics.

53. Michael Taft, *Talkin' to Myself: Blues Lyrics, 1921–1942* (New York: Rutledge, 2005), 526.

54. Flash Lyrics, "I've Got What It Takes," accessed April 2, 2021, https://www.flashlyrics.com/lyrics/bessie-smith/ive-got-what-it-takes-but-it-breaks-my-heart-to-give-it-away-61.

55. Hazel Carby, *Cultures in Babylon: Black Britain and African America* (London: Verso, 1999), 16.

56. Outhistory, "Ma Rainey's 'Prove It on Me Blues,'" accessed April 2, 2021, https://outhistory.org/exhibits/show/rainey/rainey2.

57. Protest Song Lyrics, "B.D. Woman's Blues, song lyrics," accessed April 2, 2021, http://www.protestsonglyrics.net/LGBT_Songs/BD-Womans-Blues.phtml.

58. Michael Waters, "A Pride Month Playlist, Brought to You by the Jazz Age," Atlas Obscura, June 9, 2017, accessed Dec. 17, 2021, https://www.atlasobscura.com/articles/queer-1920s-music-videos.

59. Flash Lyrics, "Dinah," accessed April 2, 2021, https://www.flashlyrics.com/lyrics/ethel-waters/dinah-84.

60. Lowell, *What's O'Clock,* 154–155.

61. Ibid., 158.

62. Ibid., 55.

63. Lowell, *Pictures of the Floating World* (New York: Houghton Mifflin, 1921), 130.

64. Lowell, *What's O'Clock,* 53.

65. Lowell, *The Complete Poetical Works of Amy Lowell*, 73.

66. Ibid., 213.

67. Lowell, *What's O'Clock,* 32–33.

68. Lowell, *The Complete Poetical Works of Amy Lowell*, 222.

69. Lowell, *Pictures of the Floating World*, 211.

70. Sarah Parker, "Amy Lowell's Appetites: Food, Consumption and Homoerotic Desire in Amy Lowell's Poetry," in *Fat Sex: New Directions in Theory and Activism*, eds. Helen Hester and Caroline Walters (New York: Routledge, 2015), 171.

71. Stein, *Selected Writings of Gertrude Stein* (New York: Vintage Books, 1990), 550.

72. Ibid., 550–551.

73. Doris T. Wight, "Woman as Eros-Rose in Gertrude Stein's *Tender Buttons* and Contemporaneous Portraits," *Wisconsin Academy of Sciences, Arts and Letters* 74 (1986), 38.

74. Stein, *Selected Writings of Gertrude Stein*, 549.

75. Ulla E. Dydo, *Gertrude Stein: The Language That Rises: 1923–1934* (Evanston: Northwestern University Press, 2003), 28; and Francis Mark Mondimore, *A Natural History of Homosexuality* (Baltimore: The Johns Hopkins University Press, 1996), 64.

76. Janie Utell, *Literary Couples and 20th-Century Life Writing: Narrative and Intimacy* (London: Bloomsbury Academic, 2020), 67–68.

77. Gertrude Stein, *A Stein Reader* (Evanston: Northwestern University Press, 1993), 454.

78. Stein, *A Stein Reader*, 461.

79. Stein, *Lifting Belly*, 20.

80. Mark, Introduction to *Lifting Belly,* xxi.

81. Ibid., xi.

82. Lesley Graydon, "How Pink Is Your Melon, Joy? The Erotic, Sexual Language of Gertrude Stein," accessed March 20, 2021, https://lesleygraydon.com.

83. Stein, *A Stein Reader*, 286.

84. Ibid., 294.

85. Carolyn Allen, *Following Djuna: Women Lovers and the Erotics of Loss* (Bloomington: Indiana University Press, 1996), 2.

86. Barnes, *Collected Poems*, 86.

87. Djuna Barnes, *The Book of Repulsive Women* (New York: Bruna Chap Books, 1915), accessed December 17, 2021, https://digital.library.upenn.edu/women/barnes/repulsive/repulsive.html.

88. Quinn Gilman-Forlini, "Erasing the Grotesque: An Analysis of Djuna Barnes' Detestation for the Book of Repulsive Women," *Apollon* 9 (2019), 34.

89. Barnes, *The Book of Repulsive Women.*

90. Ibid.

91. Barnes, *Ladies Almanack*, 6.

92. Allison Elise Carey, "Domesticity and the Modernist Aesthetic: F.T. Marinetti, Djuna Barnes, and Gertrude Stein" (PhD diss., University of Tennessee, 2003), 28.

93. Jana Evans Braziel, "'Bye, Bye Baby': Race, Bisexuality, and the Blues in the Music of Bessie Smith and Janis Joplin," *Popular Music and Society* 27, no. 1 (2004), 3.

94. Miquel-Baldellou, "The Beloved Purple of Their Eyes," 74.

95. Flash Lyrics, "There'll Be a Hot Time in the Old Town Tonight," accessed April 5, 2021, https://www.flashlyrics.com/lyrics/bessie-smith/therell-be-a-hot-time-in-the-old-town-tonight-98.

96. Historical Homos, "Ma and Bessie: Queens of the Bisexual Blues," April 26, 2020, accessed Dec. 17, 2021, https://www.historicalhomos.com/cumming-to-you-live/bisexual-blues.

97. Braziel, "'Bye, Bye Baby,'" 7.

98. Ibid., 16.

99. Maria V. Johnson, "'Jelly Jelly Jellyroll': Lesbian Sexuality and Identity in Women's Blues," *Women & Music* 7 (2003), 31.

100. Flash Lyrics, "Empty Bed Blues," accessed April 5, 2021, https://www.flashlyrics.com/lyrics/bessie-smith/empty-bed-blues-56.

101. Song Lyrics, "I Need a Little Sugar in My Bowl," accessed April 5, 2021, http://www.songlyrics.com/bessie-smith/need-a-little-sugar-in-my-bowl-lyrics.

102. Stein, *Lifting Belly*, 24.

103. Flash Lyrics, "Baby Doll," accessed April 13, 2021, https://www.flashlyrics.com/lyrics/bessie-smith/baby-doll-41.

104. Lyrics Mode, "Young Woman's Blues," accessed April 5, 2021, https://www.lyricsmode.com/lyrics/b/bessie_smith/young_womans_blues.html.

105. Shayne Lee, *Erotic Revolutionaries: Black Women, Sexuality, and Popular Culture* (Lanham: Hamilton Books, 2010), xii.

106. Paul Russell, *The Gay 100: A Ranking of the Most Influential Gay Men and Lesbians, Past and Present* (New York: Kensington Books, 1995), 29.

107. Stein, *A Stein Reader*, 379.

108. Stein, *Lifting Belly*, 45.

109. Ibid., 39.

110. Ibid., 379.

111. Linda Simon, *The Biography of Alice B. Toklas* (Lincoln: University of Nebraska Press, 1991), xi.

112. Anna Linzie, *The True Story of Alice B. Toklas: A Study of Three Autobiographies* (Iowa City: University of Iowa Press, 2006), 2.

113. Lillian Faderman, "'Which, Being Interpreted, Is as May Be, or Otherwise': Ada Russell in Amy Lowell's Life and Work," in *Amy Lowell, American Modern*, eds. Adrienne Munich and Melissa Bradshaw (New Brunswick: Rutgers University Press, 2004), 59.

114. Lowell, *What's O'Clock*, 60.

115. Ibid., 59.

116. Ibid., 44.

117. Ibid., 46.

118. Ibid., 48.

119. Lowell, *The Complete Poetical Works of Amy Lowell*, 217.

120. Lowell, *What's O'Clock*, 49.

121. Ibid., 51.

122. Ibid., 52.

123. Lowell, *The Complete Poetical Works of Amy Lowell*, 213.

124. Ibid., 216.

125. Lowell, *Pictures of the Floating World*, 97.

126. Ibid., 45.

127. Lowell, *The Complete Poetical Works of Amy Lowell*, 557.

128. Carey, "Domesticity and the Modernist Aesthetic," 109.

129. Jamie Hovey, "Lesbian Chivalry in Amy Lowell's Sword Blades and Poppy Seed," in *Amy Lowell, American Modern*, eds. Adrienne Munich and Melissa Bradshaw (New Brunswick: Rutgers University Press, 2004), 81.

130. Lowell, *The Complete Poetical Works of Amy Lowell*, 60.

131. Barnes, *Collected Poems*, 71.

132. Angela Y. Davis, *Blues Legacies and Black Feminism: Gertrude Ma Rainey, Bessie Smith, and Billie Holiday* (New York: Vintage, 1998), 306.

133. Flash Lyrics, "My Man Blues," accessed April 5, 2021, https://www.flashlyrics.com/lyrics/bessie-smith/my-man-blues-09.

134. Song Lyrics, "It Won't Be You," accessed April 5, 2021, http://www.songlyrics.com/bessie-smith/it-won-t-be-you-lyrics.

135. Last FM, "'Taint Nobody's Business," accessed April 5, 2021, https://www.last.fm/music/Bessie+Smith/_/%27Tain%27t+Nobody%27s+Business+If+I+Do/+lyrics.

136. Harrison, *Black Pearls*, 6.

137. Hazel Carby, "'Woman's Era': Rethinking Black Feminist Thought," in *African American Literary Theory: A Reader*, ed. Winston Napier (New York: New York University Press, 2000), 246.

138. Davis, *Blues Legacies and Black Feminism*, 119.

139. Elaine Feinstein, *Bessie Smith: Empress of the Blues* (New York: Penguin, 1985), 29.

140. Davis, *Blues Legacies and Black Feminism*, 24.

141. Amy Lowell, *Poetry and Poets: Essays* (New York: Biblo & Tannen, 1971), 13.

142. Melissa Bradshaw, *Amy Lowell, Diva Poet* (Surrey: Ashgate, 2011), 60.

143. Bradshaw, *Amy Lowell, Diva Poet*, 58.

144. Amy Lowell, *A Critical Fable* (New York: Houghton Mifflin, 1922), 44.

145. Ibid., 45.

146. Ibid., 535.

147. Ibid., 536.

148. Lowell, *What's O'Clock*, 5.

149. Ibid., 4.

150. Ibid., 6.

151. Ibid., 13.

152. Barbara Green, "Spectacular Confessions: 'How It Feels to Be Forcibly Fed,'" *The Review of Contemporary Fiction* 13, no. 3 (1993), 70.

153. Jean Marie Lutes, *Front Page Girls: Women Journalists in American Culture and Fiction, 1880-1930* (Ithaca: Cornell University Press, 2006), 147.

154. Susana S. Martins, "Gender Trouble and Lesbian Desire in Djuna Barnes's 'Nightwood,'" *Frontiers: A Journal of Women Studies* 20, no. 3 (1999), 108.

155. Gilman-Forlini, "Erasing the Grotesque," 34.

156. Meghan C. Fox, "'Vivid and Repulsive as the Truth': Hybridity and Sexual Difference in Djuna Barnes's The Book of Repulsive Women," *The Space Between: Literature and Culture 1914–1945* 12 (2016), accessed December 17, 2021, https://scalar.usc.edu/works/the-space-between-literature-and-culture-1914-1945/vol12_2016_fox.

157. Kent, "'Lullaby for a Lady's Lady,'" 90.

158. Frances M. Doughty, "Gilt on Cardboard: Djuna Barnes as Illustrator of Her Life and Work," in *Silence and Power: A Reevaluation of Djuna Barnes*, ed. Mary Lynn Broe (Carbondale: Southern Illinois University Press, 1991), 147.

159. Fox, "'Vivid and Repulsive as the Truth.'"

160. Julie Goodspeed-Chadwick, *Modernist Women Writers and War: Trauma and the Female Body in Djuna Barnes, H.D., and Gertrude Stein* (Baton Rouge: LSU Press, 2011), 16.

161. Leigh Gilmore, *Autobiographics: A Feminist Theory of Women's Self-representation* (Ithaca: Cornell University Press, 1994), 204.

162. Mark, Introduction to *Lifting Belly*, xix.

163. Stein, *Lifting Belly*, 17.

164. Marc Stein, *Rethinking the Gay and Lesbian Movement* (New York: Routledge, 2012), 33.

Chapter Five

Political Activism
Asserting the Creative Self

Rebellious 1920s women refused to accept confinement within traditional gender roles, spurning demands for them to be submissive, modest, passive, chaste, domestic. Instead, they participated in the public sphere where they could more freely express their autonomy and individuality. Female authors supported this cultural shift by spotlighting the voices and experiences of strong, independent women. The goal was to entertain readers and spur them to reassess cultural norms and societal restrictions. These writers' creative output fostered greater self-awareness and modeled economic, social, sexual, and artistic empowerment. Some, like Nella Larsen and Amy Lowell, were highly regarded in their literary circles but fairly unknown to the masses, whereas others, like Mae West and Bessie Smith, became cultural icons and household names.

Dorothy Parker (1893–1967) is widely considered the most famous, admired, and quoted female writer-celebrity of the Jazz Age. Adored for her sharp wit and acute insights, Parker authored scathingly satiric short stories and poems, plus social commentary essays, theater reviews, wartime journalism, literary criticism, Broadway stage plays, and Hollywood screenplays. "She wrote poetry that was at least as good as the best of [Edna St. Vincent] Millay and [A.E.] Housman. She wrote some stories that are easily as good as some of [John] O'Hara and [Ernest] Hemingway."[1] Setting the standard for a generation, "Parker's stories were admired not just by the purchasing reading masses, but by other short story writers acclaimed in their own right both then and now."[2] Her compositions, often published in popular national magazines or best-selling books, challenged female readers to question the values they were taught and engage in political activism to initiate change.

In the 1920s, Parker's feminist attacks were directed outward at patriarchal attitudes and inward at simpering women, dependent on men for approval and validation. One of the main targets was flapper culture, which she believed encouraged women to be superficial, selfish, and silly. As earlier chapters attest, the flapper mentality was much more complicated than this stereotype. Though certainly image-focused and self-involved, it also called on women to respect themselves as they asserted independence in the male-dominated public sphere. What Parker wanted was to steer modern women away from the commercially packaged identity of mindless and weak-willed display, which she labeled "flapper," and push them to achieve greater mental and emotional self-possession, so they could participate in a community of action instead of compromising themselves to fit into a flawed society.

This chapter focuses on Parker's poems and stories from the 1920s (and a few from the early 1930s) that raised awareness about sexism, racism, and classism. Satire was her primary mode of criticism, but increased interest in politics caused Parker to write serious commentary and get involved herself, such as helping to organize the first trade union of Hollywood screenwriters in 1933 and co-founding Hollywood's Anti-Nazi League in 1936. She produced blistering articles that amplified her views on topics like unjust treatment of the working poor and fascism on the international stage. I include a few examples of Parker's post-1920s work to illustrate this progression in her thinking about her role as an influencer.

Like the other authors discussed in this book, Parker wrote to complicate women's thinking about the obstacles they faced and provoke them to become agents of change. While the authors in the first two chapters advocated change for the individual woman and the authors in the second two chapters advocated change for a subculture, Parker went a step further. She wanted women, particularly those who were white and middle class, to see themselves as actors on a larger stage with the power to trigger societal change. In addition to improving themselves, their activism could improve the lives of women who lacked their wealth and standing.

CREATIVE SELF-ASSERTION

The Roaring Twenties began with a seminal political event for women. Passage of the nineteenth amendment to the Constitution in 1920 prohibited the discrimination of voting on account of sex across the United States, which significantly enhanced their ability to participate in governance. Although individual women already had been acting on their own behalf to secure economic self-sufficiency and sexual liberation, they needed a unified, multigenerational political movement to attain suffrage, a prerequisite for full citizenship in any democracy. At the heart of this movement, suffragists raised their voices and sacrificed their bodies to protest an unfair system. For a decade prior to passage of the amendment, women had marched in the streets, notably wresting attention from President Woodrow Wilson's inauguration in 1913.[3] They also endured violence while incarcerated and spoke eloquently in opposition to brutal criticism from respected male leaders, all in an effort to provide women equal access and authority as official decision-makers.

At the beginning of the twentieth century, the suffrage movement signaled that women should be seen as serious, active, rational subjects, rather than silly, passive, romantic objects. From a practical standpoint, enfranchisement gave constituencies of women more standing in national and local governments, which increased the likelihood that their opinions, needs, and concerns would influence legislation. It should be noted that women of color were largely excluded from the benefits gained by the suffragists until the Voting Rights Act of 1965.[4] Injustices like this did not go unnoticed by Dorothy Parker, who contested both sexist attitudes and racial discrimination in her published works and her political activism.

Symbolically, political autonomy represented a person's expression of personal power and dignity, so getting the vote helped women (largely white, middle-class women) legitimize their civic selfhood, elevate their public standing, improve their self-esteem. This reimagining of women's public identity was prominent in Parker's writing. She satirized the roles they were forced to play, with a keen interest in how they were supposed to feel about themselves and their relationships. Her more popular stories and poems undercut the fantasy of girlish romance and sentimentality, replacing it with a clear-eyed, self-aware recognition that love is temporary, male partners are often fickle and selfish, and life satisfaction must come from within oneself.

Beneath her wit was justified anger and bitterness about how women were treated and, more pointedly, how they allowed themselves to be treated, which Parker aimed to change. She knew self-respect and self-assertion led to success in a male-controlled world. Thus, her writing intimated, when it did not outright announce, that women must steel themselves against the widespread misogyny in the United States and strengthen their self-confidence and sense of self-worth if they wanted to be taken seriously. Although Parker laughed at the absurdity of how society perceived women, she was soberly sincere about women becoming tougher and fighting for their place alongside men in every facet of public life.

The characters in Parker's stories and poems reflect the challenges she herself faced as a young writer in the post-World War I era. She had to force her way into male intellectual circles, applying her brilliant creativity to disrupt longstanding gender assumptions and expectations. As a woman and a Jew, Parker began her writing career as an outsider but soon established herself and advanced a strong literary persona. During the 1920s, she wrote cultural essays and theater reviews for popular and prestigious magazines like *Vanity Fair*, the *New Yorker*, the *Saturday Evening Post*, and *Life*, while also publishing an astonishing number of short stories and poems. She "wrote more than 330 poems and free verses in the thirty years from 1915 to 1945. She published nearly three hundred of these during the twenties, an average of more than one poem or free verse every two weeks."[5] The acclaimed author would not be denied her voice or her rightful place among the literary and cultural elite.

Known in the 1920s as the wittiest woman in the U.S., Parker was a national celebrity. Her first book of poetry *Enough Rope* (1926) quickly became a best seller, a rare accomplishment for an American poet, male or female. The book was generally well-received by respected critics like Genevieve Taggard of the *New York Herald Tribune* and Edmund Wilson of the *New Republic*.[6] In a 1927 review for *Poetry: A Magazine of Verse*, Marie Luhrs praised Parker's verses, noting that they accomplish the seemingly impossible feat of being simultaneously "slangy, vulgar, candid" and "subtle, delicate and sparkling."[7] Luhrs admired Parker for ably employing "pertness and bravado" to express "quite genuine and profound experiences."[8]

Two more poetry collections followed, *Sunset Gun* (1928) and *Death and Taxes* (1931), but they received less public fanfare. Nonetheless, the author of clever stories and provocative articles continued to be a national celebrity and an independent spirit, evident by the first lines of the vaunted Cole Porter jazz standard "Just One of Those Things" (1935): "As Dorothy Parker once said to her boyfriend, / 'Fare thee well.'"[9] At times, Parker was dissatisfied with her career and her relationships, but she did not shrink from critically examining society or herself. One might detect her sly wit and high standards in this portrait.

Figure 5.1. Dorothy Parker
Drawn by by Emily Klein

Before Mae West hit the big screen, Parker was beloved for her cutting cultural observations and short pithy aphorisms. Quotes attributed to her include, "You can lead a horticulture, but you can't make her think," "If you want to know what God thinks of money, just look at the people he gave it to," "Brevity is the soul of lingerie," and "Beauty is only skin deep, but ugly goes clean to the bone."[10] Hearing that former president Calvin Coolidge had died in 1933, she retorted "How could they tell?"[11] Parker was particularly popular for ridiculing traditional gender roles and identities. In the poem "Neither Bloody nor Bowed" (1926), she succinctly rebuffed those who attempted to control women through sexist social conventions, quipping, "Inseparable my nose and thumb!"[12] During the 1920s, Parker consistently relied on biting satire to advocate for women's rights and promote a rebellious spirit of empowerment, independence, and self-appreciation.

In addition to attacking misogyny, Parker expressed strong political opinions about class and race. She criticized the rich and powerful for their arrogance and frivolity, arguing that working-class women deserved higher wages, better working conditions, and more respect. This message intensified during the 1930s, as the Great Depression demeaned the poor in the United States and fascist regimes abused the lower classes abroad. Parker also took on racial bigotry. Early in her career, she highlighted the nation's ugly history of discrimination and cultural appropriation in theater reviews for *Vanity Fair* (1918–1920) and *Ainslee's Magazine* (1920–1923). Furthermore, she wrote pieces of fiction to express the value of African Americans and expose the hypocrisy of self-proclaimed enlightened white liberals of the 1920s.

However, the famous wit did not merely use the written word to combat social ills. Parker was a political activist who took to the streets, donated money, and founded organizations to protest hypocrisy, injustice, and intolerance. Parker gave her financial and vocal support to quite a few causes in the 1920s and 1930s: "she railed against poverty and unemployment, the segregation of blacks in the United States, and the growing clamor of anti-Semitism in Germany,"[13] as well as Franco's fascist rule of Spain. Throughout her career, Parker never hesitated to speak her mind or fight for causes she considered worthwhile.

This radical activism, though, carried a price. Parker lost her job as a theater critic for *Vanity Fair* in 1920 after criticizing Broadway's rich and powerful. She was arrested for protesting the execution of anarchists Nicola Sacco and Bartolomeo Vanzetti in 1927. Her work for anti-fascist and pro-socialist organizations resulted in her being extensively investigated by the FBI, condemned by the California Un-American Activities Committee, named a traitor during the espionage trial of Judith Coplon, branded a concealed Communist by Joseph McCarthy's House Un-American Activities Committee, and hauled before a New York State Joint Legislative Committee.[14] Parker was denied a passport when she wanted to report on World War II in Europe, and she was blacklisted by Hollywood in 1949.

Sadly, "McCarthy-ism poisoned Dorothy's personal and professional life and eventually undermined her spirit."[15] Nevertheless, she continued to use her celebrity, money, and talent for writing and public speaking to advocate for liberty, equality, tolerance, and fairness until her death. And even beyond, as Parker willed her entire estate, including the copyrights and royalties of her writing, to Dr. Martin Luther King, Jr., and upon his death to the National Association for the Advancement of Colored People.[16]

Parker sacrificed a great deal of herself to awaken readers to society's inequities and to suggest methods for improvement. Often the only woman in a professional setting, Parker had to ignore insults from competitors and withstand jealously from colleagues. Despite a confident public persona and nationwide hero status, she freely shared psychological insecurities and emotional suffering through fictional female characters. Parker dramatized her own exhaustion over having to continually prove herself to and ingratiate herself with the men in her literary circle. The stress of needing to be both an excellent writer and a "good sport" in men's eyes led to unhappy relationships, misgivings about her own talent, and deep depression. Parker experienced "the extreme self-doubt and self-deprecation, even self-hatred, that has besieged a great many women who embarked on unconventional career and life paths,"[17] which resulted in alcoholism, divorce, and several suicide attempts.

Yet, Parker stands as a major representative of the spirit of the 1920s woman, resilient and irreverent. These qualities are displayed in works like the short poem "Resume" (1926). In her inimitable style, Parker addressed depression by naming multiple methods of suicide, identifying their flaws like "Nooses give; / Gas smells awful," and concluding with a sarcastic but sincere maxim: "You might as well live."[18] Enduring severe disappointment and depression herself, Parker wanted women to discern the attitudes and institutions tyrannizing them so they would avoid contributing to their own subjugation. She wrote for the common woman, pressing readers to locate their strength, act meaningfully, and make a difference in the world.

SONGS OF SOCIAL AWARENESS

Parker knew that before a woman can advocate for others, she must empower herself. The first step is awareness about the social expectations that aim to diminish and confine her. The poem "News Item" (1926) prompts women to recognize male insecurity and not be defeated by it. The ironic play of this simple, two-line poem: "Men seldom make passes / At girls who wear glasses"[19] along with its the title news item, aka as-if-we-didn't-already-know, suggests that it is a man's short-sightedness that stops him from seeing the worth of an intelligent, capable woman. Of course, it is the woman who suffers the pain of this blow to the ego. "Inventory" (1926) asserts, "Three be the things I shall have till I die: / Laughter and hope and a sock in the eye."[20] The speaker is not pessimistic or bitter, but she is also not dazzled by girlish dreams of unending love or male promises of a carefree life. The literal and metaphorical punches she endures make her tough and world-wise. She confronts the hard realities about her relationships with men and her subordinate position in society to become master of her own destiny.

"Somebody's Song" (1926) exposes the hollowness of fairy tale vows and criticizes the happily-ever-after life that women feel obligated to cling to. The poem takes a practical look at relationships and ends with the self-protective warning that "Lovers' oaths are thin as rain; / Love's a harbinger of pain."[21] The speaker wishes relationships were different, but she bravely faces the difficult truth of men who hold a selfish and controlling attitude toward women. She is open-eyed about her current lover, "He is neither last nor first," asserting that no matter how thirsty her heart is for love, she must acknowledge her own talents and strength, ignoring social pressures to blindly submit to the stereotypical female role of passive subordinate object.

Several other poems encourage women not to enslave themselves to an unrealistic idea of love. "To a Much Too Unfortunate Lady" (1926) and "Unfortunate Coincidence" (1926) warn them about blithely following their own desire for a romantic fantasy. Trusting one's self-worth to blind sentiment is counterproductive, according to Parker, since men commonly lie, cheat, and leave.[22] The speaker in "Ballade of a Great Weariness" (1926) explains the painful lessons she has learned after many mistakes. She must live for herself and on her own terms, alerting the reader multiple times, "Scratch a lover, and find a foe."[23]

Many of Parker's poetic personae devote their intelligence and passion to developing an independent subjectivity; they construct a practical, self-reliant identity to survive and succeed as a public figure. In "Finis" (1926), the speaker locates an inner strength, employing the harsh reality of "the crowded street"[24] to recover emotionally from a failed relationship. At first, the poem suggests her break-up is a catastrophe, but the speaker realizes that she is not unlike the self-assured, forward-looking people on the street who do not shed a tear for her. The speaker shrugs off despair, concluding the poem by stating, "I might mention, my recent dear, / I've reverted to normal, too." For Parker, a woman's normal state after a relationship ends should be the same as a man's: brief disappointment followed by the normalcy of appreciating her independence and focusing on other parts of her life. Thus, the speaker does not mourn losing a man, choosing to see it an opportunity for personal growth as she rejoins the energetic stream of city life.

The street-wise speaker in "Ballade at Thirty-Five" (1926) proudly proclaims that she is no innocent girl, choosing instead to follow "ever her natural bents."[25] She enjoys her lovers without deluding herself about their intentions because she "Always saw what the end would be." Her insights about men make her careful with her affections: "I loved them until they loved me." Similarly, the speaker in "The Red Dress" (1928) indicates she has outgrown the role of silly young girl. She is no longer beholden to empty promises of romance and the absurd belief she will find a man "with stars behind his eyes . . . and lips too warm for lies."[26] She has gladly "grown to womanhood," which has provided the maturity to recognize the childhood dreams she was fed had limited her mental and emotional development. Achieving a different type of freedom than she expected, the speaker relinquishes her adolescent desire to wear a red dress and try to attract the perfect man, preferring to free herself of romantic delusion.

In addition to ridiculing the dreamy romance mythology itself, Parker sought to expose the psychology behind young women's self-abnegation. For example, "I Know I Have Been Happiest" (1926) criticizes the masochistic devotion men expect of women, "the need of woman, this his curse: / To range her little gifts, and give, and give."[27] The implication is that men feel justified to take and take from women, who are traditionally society's givers. This taking includes siphoning women's emotional energy without reciprocation. The poem's speaker knows this is harmful and jokes, "My gift [to a man] shall be my absence." Similarly, the poem "For an Unknown Lady" (1926) condemns ladies who come running when a lad merely whistles.[28] Parker warned against trusting the false words men speak, for women must keep their hearts and their selfhoods as their own, not giving them away rashly or losing themselves in a man.

"Song of One of the Girls" (1926) counteracts female passivity by placing the speaker alongside strong, heroic, rebellious women from mythology and history, such as Dido, Eve, and Kitty O'Shea.[29] Presumably speaking for all women, the speaker declares herself a glamorous lady, "At whose beckoning history shook. / But you are a man, and see only my pan, / So I stay at home with a book." Her staying at home is likely more symbolic than literal, choosing self-respect and self-improvement above degrading herself for a man who cannot see beyond her appearance. Taking her place among the great women, the speaker participates in the public sphere as an active subject who shakes up accepted norms and reshapes history.

Likewise, the female speaker in "Indian Summer" (1926) transitions from the dutiful, self-sacrificing, subordinate object of male desire to a self-possessed, self-aware actor in her own life.[30] She proudly vows, "But now I know the things I know, / And do the things I do," indicating she has learned to appreciate who she is and think for herself. As a result, she does not care about her partner's objections, announcing that if he cannot accept her for who she is, "To hell, my love, with you!" Moreover, Parker's "Men" (1926) warns women in no uncertain terms that they are treated poorly because they bow to male assumptions. By obeying these assumptions, women relinquish control of their selfhood to men, and "once [the men] have you, safe and sound. . . . They'd make of you another person."[31] The poem concludes with Parker being sick and tired of men trying to control and remake women. The speaker implores women to govern their own lives and resist men's selfish need to "influence and educate."

One of Parker's trademarks was putting a revelatory and often feminist stinger in a poem's last line or two. For instance, throughout "Folk Tune" (1926) the speaker wistfully presents her lover with a number of ways he is deficient compared to other men. However, instead of concluding the poem with a romantic I-love-you-despite-your-faults sentiment, the speaker states, "Why, ah why, then, should I love you? / Naturally, I do not."[32] In "Renunciation" (1926), the speaker attests that women should prefer being alone to remaining in bad relationships. Early in the poem, she notes her lover's frequent glances at other attractive women. She ultimately does not respond with pathetic pleas or an attempt to lure him back. Instead, she finishes with the sober retort, "Don't you think it's time we parted? . . . / Fair enough!"[33] The ellipse is in the poem, taking the place of the man's reply and giving the woman authority in her own decision-making. The final phrase shows she has the emotional maturity and strength (note the exclamation point) to accept a difficult truth and move on.

These poems normalize a woman's refusal to compromise her strength, intelligence, or independence to be what a man wants or society expects. Sometimes it reduces the likelihood of an imbalanced relationship. "Day-Dreams" (1926) tells a story of a woman who fantasizes about reducing herself to a cook and laundress through marriage in order to live what she has been led to believe would be the perfect life. The last stanza begins by rhapsodizing a "model life"[34] the man and woman would enjoy if they were united as one, which requires the woman to subsume her selfhood to her husband's. The final lines, however, revoke this vision of their future: "And so I think it best, my love, / To string along as two." The speaker prefers maintaining her dignity to a wife's position of confinement and self-denial. This commitment to independence is also the main theme of "Men I'm Not Married To"

(1922). The speaker keeps her distance from the handsome young men she sees walking the city streets to maintain her own name and identity: "'but for heaven's grace,' I cry, / 'There goes the guy whose name I'd wear!'"[35] In a gender reversal, the female speaker exerts the social power and controls men with her gaze. She judges their attractiveness without sacrificing her agency, "They're fair to see—but only fair."

In addition to avoiding the wrong relationship, refusing to compromise one's identity and self-worth might ensure the right partnership. "Interview" (1926) alludes to men who privately appreciate self-possessed and even rebellious women. Unlike the common views shared in polite society, such as men favoring demure and prudish ladies, the speaker trumpets that she has had no complaints from admirers or lovers about her swearing freely, staying out late, reading erotic poetry, responding to sexual overtures, and wearing cosmetics.[36] For the liberated woman, a satisfactory life requires breaking conventions and exhibiting her true self in public.

Readers had the opportunity to learn from Parker's perceptive observations and personal experiences, not to spare them the difficulties of life but to guide their speedy recovery. "Now at Liberty" (1926) suggests that lonely, brokenhearted women need not hide in their homes, defeated and destitute. The abandoned woman should move forward, evident in the poem's many parenthetical remarks, such as the line after mourning a forsaken heart: "(Whom shall I get by telephone?)"[37] and the line after expressing yearning: "(Nevertheless, a girl needs fun.)" The speaker betrays her practical, unromantic nature, insisting that rejection will not stop her from eating, living, or having fun. She also asserts greater sexual and social agency, excited to contact other boys to secure a new lover.

Several poems challenge the subjugation of women by a male literary tradition, which influences the way actual women are assessed and treated. "Verse Reporting Late Arrival at a Conclusion" (1926) criticizes the many novels and plays that portray women as "reckless in love,"[38] indicting women who blissfully envelop themselves in a dream of romance. The poem's speaker is bitter that women are hounded into adopting this attitude, which causes them to believe they have done something wrong when confronted by life's harsh realities: "The thorn, so to say, is revealed by the rose. / The best that she gets is a sock in the nose." Parker proclaimed that the falsity of a happily-ever-after "rose" fantasy damages women, urging authors and playwrights to present a more realistic version of a woman's life and prospects.

Finally, "Song of Perfect Propriety" (1926) criticizes the limitations put on female authors. The speaker wishes to be a rough pirate who travels the world in search of adventure, wealth, violence, and power. She objects to the fate assigned women at the time, preferring to "strut and curse . . . to dance and laugh. . .and rip the hearts of men in half."[39] Unfortunately, such desires remain dreams because the speaker is reduced to "writing little verse, / As little ladies do." Parker, though, successfully affected a buccaneer-like persona, attacking social mores to rob them of their authority and sharing the spoils with other brash, fearless women. The conservative male authorities were no match for Parker's saber-like pen and because of her, many women found their voice and declared their independence.

SATIRIZING SEXISM

Parker wanted women to be valued as intelligent, capable adults who cared about political issues and acted on their own behalf. In the 1956 interview "Writers at Work" conducted by *The Paris Review*, Parker indicated she was an activist early in her writing career, "I'm a feminist, and God knows I'm loyal to my sex, and you must remember that from my very early days, when this city was scarcely safe from buffaloes, I was in the struggle for equal rights for women."[40] She also explained that despite the humorous tone of her writing, she engaged serious issues in a meaningful way, unlike some female writers: "The purpose of the writer is to say what he feels and sees. To those who write fantasies—the Misses [Faith] Baldwin, [Edna] Ferber, [Kathleen] Norris—I am not at home." Parker refused to indulge in the romantic or sentimental fantasies that women were expected to write and read; instead, she exposed readers to life's hard realities and urged them to work for a better future.

"The Garter" (1928) is an autobiographical story that attacks the sexualization and disrespect experienced by professional women. Protagonist "Dorothy Parker" must contend with a broken garter at a party, which she is meant to view as a disaster. Although Parker pokes fun at her own public image, the story has a serious undertone, advocating for the same respect male writers and public figures receive. Not passive or romance-obsessed, the character is liberated and well-read, quoting Charles Dickens. A professional, she disdains those who seek to reduce her authority or self-respect: "All they see is this unfortunate exterior. There's a man looking at it now. All right, baby, go on and look your head off. . . . Look pretty silly, don't I, sitting here holding my knee? Yes, and I'm the only one that's going to hold it, too. What do you think of that, sweetheart?"[41] Beyond this strong expression of self-possession, the protagonist makes fun of romance, laughing at the assumption that she would like to cry because she cannot meet new men or dance once her garter has broken. The story ends hopefully with "the dream of gendered cooperation in the professional sphere."[42] An author with respected public status and financial independence, "Parker appropriates masculine professional privilege" to rewrite how the public viewed her and the issues she considered important.

She also used her personal experience in stories that tackle taboo topics like divorce, alcoholism, suicide, and abortion. For example, the distress felt by the female protagonists who ended their pregnancies in "Mr. Durant" (1924) and "Lady with a Lamp" (1932) echoed Parker's depression following her own abortion in 1922. The pregnancy was the result of an extramarital affair with Charles MacArthur, playwright and fellow member of the Algonquin Round Table, a famed literary and cultural clique. When he ended their relationship, Parker attempted suicide and then cast him as the monstrous title character in "Mr. Durant," a family man who seduces a young woman and callously discards her once her "condition"[43] is taken care of. Among her friends, Parker criticized MacArthur's inconstancy and acknowledged her own miscalculation by stating, "It serves me right for putting all my eggs in one bastard."[44]

Parker aimed to undermine the patriarchy's hold over women, but her poems and stories did not always attack men and their sense of superiority directly. Instead, she sometimes chose to criticize the oppressive archetypes of femininity by ridiculing the women who upheld them. For example, "Women: A Hate Song" (1916) begins with the contention that she hates women who obey sexist stereotypes, stating, "They get on my Nerves. / There are the Domestic ones. / They are the worst."[45] Parker's penetrating humor most often targeted women clinging to conventional attitudes or women embracing the more superficial characteristics and material trappings of flapper culture. She knew that women like herself were tired of the limited choices they had and the poor female role models popular in the 1920s.

Faithful readers understood and appreciated the message thinly veiled in Parker's satirical fiction: reject the unsatisfactory female traits male society desired and only take part in a version of womanhood that embodies intelligence, competence, action. Thus, her use of parody and mockery actually "encourages sisterly bonding and welcomes real women, who are misrepresented by compulsory feminine images of happy domesticity or deviant sexual availability."[46] Instead of permitting women to accept domination or wallow in a sense of victimhood, Parker pushed women to become more self-aware and fight for their rights as citizens and as human beings. For them to become activists.

This encouragement occurred at an important time of cultural transition. While Parker worked for change, many women remained convinced that traditional gender roles served their best interests and supplied everything they needed. These conventional women were unwilling or unable to challenge their second-class status in the family or in public society. For instance, political scholars have noted that during the early years of enfranchisement many women did not become independent voters. "To the surprise of some suffragists, a female voting bloc had not emerged."[47] Some simply did not vote, while others parroted the choices made by husbands or fathers. Few women were elected to office, nationally or locally, and issues championed by feminists were not being addressed. Unfortunately, "having struggled for so long for one elusive victory, some women suffered a failure of imagination about what should come next."[48]

Parker, though, had considerable imagination. She worked to increase women's rights and defeat the assumption that women were too weak or emotional to get involved in politics and social change. Her literature subverted what she considered the failings of the older Victorian stereotypes and the new flapper generation. As I stated earlier, the flapper was an important counterculture icon, instrumental in women's rebellion against outdated morals and manners. This figure challenged conventional norms and stood for sexual freedom and financial independence. However, Parker and other activists disparaged the flapper as a self-interested hedonist who preferred to indulge in 1920s consumerism rather than do the hard work of feminism like marching for voting rights, publicly demanding access to contraception, and rallying support for the Equal Rights Amendment. Parker made fun of "the contemporary vision of the liberated woman" by mocking "the infantilism of the flapper" and the "valorization of devil-may-care glamour girls."[49] Parker decided that in order to promote a new femininity of strength, wit, capability, and action, she first had to discredit the apolitical flapper and the helpless glamour girl for contributing to their own captivity.

Several short stories, such as "The Sexes" (1927) and "From the Diary of a New York Lady" (1933), satirize the superficiality, vanity, and purposelessness Parker saw in flapper culture. The shallow, childish female characters in these stories are ignorant of the fact that they are not in control of their empty, pointless lives. The protagonist in "From the Diary of a New York Lady" focuses considerable attention on fashion, gossip, and well-manicured fingernails. This young socialite must expend so much energy keeping up appearances that she cannot be bothered to read mind-improving literature. She writes on Monday, "Started to read a book, but too nervous," and then on Thursday, "Began to read a book, but too exhausted."[50] For Parker, reading is a sign of a character's ability to be critical of society and, perhaps more importantly, critical of the role she has accepted in that society.

Another of character who tries and fails to read is the protagonist in "The Telephone Call" (1930). This young woman is paralyzed by her need for attention and affection, incapable of sustained thought while waiting for a telephone call from a male admirer. Even if she could focus on reading a novel, she laments that "all the books are about people who love each other, truly and sweetly."[51] Parker's story teaches "that an obsessive preoccupation with romance is often self-defeating."[52] The protagonist is unsympathetic because she reduces her whole existence to a pathetic need for romance, neurotically worrying that some man might not care for her and demeaning herself as she repeats a prayer dedicated to her desperation: "Please let me see him again, God. Please, I want him so much."[53]

The character admits that this obsession is unhealthy, a means of putting herself in hell, but she will not consider speaking her mind or making herself an equal partner in the relationship. She hides her true self and bemoans her confinement in a gender role, "[men] hate you whenever you say anything you really think. You always have to keep playing little games."[54] Parker ridiculed this helplessly passive woman, so paralyzed by concern about how she is perceived that she cannot take the initiative to call the man herself or, better yet, live her own life free of his influence.

These stories deride weak, unimaginative women who subserviently obey the image-driven and romance-obsessed identity modern culture imposes on young women. Other Parker stories, though, offer heroic women that portray a more intellectually and socially independent identity as they confront unfair gender codes. For example, the self-aware main character in "The Little Hours" (1933) uses intelligence and humor in her interior monologues to lambaste the circumstances she and other women regularly face. The protagonist, unable to sleep, seriously considers the challenges of being a woman in "a man's world."[55] She despises society for not following her lead and forcing women to conform, leading to the astute critique, "If that isn't the woman of it for you! Always having to do what somebody else wants, like it or not."[56]

Unlike the glamour girls who mindlessly devote themselves to male attention, the self-possessed woman in "The Little Hours" reads voraciously, lauding poets like lauding poet Charles Baudelaire and philosopher Thomas Carlyle. Countering the assumption that a woman needs sentimental and idealized love, the protagonist condemns the flood of popular romance fiction and agrees with François La Rochefoucauld's sarcastic quip that "if nobody had ever learned to read, very few people would be in love."[57] She adds her own maxim about the problematic connection of sex and a fiction of fairy-tale romance by joking, "If nobody had ever learned to undress, very few people would be in love."[58] Not wanting sex confused with love, she asks men to consider their partners' intellect and treat women as their equal. Therefore, if getting a good night's sleep means conforming "to the rotten little standards of this sluggard civilization,"[59] a woman should continue to wrestle her midnight demons to find her true self.

Another character who is true to herself, at least internally, is the protagonist of "The Waltz" (1933). In this satire, a frustrated woman escapes into her intellect and imagination to defy society's rotten, petty standards. Although she smiles and acquiesces, as is expected of a woman at a public dance, her thoughts explode gender stereotypes and demonstrate superiority over her inept male dance partner. The narrator is able to create a "pleasurable psychological detachment from the restrictive social circumstances,"[60] because "her creativity is an assertion of autonomy within the story. Humor provides 'a room of her own.'" As pioneering author and feminist Virginia Woolf notes in her famous essay "A Room of One's Own" (1929), a private space, along with a personal income, is essential for female independence. Parker's protagonist in "The Waltz" is another well-read woman who references Poe's "The Fall of the House of Usher," as well as contemporary author and drama critic George Jean Nathan.

Broadening her feminist message, Parker's "The Waltz" speaks to the reader on multiple levels. For instance, the protagonist's reaction to the man asking her to dance, "Why can't he let me lead my own life?"[61] acts as the dismissal of a single bad dancer and a rebuke against male-dominated society's attempt to control women. Unable to politely decline the man's invitation to dance, she remarks that public life is a trap for women who desire access but lack agency. Using dance as a metaphor, the woman alludes to the problem of allowing men to take the lead in women's lives and identities. She declares that she embodies "Outraged Womanhood,"[62] yet she chooses to bite her tongue and bide her time, suggesting that she needs female readers to unite if they wish to keep the patriarchy from stepping on their toes.

RE-EXAMINING RACISM

One type of unification Parker fostered was between white and African American women, with the goal of addressing widespread racial injustice and violence. Several poems and stories feature an African American protagonist, the speaking subject who invites the reader into her thoughts, emotions, and experiences. Other compositions use a white protagonist to challenge the unconscious racism that exists in the beliefs and language of white America. An example is a detestable comment about service in a nightclub from "A Terrible Day Tomorrow" (1928): "What's the matter, can't I get a drink here? Am I a nigger, or something?"[63] In the story, these words are meant to contribute to the reader's dislike of an arrogant and privileged white character. Outside of the story, the epithet bespeaks the casual racism in U.S. society during the 1920s, which Parker wanted to bring to people's attention and no longer condone.

Chapter 3 of this book examines race from the perspective of authors who were themselves women of color. Novelists Nella Larsen and Mourning Dove described the physical and psychological attacks on the African American and Native American communities, as well as white society's fetishistic fascination and appropriation of their cultures. Aware of her white privilege, Parker realized the necessity of addressing racial prejudice and discrimination head on, detailing the plight of minorities and demanding accountability from her white readers. Parker wrote about racial inequality because she felt "irritation with those who remain complacent about status quo politics as long as they have their own 'peace o' mind.'"[64] Devoted to this cause, Parker made a "lifelong commitment to equality and justice"[65] that included intense respect and admiration for civil rights leaders like Dr. Martin Luther King, Jr. Parker drove white, middle-class women to recognize their power and broaden their political views on race and class.

During the push for suffrage, female activists of all races had united to gain voting rights. However, it was a tenuous coalition, and women of color ultimately were denied the full realization of their civil rights. The National Woman's Party (NWP) did little to protect these rights, choosing to "ignore the disfranchisement of black voters as a condition of Southern states ratifying the 19th amendment."[66] African American activists were disillusioned when NWP's founder and leader Alice Paul "dismissed race discrimination as tangential to the cause of women's equality." The activists were further disappointed that a growing number of white women, including some former suffragists, "became active in racial supremacist movements."[67] It appeared that many white women were no more interested than white men in relinquishing their sense of racial superiority and entitlement.

Parker was decidedly disturbed by the prejudice and discrimination perpetrated by her white countrymen. Early in the 1920s, she used her theater column in *Ainslee's Magazine* to criticize how race was portrayed in Broadway productions. Parker "abhorred the racial stereotypes prevalent of the era; there are numerous reviews where she casts a withering gaze at blackface actors (and even black actors in white paint)."[68] For example, Parker's October 1920 column, "Words and Music," critiqued the play *Come Seven*, a comedy written by Octavus Roy Cohen that was "based on his *Saturday Evening Post* stories of negro life."[69] In the review, Parker shrewdly surmises, "The actors' portrayal of the negro race goes only as deep as a layer of burnt cork, and so, one cannot help but feel, does the author's." The scenes are "less a picture of the negro than a picture postcard,"[70] and the characters "are not of the colored race, but of the blackface race—the typical stage negroes, lazy, luridly dressed, addicted to crap shooting, and infallibly mispronouncing every word of more than three syllables." A few months later in a column titled "Standing Room Only, and Very Little of That" (1921), Parker further criticized the limitations placed on African American performers: "In no way are our producers more wasteful of genius than in their disregard of negro actors."[71]

This dissatisfaction with racism was also the theme of several creative pieces. The poem "The Dark Girl's Rhyme" (1926) identifies societal stereotypes about race, as well as the damage they do to individuals. Setting aside her typical humorous tone, Parker used pathos to alert and shame the reader. The poem's speaker, an African American woman, opens with a question about herself and her white lover, stating that everyone who sees them together exhorts him to flee from her. She realizes that the visibility of their racial difference makes every person they encounter a potential enemy to the success of their relationship. Her happiness is under continuous assault, causing her to question its permanence. The speaker also deplores the burden of U.S. racial history, which proclaims her inferiority and forever separates people of different races even if they love each other. As the speaking subject, this African American woman is empowered to decry how ignorant and abusive attitudes of the past unfairly confine and condemn people of color in the present.

The speaker worries about white resistance to her interracial relationship and knows her mate, who comes from a privileged white background, is ill-equipped to deal with the backlash. Blessed as part of the privileged race, the man is associated with active verbs as he rules the marketplace, farms his ancestral land, accumulates wealth, and enjoys life without a care in the world. The speaker, on the other hand, has endured brutal treatment, denied respect as a irredeemable sinner even before she was born. She must perform to the satisfaction of white society, continually fiddling the white folks' tune and kissing their feet, just to acquire the basics like food and shelter. As a result, she reiterates that white society would gladly help her lover abandon her, since they were irate that there could be a child with the "Blood of him and me."[72]

As I explained in chapter 3, blood played a major role in racist attitudes of the time. The one-drop rule, in which a single African American ancestor made a person Black and inferior no matter her skin color, led white society in the 1920s to fear having what they considered the tainted blood of African Americans enter a pure white family line. This possibility caused white blood to rise in anger and hate, which created bad blood between the races and resulted in blood-letting when whites attacked and lynched African Americans.

"The Dark Girl's Rhyme" ends as it began with the speaker questioning the future of her relationship and the difficulty of positive social change. The major challenge is to reconcile the love a couple feels and the hate encouraged by common stereotypes and prejudices. Instead of welcoming diversity and promoting racial harmony, the prevailing ideology intensifies the divide, as stated in the final lines: "Living for a hating, / Dying of a love?"[73] These lines are posed as a question to cast doubt about the hate and death that white elites have instituted from a sense of superiority, with the intension of desta-bilizing the certainty of a racist, inhuman ideology. Readers are meant to see the absurdity of supporting an attitude that encourages hate and ensures the death of love.

The story "Arrangement in Black and White" (1927) again draws upon Parker's signature wit and satirical prowess. The setting is a dinner party where the blond-haired protagonist eagerly wants to meet Walter Williams, a famous African American singer.[74] The story's humor springs from the woman's total lack of self-awareness, as she claims to be tolerant and broad-minded, yet her comments and behavior reveal subconscious prejudice. The protagonist is not named, suggesting her hypocrisy is common among whites who want to be seen as progressive. They do not realize the hollowness of professed ideals that lack self-examination and true understanding of racial issues or white people's role in them. Parker's complaints echoed popular 1920s African American writers like Jean Toomer and Angelina Grimke who highlighted "the catastrophic effects that white hypocrisy has on black lives."[75] Parker's hypocritical protagonist fails as an ally, doing nothing to forsake her own privilege and power, or curb the rampant discrimination and violence perpetrated by others of her race.

Parker made her protagonist's superficial and ignorant attitude more glar-ing by having the woman brag that she approaches race better than her hus-band, who refuses to attend the party. She says, "he's just the other way. Well, you know, he comes from Virginia, and you know how they are."[76] Neverthe-less, she defends his refusal to hire white servants, incorrectly thinking his need to play the role of master is actually love and respect for the "regular old nigger mammy" they employ. The protagonist is blind to her husband's sense of racial superiority and his attempts to belittle and restrict African Ameri-cans, stating proudly, "he hasn't got a word to say against colored people as long as they keep their place." She even seems to admire his arrogance and unearned privilege when giving servants his old clothes, which becomes a major issue in another of Parker's stories: "Clothe the Naked." The protago-nist in "Arrangement in Black and White" does take issue with her husband's refusal to sit down to dinner with African Americans, but she rebukes herself for criticizing him, stating unironically, "I'm just terrible to him. Aren't I ter-rible?" Although the host affirms she is not terrible, the reader realizes the woman's superficial performance of support for African Americans masks a terrible mindset that complements her husband's bigotry.

The protagonist repeats the self-congratulatory platitude that race means nothing to her, stating, "I don't see why on earth it isn't perfectly all right to meet colored people."[77] However, she soon reveals her true nature. As she begs the host for an introduction to Mr. Williams, she immediately frames him as untouchable, perhaps even inhuman. She also expresses her belief that he and fellow African Americans are "just like children—just as easygoing, and always singing and laughing and everything."[78] This white woman assumes the famous African American singer must be immensely grateful that he has been invited to this dinner party and introduced to so many "marvelous" white people. The host replies, "I hope not,"[79] which emphasizes the error of this thinking to the reader, even if the protagonist cannot recognize it. By fervently insisting on a tolerance for African Americans in general and a respect for this man in particular, the protagonist betrays her willful act of being oblivious to the intolerance indicated by her words and the disrespect inherent in her actions.

The character expresses another problematic white attitude by using the Black man's artistic talent to remove him from his race. She suggests that his exceptionalism helps him escape the negative characteristics she believes plagues all African Americans. She appreciates his nice manners, contrasting them to "so many colored people, you give them an inch, and they walk all over you."[80] She assumes this public figure "doesn't try any of that" because "he's got more sense" than to overstep and falsely paint himself as an equal to members of white high society, those who consume his work and patronize his humanity. She also references the so-called positive stereotype that all African Americans have an innate, genetic musical ability: "Isn't it marvelous, the way they all have music in them? It just seems to be right *in* them."[81] She briefly considers inviting the great singer to her home, but only because he is exceptional and only if he consents to sing for her like a trained bird. Her continued efforts to praise the man only exposes the woman's deep-seated distrust and dislike for the rest of his race.

When she is finally introduced to him, the protagonist is unsure whether to shake his hand as she would a white man. She speaks volumes in the words she almost says. First, she states that her angry husband "looks just as black as the ace of—Well. Tell me, where on earth do you ever get all those songs of yours?"[82] Then, she comments about a white actor in the room, stating, "I had no idea she was so terribly dark. Why, she looks almost like—Oh, I think she's a wonderful actress!" She later admits to the host, "I was just going to say Katherine Burke looked almost like a nigger. I just caught myself in time. Oh, do you think he noticed?"[83] The host says no, but the point is that the reader noticed. The story ends with the protagonist marveling at the fact that she called an African American "Mister!" with a straight face. Obviously, the reader is meant to laugh at this woman and, unlike her, recognize how her beliefs harm everyone, Black and white.

The most anthologized of Parker's stories, "Big Blonde" won the O'Henry Prize as the best short story of 1929. It has three African American characters that symbolize the connection between commerce and sex in a culture that metaphorically enslaves white women: "In the context of Parker's story, blonde is connected to black through the vulnerability of the body."[84] The big blonde, Hazel Morse, is a mere commodity, a body for display and male enjoyment. Her relationships are shallow and her identity is not her own, causing her to feel exploited and isolated. When Hazel attempts suicide, it is the African American characters who prevent it. On the one hand, their act of kindness connects her plight to their experience of racial subjugation; however, it also isolates her further through the reinforcement of racial difference. The story requires this difference because making the three characters white would result in Hazel being seen as "less white, less innocent, less alone. She would be less effective in dramatizing her story of estrangement and alienation, and less able to contain and isolate the germ of another idea: That all American freedom is broadly and historically conditional." Thus, Hazel's alienation does double duty, highlighting the subjugation of women and insinuating that race determines freedom and respect. One could certainly criticize Parker for appropriating the African American experience of racial domination and abuse to serve her white protagonist, but her goal was to make white readers feel ashamed at both sexism and racism.

Returning to the pathos of "The Dark Girl's Rhyme," Parker's story "Clothe the Naked" (1938) shows the injustices in U.S. society from the perspective of the despised underclass by again making an African American woman the protagonist. Big Lannie cleans clothes for white ladies of leisure, doing hard labor for nominal pay. Strong and self-sufficient, she does not complain about either the physical pain or the social subordination she suffers. Despite the death of her beloved husband and all of her children, Big Lannie "did her work perfectly; some of the ladies even told her so."[85] This recognition and praise shows her value, yet the privileged white ladies do not consider her a human being.

Oblivious to her needs or feelings, the white employers are outraged when she quits her jobs to care for her newborn blind grandson. Unable to abide this imposition on their selfish wants, the ladies lash out at Big Lannie with hatred and self-pity. Secure in their own superiority, the white women immediately revert to the worst stereotyping about African Americans: "'Honestly, those niggers!' each said to her friends. 'They're all alike.'"[86] Presenting the story from an African American perspective demonstrates just how harsh and unwarranted these insults are. Big Lannie's personal dedication to her work and her family disprove her employers' stereotypes of sloth, selfishness, and unreliability.

The protagonist tries to protect her grandson Raymond, wanting him to avoid the burden of poverty and belittlement that has dominated her. When his clothes become too worn for her to mend, Big Lannie swallows her self-respect and begs her white employer for some old clothes. Mrs. Ewing condescends to give a suit of her husband's, but only after complaining that she already does extensive charity work for local organizations and cautioning her servant against expecting future handouts. The story demonstrates how Mrs. Ewing's moral superiority is a form of abuse, as she uses wealth and status to dominate and diminish. After receiving the cast-off suit, Raymond leaves their apartment where he is introduced to ridicule and denigration: "It was like great flails beating him flat, great prongs tearing his flesh from his bones. It was coming at him, to kill him."[87] The formal suit does not fit him, literally and figuratively. He is reduced to a caricature, an African American man trying but failing to fit into the white-man's world. In the street, "he lay screaming, in blood and dust and darkness," and when his grandmother returns home she finds him "on the floor in the corner of the room, moaning and whimpering" like a whipped dog. Parker aimed to tear the reader's heart, just as Big Lannie's heart is torn, and to feel shame at her claims that "everything's all right,"[88] which "neither he nor she believed."

In these stories, Parker challenged middle-class white readers to consider the gross inequities and the daily indignities faced by African Americans. She entreated white women to understand the power they held over women of color. For instance, Big Lannie does not have job security, made plain when her employer threatens to hire a younger, faster worker. Fearing for her and her family's survival, the African American servant must express deference and gratitude no matter how she is treated. Whether they know it or not, white women have privileges and opportunities for themselves and their families that are denied African Americans. Parker did not sentimentalize this inequality, but she did illustrate the material and psychological damage it can cause. She asked white readers to examine their own thoughts and actions, so they might feel compassion for human beings that are devalued and disadvantaged.

Parker believed that those with white privilege should help those without, not because they are superior, but because unearned access to wealth and power demands it. From this standpoint, the title "Clothe the Naked" is a call to action. The deeper implications of this principle are that the people lucky enough to be born into financial and social affluence should not merely give cast-off clothing; they should also fight for social justice and racial equality. They must "clothe" the abused and forgotten with human dignity and a chance for success.

SPEAKING FOR THE POOR

Throughout her writing career, Parker spoke up for the working class of all races and ethnicities, criticizing the abuses of employers and society's refusal to assist those in poverty. In her 1926 poem "Symptom Recital," she admitted, "I'm disillusioned, empty-breasted. / For what I think, I'd be arrested."[89] A year later she was arrested for protesting the execution of anarchists Sacco and Vanzetti, causing her political activism to take a more radical turn. After that, Parker frequently spoke out, joined anti-fascist organizations, and established Hollywood's first union for screenwriters. "In 1934, Parker, responding to the promise of Communism to feed the hungry and clothe the poor, had declared herself a Communist."[90] Her politics did have a negative impact on the production of her stage plays and her screenwriting career. Nevertheless, Parker continued to advocate for the ignored and underserved at home and abroad.

Her stories of working women show the strain of maintaining a positive self-image in the face of a capitalist-consumer culture that values a person based on how she looks and what she owns. In the 1920s, it was expensive to maintain a stylistic appearance and an indulgent lifestyle; one needed an attractive, athletic physique adorned with the proper clothing, jewelry, cosmetics, automobile, and home. The question, of course, is who sets the standard and who benefits. The answer, not surprisingly, is men. Advertisers and business owners in the 1920s established the frivolous glamour girl as a feminine ideal to cause women, young and old, to pay "sky-rocketing costs"[91] for "popularity and self-esteem." The price of acceptance and success could bankrupt a woman's pocketbook and her soul, as appearance became more important than substance and one's character was subsumed by one's image. Parker complained that the glamour girl, who she aligned with the flapper, was not only vain, vapid, and ultimately unfulfilled, but she also tacitly subscribed to the gender stereotypes and inequalities underlying popular culture. "Parker's irritation with the flapper's girlish ways reflects her reservations about feminine roles that substituted a cult of the body for intellectual development and narcissism for ambition."[92]

Working women who bought into the cult of the body tried to remake themselves in the image of the silly, superficial glamour girl, adopting the self-image of a passive object, dependent on male attention and care. Parker's "Big Blonde" features a working-class protagonist, Hazel, who struggles financially and emotionally to survive in the modern world. She must make herself attractive to supplement her meager income and reduce her loneliness and boredom. The men she meets can buy what and who they wish, but a woman must maintain her beauty, continually flatter the men, and be "a good sport"[93] to live a comfortable life. Hazel follows the rules and happily gets married, finally able to relax and drop the exhausting glamour girl role assigned by society. However, after the honeymoon, her husband wants her to reassume the stereotype and behave like an amusing, compliant girl. Hazel's refusal causes the couple to shift from being lovers to becoming enemies, resulting in him leaving her.

On her own, Hazel has little choice but to re-adopt feminine stereotypes, dragging herself to a neighbor's drinking parties for a group of middle-aged men she calls, "The Boys."[94] Diminished and helpless, she must perform again as a "girl," becoming the "dizzy blonde"[95] who is always jolly while drinking and flirting. When one of the "boys" takes her as his "doll," she must play the good sport even more. His proprietorship forces her to hide feelings of depression deep inside, prompting her to hate her life and herself. She drinks to excess and eventually takes pills in a suicide attempt. When she regains consciousness, she feels a "saturating wretchedness" and prays to remain "always drunk."[96]

The Big Blonde's misery reflects her subjugation as a woman and as a member of the working class. She is victimized by the male commerce of female bodies and the social dictum that women must be what men want or men will ignore, abuse, and divorce them. A Marxist might state that this capitalistic relationship puts men in charge of the means of production and alienates women from their bodies, their humanity, economic self-sufficiency, positive self-identity, and social agency. In the end, Hazel would rather destroy her body than continue to allow it to remain outside of her control and in service to male interests.

Even the choice of self-destruction is denied by a man, the doctor who saves her life. When confronted with Hazel's comatose body, the doctor pulls back her nightgown and cruelly pinches her legs, exposing her half-naked body to public display without her consent. The elevator operator chuckles as he watches this rough examination of Hazel's unconscious body. It appears to him like the doctor is "tryin' to push her right on th'ough the bed."[97] The sexual overtones of this comment remind the reader that the doctor reluctantly left his own bedroom and the prostitute he engaged to attend to Hazel. Parker's story shows how common it is that a woman loses authority over her life, and her death, in a male-controlled society.

One might wonder how Hazel falls victim to the patriarchy when Anita Loos's ditzy blonde Lorelei Lee does not. The difference: "Despite all of

Lorelei's apparent errors, she is always aware of the power dynamics that shape the relations between men and women; Lorelei uses her insights about human nature to alter this dynamic, have fun, and best the men who woo her. In contrast, Hazel gets attention wherever she finds it, without questioning the sexist intentions of her suitors."[98] Hazel lacks Lorelei's insight or her confidence. Suicide is Hazel's only recourse, whereas Lorelei murders an unfaithful suitor and manipulates a male jury into acquitting her. She then exploits wealthy men and initiates a marriage on her own terms. A courageous Lorelei constructs and manages the spectacle of her femininity and sexuality—she controls the means of production. Empowered, Lorelei dominates her husband and her destiny. On the other hand, a bewildered Hazel cannot avoid becoming a spectacle that the male gaze controls. Passive and despondent, she is exploited and discarded by men, which "attracts pity rather than sympathy" from women readers. Both stories satirize society and the men who run it; however, Loos's is a romp with a happy ending, while Parker's demonstrates the brutal consequences of misogyny on a woman's body, psyche, and spirit.

A later story that continues Parker's analysis of the psychological and emotional burden carried by working-class women is "The Standard of Living" (1941). The main characters are two New York City stenographers who live at home and pay half of their salaries to support their families.[99] They live mundane lives except for a game they play of pretending to receive a million dollars, with the stipulation they spend it entirely on themselves. They promenade around the city with a regal air, imagining themselves as rich ladies of leisure. However, their self-image is punctured when they visit a posh Fifth Avenue shop and learn that a string of pearls costs $250,000. Upon leaving the shop, "their shoulders dropped and they dragged their feet; they bumped against each other, without notice or apology, and caromed away again. They were silent and their eyes were cloudy."[100] The women soon resume their game, but it is clear they feel the emptiness of this fantasy, knowing they will always be denied the sense of self-worth and respect that accompanies wealth and status.

In addition, Parker wrote essays expressing her political views, often using a serious tone rather than her trademark wit. One example is "Not Enough," published in *New Masses* on March 14, 1939. Writing in the first person, Parker began by chiding her childhood self for not protesting when her rich aunt, "a horrible woman then and now,"[101] callously disregarded the plight of the working class, ignoring the fact that the men shoveling snow in a blizzard are not paid enough to buy adequate shoes and are denied work when the weather is tolerable. Even though young Parker said nothing, she felt "wild with the knowledge of injustice and brutality and misrepresentation," especially since "I knew it need not be so." Witnessing what rich people say and do, she preferred to associate herself with "the masses," as she was "proud of being a worker, too." As the only group worthy of her respect, blue-collar workers defy stereotypes by frequently demonstrating they are serious, conscientious, supportive, interesting, and spirited.

During the 1920s, Parker used biting satire to express her concerns, but in the 1930s she converted her beliefs into action. She revealed in "Not Enough" that her political activism truly began in Hollywood, exalting screenwriter Donald Ogden Stewart as her inspiration and co-conspirator. Together, they served on the Screenwriters Guild's board of directors and formed the Anti-Nazi League. In addition, Parker visited Spain and described first-hand the danger and self-sacrifice of a people fighting against fascism. She asserted, "I think that order, of course, should be inverted."[102] The experience excited her desire to fight for human decency in her own nation and caused her to realize, "the only possible thing for mankind is solidarity."

Feeling that writing was not enough, Parker started giving public speeches to raise money for anti-fascist causes. She chose to be "unpleasant"[103] instead of comical, so neither the issues nor her views could be disregarded. She published articles in magazines read by intelligent, influential people who had retreated to "that dreary ivory tower" to ignore the world's problems. "Not Enough" concludes by committing to the oppressed, impoverished outcasts across the globe and demanding the privileged own up to their responsibility to help hardworking men and women in the United States who cannot earn enough to feed their children. By publicly commanding herself to do more to assist those in need, Parker suggested that her readers must face the hard truths and act to make the world better.

She opposed the rich and powerful, but she also was not shy about criticizing herself and fellow "light-verse writers"[104] of the 1920s for being oblivious to the serious issues in society. The article "Sophisticated Poetry—And the Hell with It" (1939), published in *New Masses*, pokes fun at her early ambition to become a "sophisticate" author.[105] Defining the sophisticate as a low-rent cynic, Parker denounced her naïve and self-centered 1920s self as "dashing and devil-may-care," at best, and "dowdy," at worst. She claimed that she began her career with the aspiration to write well-constructed, humorous, smart verse that demonstrated a carefree and fanciful attitude. Unfortunately, she and her fellow authors remained in the immature "smarty-pants"[106] phase of life too long. Hard-won intellectual and artistic maturity caused her to replace "I" with "we" in her writing because, as Parker argued, "you cannot find yourself until you find your fellow man. . . . It is no longer the time for personal matters—thank God! Now the poet speaks not just for himself but for all of us—and so his voice is heard, and so his song goes on."

The essay lauded the new generation of politically conscious writers who stepped outside of their self-interest to organize, protest, and create change. With a better-late-than-never self-scolding, Parker expressed pride that she had committed to writing in defense of the poor and neglected, unconcerned about the feathers she might ruffle among well-to-do socialites or anti-communist politicians.

NOT GIVING A DAMN

Parker created a defiant attitude for 1920s women, stating in her poem "Observation" (1926): "But I shall stay the way I am, / Because I do not give a damn."[107] Standing up for what she believed, Parker earned the respect of contemporaries and the praise of critics, who admired her unique talent and enjoyed her brash personality. Celebrated columnist and fellow Algonquin Round Table member Franklin Pierce Adams once called her "the only limited-edition girl I know, by which I mean there is nobody like her, nor ever was."[108] Literary and cultural critic Edmund Wilson proclaimed in "A Toast and a Tear for Dorothy Parker" (1944) that "she has put into what she has written a voice, a state of mind, an era, a few moments of human experience that nobody else has conveyed."[109] Accomplished screenwriter Nora Ephron related being inspired by the legend of Parker's wit and social conscience: "I grew up on it and coveted it desperately. All I wanted in this world was to come to New York and be Dorothy Parker."[110]

A celebrity and an icon, Parker was the voice of a generation attempting to overturn the status quo. Her cynical and scornful literary style was attractive to female readers in the 1920s, for it articulated their dissatisfaction with being the passive objects of male consumption. In the face of restrictive traditional values on one side and narcissistic glamour girl culture on the other, many women sought to do more than complain. Parker modeled finding strength in oneself and actively fighting for change in the larger society. She bravely showed that disputing the sexism, racism, and classism inherent in the establishment meant using one's intellect to identify and discard the self-destructive identities assigned to women, minorities, and the poor. The goal was to make readers more self-conscious, so they would note the inequalities limiting their advancement and stop meekly accepting anything less than the rights and respect due them.

Parker, like all successful humorists, relied on a "magnificent disregard"[111] of society's expectations, hoping that the readers would follow her lead but refusing to compromise her message or her tone if they did not. She encouraged women to speak their minds and upend what was considered the normal, acceptable feminine identity and behavior. She purposefully displayed a strength of mind and will that possessed a "cosmopolitan, cognitive superiority to the leaky, fraying, diminishing sentimentality Parker associates with the fantasy-saturated practices of normative femininity."[112] Although publicizing her political views at the height of her career cost Parker professionally and personally, she nonetheless valiantly thumbed her nose at critics and inspired others to do the same.

Parker claimed years later that her 1920s verses had become "terribly dated" and were "no damn good."[113] This evaluation may or may not be true, but certainly the ideas she forwarded and the actions she espoused resonated with female readers. A self-aware subject, Parker laughed at convention and sentimentality, urging solidarity among all women in the fight against the patriarchy and the weapons it wielded. Parker exhorted her readers to be aware of their potential and avoid being reduced to an afterthought. As she attests in the poem "Chant for Dark Hours" (1926), modern women must not fall into the same trap as previous generations: "All your life you wait around for some damn man!"[114]

NOTES

1. John Keats, *You Might as Well Live: The Life and Times of Dorothy Parker* (New York: Simon and Schuster, 1990), accessed December 17, 2021, https://books.google.com.

2. Ken Johnson, "Dorothy Parker's Perpetual Motion," in *American Women Short Story Writers: A Collection of Critical Essays*, ed. Julie Brown (New York: Rutledge, 2000), 252.

3. National Organization for Women, "History of Marches and Mass Actions," accessed August 26, 2020, https://now.org.

4. Anthony Brown, Joanna Batt, and Esther June Kim, "Beyond the 19th: A Brief History of the Voter Suppression of Black Americans," *Social Education* 84, no. 4 (2020), 204; and Emily Baxter, Kaitlin Holmes, and Rob Griffin, "The Importance of Women of Color Voters: Then and Now," Center for American Progress, accessed August 25, 2020, https://wnywomensfoundation.org.

5. Stuart Y. Silverstein, Introduction to *Not Much Fun: The Lost Poems of Dorothy Parker* (New York: Scribner, 2009), 69.

6. Genevieve Taggard, "You Might as Well Live," *New York Herald Tribune Books*, March 27, 1927, 7; and Edmund Wilson, "Dorothy Parker's Poems," *New Republic*, January 19, 1927, 256.

7. Marie Luhrs, "Fashionable Poetry," *Poetry* 30, no. 1 (1927), 53.

8. Luhrs, "Fashionable Poetry," 54.

9. Cole Porter, "Just One of Those Things," *Poets.org*, accessed April 7, 2021, https://poets.org/poem/just-one-those-things.

10. Stephen M. Silverman, *Funny Ladies* (Boston: New World City, 2018), accessed Dec. 17, 2021, https://books.google.com; and Jonathan L. Entin, "A Civil Rights Life: Nathaniel R. Jones. Answering the Call: An Autobiography of the Modern Struggle to End Racial Discrimination in America. New York: The New Press, 2016," *Case Western Reserve Law Review* 68, no. 2 (2017), 657.

11. David Greenberg, *Calvin Coolidge: The American Presidents Series: The 30th President, 1923–1929* (New York: Henry Holt and Company, 2006), 9.

12. Dorothy Parker, *The Portable Dorothy Parker* (New York: Penguin, 2006), 117.

13. Milly S. Barranger, "Dorothy Parker and the Politics of McCarthyism," *Theater History Studies* 26 (2006), 9.

14. Barranger, "Dorothy Parker and the Politics of McCarthyism," 10–12.

15. Marion Meade, *Dorothy Parker: What Fresh Hell Is This?* (New York: Penguin, 1989), 61.

16. Amelia Simpson, "Premium Swift: Dorothy Parker's Iron Mask of Femininity (1996)," in *The Critical Waltz: Essays on the Work of Dorothy Parker*, ed. Rhonda S. Pettit (Madison, NJ: Fairleigh Dickinson University Press, 2005), 209.

17. Brett Candish Miller, *Flawed Light: American Women Poets and Alcohol* (Champaign: University of Illinois Press, 2009), 19.

18. Dorothy Parker, *Enough Rope* (New York: Boni and Liveright, 1926), 61.

19. Parker, *Enough Rope*, 85.

20. Ibid., 53.

21. Ibid., 24.

22. Ibid., 28, 51.

23. Ibid., 60.

24. Ibid., 82.

25. Ibid., 74.

26. Parker, *The Portable Dorothy Parker*, 212.

27. Parker, *Enough Rope*, 40.

28. Ibid., 80.

29. Ibid., 86.

30. Ibid., 78.

31. Ibid., 84.

32. Ibid., 68.

33. Ibid., 62.

34. Ibid., 63.

35. Dorothy Parker, *Men I'm Not Married To* (New York: Doubleday, 1922), 1.

36. Parker, *Enough Rope*, 106.

37. Ibid., 54.

38. Ibid., 52.

39. Ibid., 70.

40. Parker, *The Portable Dorothy Parker*, 577.

41. Ibid., 558–559.

42. Catherine Keyser, *Playing Smart: New York Women Writers and Modern Magazine Culture* (New Brunswick: Rutgers University Press, 2010), 71.

43. Parker, *The Portable Dorothy Parker*, 39.

44. Silverstein, Introduction to *Not Much Fun*, 33.

45. Dorothy Parker, "Women: A Hate Song," *Vanity Fair*, August 1916, accessed December 17, 2021, https://www.vanityfair.com/news/1916/08/women-a-hate-song.

46. Francisco Jose Cortes Vieco, "'I Hate Women. They Get on My Nerves': Dorothy Parker's Poetry of Female Sympathy," *ES Review: Spanish Journal of English Studies* 38 (2017), 65.

47. David Joseph Goldberg, *Discontented America; The United States in the 1920s* (Baltimore: Johns Hopkins University Press, 1999), 53.

48. Annelise Orleck, *Rethinking American Women's Activism* (New York: Routledge, 2015), 29.

49. Catherine Keyser, "The Macabre Magazine: Dorothy Parker, Humor, and the Female Body," in *Death Becomes Her: Cultural Narratives of Femininity and Death in Nineteenth-Century America*, eds. Elizabeth Dill and Sheri Weinstein (Newcastle: Cambridge Scholars, 2008), 148, 132.

50. Parker, *The Portable Dorothy Parker*, 327, 330.

51. Ibid., 123.

52. Joseph L. Coulombe, "Performing Humor in Dorothy Parker's Fiction," *Studies in American Humor* 3, no. 28 (2013), 55.

53. Parker, *The Portable Dorothy Parker*, 120.

54. Ibid., 122.

55. Ibid., 255.

56. Ibid., 256.

57. Ibid., 254.

58. Ibid., 255.

59. Ibid., 256.

60. Coulombe, "Performing Humor in Dorothy Parker's Fiction," 52.

61. Parker, *The Portable Dorothy Parker*, 47.

62. Ibid., 49.

63. Dorothy Parker, *Complete Stories*, ed. Colleen Breese (New York: Penguin, 1995), accessed December17, 2021, https://books.google.com.

64. Rhonda S. Pettit, *A Gendered Collision: Sentimentalism and Modernism in Dorothy Parker's Poetry and Fiction* (Madison, NJ: Fairleigh Dickinson University Press, 2000), 62.

65. Pettit, *A Gendered Collision*, 64.

66. Orleck, *Rethinking American Women's Activism*, 31.

67. Ibid., 30.

68. Kevin C. Fitzpatrick, "Introduction: In the Aisle Seat with Dorothy Parker," in *Dorothy Parker: Complete Broadway, 1918–1923*, ed. Kevin C. Fitzpatrick (Bloomington: iUniverse, 2014), xxiii.

69. Dorothy Parker, *Dorothy Parker: Complete Broadway, 1918–1923*, ed. Kevin C. Fitzpatrick (Bloomington: iUniverse, 2014), 161.

70. Parker, *Dorothy Parker: Complete Broadway, 1918–1923*, 162.

71. Ibid., 197.

72. Parker, *Enough Rope*, 19.

73. Ibid., 19.

74. Parker, *The Portable Dorothy Parker*, 19.

75. Susan Edmunds, *Grotesque Relations: Modernist Domestic Fiction and the U.S. Welfare State* (Oxford: Oxford University Press, 2008), 76.

76. Parker, *The Portable Dorothy Parker*, 20.

77. Ibid., 19.

78. Ibid., 20.

79. Ibid., 19.

80. Ibid., 23.

81. Ibid., 21.

82. Ibid., 22.

83. Ibid., 23.

84. Amelia Simpson, "Black on Blonde: The Africanist Presence in Dorothy Parker's 'Big Blonde,'" *College Literature* 23, no. 3 (1996), 113.

85. Parker, *The Portable Dorothy Parker*, 358.

86. Ibid., 359.

87. Ibid., 366.

88. Ibid., 367.

89. Parker, *Enough Rope*, 92.

90. Barranger, "Dorothy Parker and the Politics of McCarthyism," 9.

91. Zeitz, *Flapper*, 208.

92. Keyser, *Playing Smart*, 52.

93. Parker, *The Portable Dorothy Parker*, 187.

94. Ibid., 193.

95. Ibid., 194.

96. Ibid., 208, 210.

97. Ibid., 207.

98. Laurie J.C. Cella, "Narrative 'Confidence Games': Framing the Blonde Spectacle in *Gentlemen Prefer Blondes* (1925) and *Nights at the Circus* (1984)," *Frontiers: A Journal of Women Studies* 25, no. 3 (2004), 53.

99. Parker, *The Portable Dorothy Parker*, 29.

100. Ibid., 34.

101. Ibid., 462.

102. Ibid., 464.

103. Ibid., 465.

104. Ibid., 561.

105. Ibid., 560.

106. Ibid., 562.

107. Parker, *Enough Rope*, 91.

108. Marion Meade, *Bobbed Hair and Bathtub Gin: Writers Running Wild in the Twenties* (Orlando: Houghton Mifflin Harcourt, 2004), 271.

109. Edmund Wilson, *Classics and Commercials: A Literary Chronicle of the Forties* (New York: Macmillan, 1950), accessed December 17, 2021, https://books.google.com.

110. Nora Ephron, *Crazy Salad and Scribble Scribble: Some Things about Women and Notes on Media* (New York: Vintage, 2012), 168.

111. Marion Meade, Introduction to *The Portable Dorothy Parker* (New York: Penguin, 2006), xiv.

112. Lauren Berlant, *The Female Complaint: The Unfinished Business of Sentimentality in American Culture* (Durham: Duke University Press, 2008), 211.

113. Parker, *The Portable Dorothy Parker*, 576.

114. Parker, *Enough Rope*, 50.

Conclusion

Identity Affirmation

The eleven authors I have chosen to discuss made names for themselves in the 1920s by endorsing and amplifying the cultural upheaval rippling across the United States at the time. Poet or playwright, novelist or blues lyricist, each author attracted a loyal following of women who recognized themselves in the fiction. Set in the raucous Jazz Age, the stories and lyrics not only reflected who the primary reader was, an ambitious and hard-working woman confronting overwhelming obstacles, but they also revealed who the reader aspired to be, an accomplished and self-actualized modern woman. The protagonists in these texts promoted personal growth and social activism, forcing their way into male-only careers and public spaces. They prodded readers to act on their own behalf as they celebrated a woman's creativity, intellect, competence, humor, resourcefulness, and sexual autonomy.

I study these authors to understand the influence they had in the twenties and the impact they might have today. Their works tapped into a discontent women felt about the roles they were obliged to perform and modeled several versions of femininity that subverted the status quo of male dominance and female subservience. The preferred outcome was for women to gain personal satisfaction and admission to public life.

One 1920s identity that led women toward self-determination and gender equality was the capable, confident New Woman. Authors Anzia Yezierska and Mourning Dove exemplified this type of womanhood, calling out injustice and misogyny in their novels about women who doggedly argue that their ability to do the work of a man necessitates they be given the same opportunities and respect. Their fictional protagonists did not embody a new persona, as the New Woman had been developing since the turn of the century; however, they did validate those who were trying this persona on for size, showing the strength of character and upward mobility it fostered.

173

These self-made women overcome hardship and abuse to support themselves financially and emotionally. Readers cheer for self-aware characters who own their bodies, empowered to control the profit of their labor and the recipients of their sexual interest. They have strong moral convictions and refuse to undersell their value as human beings, lessons that resonated with readers who faced pressure to compromise themselves as daughters, wives, employees, and community leaders.

A wildly popular version of womanhood in the 1920s was the flapper, a figure who undermined male domination through her liberated, devil-may-care approach to life. Adopting a flapper identity enabled women to shrug off gender expectations and live as they wished, symbolized by bobbing their hair, shortening their skirts, wearing make-up, drinking bathtub gin, and dancing with men. Authors Anita Loos, Josephine Lovett, and Mae West displayed this attitude, injecting flagrant rule-breaking and shameless sexuality into their stories about strong-willed, self-reliant women who will not be tamed by men or their outdated social mores.

Just like the New Women, the flappers ruled their own bodies, spoke their minds, and loved themselves. Readers are meant to emulate these honest and outgoing characters, in contrast to the stories' unhappy female antagonists who repress their sexuality and passively obey patriarchal edicts for the promise of wealth and status. Furthermore, readers admired flapper characters for refusing to be confined by marriage and choosing, just as Yezierska and Mourning Dove's protagonists ultimately do, to marry men that respect their personhood and do not stop a wife from being her own boss, a partner rather than a subject to her husband.

These versions of femininity fit into the 1920s feminist counter-narrative of women adopting a strong identity to serve the needs and accomplish the goals they have as individuals. In addition, the authors asked readers to identify themselves as part of a group, working for cultural diversity and against the compounding of oppression through racism, classism, homophobia, and sexism.

Women of color made sizable contributions and sacrifices for suffrage, yet they did not reap the benefits of enfranchisement for generations. Instead, they found themselves diminished within the feminist movement and excluded from many areas of mainstream society. In response, authors Nella Larsen, Mourning Dove, and Dorothy Parker directly challenged racial and ethnic prejudice, illustrating its detrimental effects on minority women. Their novels and short stories dramatized the rampant bigotry of mainstream white society, encouraging women of color to support each other and urging white women to recognize both their perpetuation of individual injustices and their tacit approval of systemic inequities. The presentation of racial pride (and white shame) alerted readers that this issue deserved their attention, important at a time of racial unrest and violence as the growth of progressive thinking provoked brutal backlash from individual white supremacists and organized hate groups like the Ku Klux Klan.

Racial and ethnic minorities were not the only group identities championed by authors of the Roaring Twenties. Lesbians were another community fighting for acceptance and equal rights. Although sexuality is a key aspect of one's individual identity, sexual orientation has long been a standard by which U.S. society determines whether to include or exclude someone. As with men and women or whites and people of color, heterosexuals and homosexuals were not accorded the same privileges or respect in the 1920s. Seeking change, authors Djuna Barnes, Amy Lowell, Bessie Smith, and Gertrude Stein wrote poetic and blues lyrics that defended female alliances and same-sex desire. Their works charmed (and scandalized) the cultural elites and the masses, an effort to redefine and normalize lesbianism. Audiences were given positive representations of lesbians exploring their sexuality, forming committed relationships, and speaking out publicly. During an era when women's heterosexual passion was more open and accepted, women-loving women were raising their profile and, with the help of conscientious authors, claiming a spot in mainstream culture.

The texts studied here taught 1920s women that they had viable routes to realizing who and what they wanted to be as individuals and citizens in U.S. society. The fictional works honored a woman's individual dreams and desires, offering a sense of purpose based on her talent and resolve instead of gendered assumptions. Stories of women enjoying professional careers and sexual freedom, while commonplace today, were a revelation to many 1920s readers. Their availability through popular magazines, blues records, movie houses, and neighborhood bookstores created an imagined community for those who felt alone and unsupported, connection to a knowing authorial voice and entry into a national sisterhood. The authors outlined the benefits and obligations of being an activist, suggesting women publicly insist on the rights and recognition they deserved as human beings. The stories jolted readers out of their complacency or hopelessness, inspiring perseverance and strengthening a sense of self-worth.

These authors were leading voices for women's liberation in the 1920s, but what is their impact today? Several waves of feminism have swept through U.S. society since then, so recent texts are perhaps more relevant to contemporary readers. However, lessons from the past are relevant today. Authors like Dorothy Parker, Mae West, and Gertrude Stein have maintained a following, while others, like Nella Larson, Mourning Dove, and Anzia Yezierska, have been rediscovered, regaining some of their former literary and cultural status.

Parker is the author from the twenties who probably has the most cachet for women today. Many of her works have never gone out of print; plus, quotes attributed to her swirl through popular discourse. Her reputation is aided by the Dorothy Parker Society, which maintains and updates a website devoted to the author.[1] Parker is respected as "a woman who had been courageously outspoken about many aspects of the female experience, including her own, which were not commonly addressed in public."[2] The cultural rebel did not shy away from her own failures and self-doubt, centering stories and poems around her own experience with abortion and suicide attempts. Simone de Beauvoir recognized Parker's worth as an author and activist, praising her in the introduction to her seminal feminist work *The Second Sex* (1949). De Beauvoir lauded Parker's impact on gender equality, epitomized by this quote she took from Parker's review of *Modern Woman: The Lost Sex* (1947), "I cannot be fair about books that treat women as women. My idea is that all of us, men as well as women, whoever we are, should be considered as human beings."[3]

This goal of ending gender segregation has been part of the feminist agenda for decades. The use of differences between the sexes creates a hierarchical binary that subordinates women to an inferior cultural position. A major contingent of feminists believe vanquishing gender inequality requires "not just the elimination of male *privilege* but of the sex *distinction* itself: genital differences between human beings would no longer matter culturally."[4] Recent calls for "a feminist degendering movement"[5] would improve women's standing in employment, cultural production, and the larger social order. As Parker prophesized, the termination of gender divisions leads to parity and equality, "undercutting the subordination of women by men."[6]

Supporters of this movement recognize that dismantling the binary structure would also reduce the sexual objectification and abuse of women and the discrimination of lesbians and transgendered people.[7] Poems and blues lyrics by Djuna Barnes, Amy Lowell, Bessie Smith, and Gertrude Stein, along with plays by Mae West and Josephine Lovett mirror the battles lesbians and heterosexual women wage to procure sexual independence. The 1920s texts imbued a woman's sexual desire with social power, making her a speaking subject rather than an object of male attention and control. Twenty-first-century women face some of the same stereotypes as the characters in these stories, attacked for unapologetically expressing their sexual self. The lessons taught a century earlier, such as women embracing their genuine passions and expressing them freely, bolster present-day feminist directives for women to reclaim their bodies and assert personal agency. The 1920s authors were ahead of their time, alerting readers that sexual autonomy for homosexuals and heterosexuals is a fundamental human right.[8]

Nella Larsen and Mourning Dove are two recently rediscovered authors currently making an impact on readers and scholars. Their novels remain relevant because race is still contested in U.S. society and women of color continue to be disempowered, their humanity routinely denied. In terms of civil rights and legal protections, minority women face an alarming level of violence to their bodies and their identities. Moreover, feminist scholars analyze the "intersectional relationship between race, ethnicity, gender, sexuality, class, and nation."[9] This "interlocking nature of various axes of exclusion" victimizes non-white women at much higher rates than any other group. Larsen and Mourning Dove invented protagonists that experience multiple axes of exclusion, drawing attention to the unfair and artificial constructions of race and gender by being biracial and winning the respect of the men in their lives. Thus, one could argue that these authors' strategies for overthrowing racist power structures "can be recovered for modern readers."[10]

Finally, the novels by Anzia Yezierska and Anita Loos remain relevant because women continue to struggle with establishing themselves as working professionals and respected community leaders. Their protagonists seek to learn the rules of the system and insert themselves, so they may attain a career that allows them to support and govern themselves. Although some feminists today advocate a revolution against the system, others ask for the system to provide equal opportunity and access. Women who play the game can seize a position alongside or above the men in their field, ably performing to the standards set by men. Yezierska and Loos exposed the unfairness of the current rules by showing what a woman can do if given the chance, confirming the absurdity of gender stereotypes and the damage they can do.

In conclusion, works by women authors of the Jazz Age speak to significant gender, race, and class issues at the heart of U.S. society, then and now. Their stories contribute to a long feminist tradition that has inspired women to reject the life they were told to want and fight for the life they desire and deserve. The Roaring Twenties was a time of transition from traditional feminine identities to economic self-sufficiency, sexual freedom, political action, and artistic creativity. Acutely aware of the seismic shift underway, a circle of brilliant women authors renounced ballads of passivity and romance. They dove into taboo topics, exposing hypocrisy and agitating for a new social order. This approach is plain in Dorothy Parker's "Prologue to a Saga" (1931), where a strong-minded, rebellious speaker derides the "pretty dears"[11] weeping for lost love. Energized, she announces, "Gangway, girls: I'll show you trouble." For Parker and her compatriots, charging ahead and getting into "trouble" was the only righteous choice.

NOTES

1. Dorothy Parker Society, "About," accessed August 7, 2020, https://dorothyparker.com.

2. Sandra J. Gall, "Seymour Barab's Songs of Perfect Propriety Volumes I and II: The Relationship between Barab's Music and Words by Dorothy Parker" (PhD diss., University of Oklahoma, 2000), viii.

3. Simone de Beauvoir, *The Second Sex*, trans. Constance Borde and Sheila Malovany-Chevallier (New York: Vintage, 2011), 4.

4. Shulamith Firestone, *The Dialectic of Sex: The Case for Feminist Revolution* (New York: Bantam, 1972), 11.

5. Judith Lorber, "Using Gender to Undo Gender: A Feminist Degendering Movement," *Feminist Theory* 1, no. 1 (2000), 80.

6. Lorber, "Using Gender to Undo Gender," 81.

7. Lena Holzer, "Smashing the Binary? A New Era of Legal Gender Registration in the Yogyakarta Principles Plus 10," *International Journal of Gender, Sexuality and Law* 1, no. 1 (2020), 101.

8. Dana-Sophia Valentiner, "The Human Rights to Sexual Autonomy," *German Law Journal* 22, no. 5 (2021), 703.

9. Renya K. Ramirez, "Learning across Differences: Native and Ethnic Studies Feminisms," *American Quarterly* 60, no. 2 (2008), 305.

10. Clifton Frei, "Nella Larsen's *Passing* and the Tragedy of the Oppressed: Trauma, Race, Identity, and Reading Resistance," *NEIU 27th Annual Student Research and Creative Activities Symposium*, 2019.

11. Parker, *The Portable Dorothy Parker*, 315.

Bibliography

Adair, Vivyan C. "Of Home-Makers and Home–Breakers: The *Deserving* and the *Underserving* Poor Mother in Depression Era Literature." In *The Literary Mother: Essays on Representations of Maternity and Child Care*, edited by Susan C. Staub, 48–68. Jefferson: McFarland & Company, 2007.

Aleman, Ana M. Martinez and Kristen A. Renn. *Women in Higher Education: An Encyclopedia.* Santa Barbara: ABC-CLIO, 2002.

Aliaga–Buchenau, Ana-Isabel. *The Dangerous Potential of Reading: Readers & the Negotiation of Power in Nineteenth-Century Narratives.* New York: Routledge, 2004.

Allen, Carolyn. *Following Djuna: Women Lovers and the Erotics of Loss.* Bloomington: Indiana University Press, 1996.

Allen, Frederick Lewis. *Only Yesterday: An Informal History of the 1920's.* New York: Harper, 1931.

Automotive News. "1920s." Accessed October 22, 2020. https://www.autonews.com/article/20000828/ANA/8280853/1920s.

Bachhofer, Aaron. "Smith, Bessie" In *LGBTQ Americans in the U.S. Political System*, edited by Jason Pierceson. Santa Barbara: ABC-CLIO, 2019.

Banet–Weiser, Sarah and Kate M. Miltner. "#MasculinitySoFragile: culture, structure, and networked misogyny." *Feminist Media Studies* 16, no. 1 (2015): 171–174.

Barlow, William. "Black Music on the Radio During the Jazz Age." *African American Review* 29, no. 2 (1995): 325–328.

Barnes, Djuna. *The Book of Repulsive Women.* New York: Bruna Chap Books, 1915. Accessed Dec. 17, 2021. https://digital.library.upenn.edu/women/barnes/repulsive/repulsive.html.

———. *Collected Poems.* Madison: University of Wisconsin Press, 2005.

———. *Ladies Almanack.* New York: New York University Press, 1992.

Barranger, Milly S. "Dorothy Parker and the Politics of McCarthyism." *Theater History Studies* 26 (2006): 7–30.

179

Barrett–Fox, Jason. "Rhetorics of Indirection, Indiscretion, Insurrection: the 'Feminine Style' of Anita Loos, 1912–1925." *JAC: Journal of Advanced Composition* 32, no. 1 (2012): 221–249.

Baxter, Emily, Kaitlin Holmes, and Rob Griffin. "The Importance of Women of Color Voters: Then and Now." *Center for American Progress*. Accessed August 25, 2020. https://wnywomensfoundation.org.

Beauvoir, Simone de. *The Second Sex*. Translated by Constance Borde and Sheila Malovany-Chevallier. New York: Vintage, 2011.

Berch, Bettina. *From Hester Street to Hollywood: The Life and Work of Anzia Yezierska*. New York: Sefer International, 2009.

Berlant, Lauren. *The Female Complaint: The Unfinished Business of Sentimentality in American Culture*. Durham: Duke University Press, 2008.

Bhusal, Ashok. "The Rhetorical of Racism and Anti-Miscegenation Laws in the United States." *IAFOR Journal of Arts & Humanities* 4, no. 2 (2017): 83–89.

Bowser, Aubrey. "The Cat Came Back." *The New York Amsterdam News*, June 5, 1929.

Bradshaw, Melissa. *Amy Lowell, Diva Poet*. Surrey: Ashgate, 2011.

Braziel, Jana Evans. "'Bye, Bye Baby': Race, Bisexuality, and the Blues in the Music of Bessie Smith and Janis Joplin." *Popular Music and Society* 27, no. 1 (2004): 3–26.

Brody, Jennifer Devere. "Clare Kendry's 'True' Colors: Race and Class Conflict in Nella Larsen's *Passing*." *Callaloo* 15, no. 4 (1992): 1053–1065.

Brown, Anthony, Joanna Batt, and Esther June Kim. "Beyond the 19th: A Brief History of the Voter Suppression of Black Americans." *Social Education* 84, no. 4 (2020): 204–208.

Bushnell, Candace. Introduction to *Gentlemen Prefer Blondes*. New York: Liveright, 1998.

Cahn, Susan K. *Coming on Strong: Gender and Sexuality in Twentieth–century Women's Sport*. Cambridge: Harvard University Press, 1994.

Calverton, Victor Francis. "Careers for Women—A Survey of Results." *Current–History* 29 (1929): 633–638.

Carby, Hazel. *Cultures in Babylon: Black Britain and African America*. London: Verso, 1999.

———. "'Woman's Era': Rethinking Black Feminist Thought." In *African American Literary Theory: A Reader*, edited by Winston Napier, 242–256. New York: New York University Press, 2000.

Carey, Allison Elise. "Domesticity and the Modernist Aesthetic: F.T. Marinetti, Djuna Barnes, and Gertrude Stein." PhD diss. University of Tennessee, 2003.

Castillo, Susan. "Narratives of Blood." *Early American Literature* 41, no. 2 (2006): 339–345.

Cella, Laurie J.C. "Narrative 'Confidence Games': Framing the Blonde Spectacle in *Gentlemen Prefer Blondes* (1925) and *Nights at the Circus* (1984)." *Frontiers: A Journal of Women Studies* 25, no. 3 (2004): 47–62.

Chauncey, George. *Gay New York: Gender, Urban Culture, and the Making of the Gay Male World 1890–1940*. New York: Basic Books, 1994. Accessed December 17, 2021. https://books.google.com.

Chenier, Elsie. "Conjugal Misconduct: Defying Marriage Law in the Twentieth–Century United States by William Kuby (review)." *Journal of the History of Sexuality* 29, no. 1 (2020): 121–124.

Childs, Peter. *Modernism*. New York: Routledge, 2000.

Chopin, Kate. "The Story of an Hour." *The Kate Chopin International Society*. Accessed March 30, 2021. https://www.katechopin.org/story-hour.

Cohen, Steve. "The Captive, a Pioneering Play about a Lesbian." *The Cultural Critic*. Accessed April 2, 2021. https://theculturalcritic.com/the-captive-a-pioneering-play-about-a-lesbian.

Coleman, Victoria H. and M. M. Carter. "Biracial Self–Identification: Impact on Trait Anxiety, Social Anxiety, and Depression." *Identity: An International Journal of Theory and Research* 7, no. 2 (2007): 1–12.

Conor, Liz. *The Spectacular Modern Woman: Feminine Visibility in the 1920s*. Bloomington: Indiana University Press, 2004.

Cope, Edward Drinker. "E. D. Cope to Julia Cope, March 27, 1888," KIC Document 53, American Museum of National History Library.

———. "Two Perils of the Indo–European." *The Open Court* 3, no. 127 (January 30, 1890): 2070–2071.

Cornes, Judy. *Sex, Power and the Folly of Marriage in Women's Novels of the 1920s: A Critical Study of Seven American Writers*. Jefferson: McFarland & Company, 2015.

Cott, Nancy. *The Grounding of Modern Feminism*. New Haven: Yale University Press, 1987.

Coulombe, Joseph L. "Performing Humor in Dorothy Parker's Fiction." *Studies in American Humor* 3, no. 28 (2013): 45–57.

Cover, Robert M. *Auto Mania*. New Haven: Yale University Press, 2007.

Cruea, Susan M. "Changing Ideals of Womanhood during the Nineteenth–Century Woman Movement." *ATQ: 19th century American literature and culture* 19, no. 3 (2005): 187–204.

Dalley, Lana L. and Jill Rappoport. *Economic Women: Essays on Desire and Dispossession in Nineteenth-Century British Culture*. Columbus: Ohio State University Press, 2017.

Daniel, Lucy. *Gertrude Stein*. London: Reaktion, 2009.

Davies, Margery. *Woman's Place Is at the Typewriter*. Philadelphia: Temple University Press, 2010.

Davis, Angela Y. *Blues Legacies and Black Feminism: Gertrude Ma Rainey, Bessie Smith, and Billie Holiday*. New York: Vintage, 1998.

Deer, Sarah. "Toward an Indigenous Jurisprudence of Rape." *Kansas Journal of Law & Public Policy* 14 (2004–2005): 121–154.

De Roche, Linda. *The Jazz Age: A Historical Exploration of Literature*. Santa Barbara: ABC–CLIO, 2015.

Dewey, John. "Professional Spirit Among Teachers." *American Teacher* 2 (1913): 114–116.

Diner, Hasia R. *The Jews of the United States, 1654 to 2000*. Berkeley: University of California Press, 2004.

Doan, Laura. "Passing Fashions: Reading Female Masculinities in the 1920s." *Feminist Studies* 24, no. 3 (1998): 663–700.

Doherty, Thomas. *Pre–Code Hollywood: Sex, Immorality, and Insurrection in American cinema, 1930–1934*. New York: Columbia University Press, 1999.

Dorr, Lisa Lindquist. "Arm in Arm: Gender, Eugenics, and Virginia's Racial Integrity Acts of the 1920s." *Journal of Women's History* 11, no. 1 (1999): 143–166.

Dorothy Parker Society. "About." Accessed August 7, 2020. https://dorothyparker .com.

Doughty, Frances M. "Gilt on Cardboard: Djuna Barnes as Illustrator of Her Life and Work." In *Silence and Power: A Reevaluation of Djuna Barnes*, edited by Mary Lynn Broe, 137–155. Carbondale: Southern Illinois University Press, 1991.

Dove, Mourning. *Cogewea: The Half–Blood*. Lincoln: University of Nebraska Press, 1981.

———. *Mourning Dove: A Salishan Autobiography*, edited by Jay Miller. Lincoln: University of Nebraska Press, 1990.

Dreifus, Erika. "A Room of Anzia Yezierska's Own." *JBooks.com: The Online Jewish Book Community*. 2009. Accessed December 17, 2021. http://jbooks.com/inter views/index/IP_Dreifus_Yezierska.htm.

Du Bois, W.E.B. "Passing." *The Crisis* 36 (1929): 234, 248–250.

———. *The Souls of Black Folk*. New York: Norton, 1999.

Dumenil, Lynn. *The Modern Temper: American Culture and Society in the 1920s*. New York: Hill and Wang, 1995.

Dydo, Ulla E. *Gertrude Stein: The Language that Rises: 1923–1934*. Evanston: Northwestern University Press, 2003.

Edmunds, Susan. *Grotesque Relations: Modernist Domestic Fiction and the U.S. Welfare State*. Oxford: Oxford University Press, 2008.

Entin, Jonahtan L. "A Civil Rights Life: Nathaniel R. Jones. Answering the Call: An Autobiography of the Modern Struggle to End Racial Discrimination in America. New York: The New Press, 2016." *Case Western Reserve Law Review* 68, no. 2 (2017): 651–673.

Ephron, Nora. *Crazy Salad and Scribble Scribble: Some Things about Women and Notes on Media*. New York: Vintage, 2012.

Evans, Nicholas M. *Writing Jazz: Race, Nationalism, and Modern Culture in the 1920s*. New York: Routledge, 2016.

Faderman, Lillian. "Lesbian Chic in the '20s." *UCLA Film and Television Archive*. 1990. Accessed December 17, 2021. https://www.cinema.ucla.edu/sites/default/ files/Lesbian%20Chic%20Lillian%20Faderman%201990.pdf.

———. *Odd Girls and Twilight Lovers: A History of Lesbian Life in Twentieth–Century America*. New York: Columbia University Press, 2012.

———. "'Which, Being Interpreted, Is as May Be, or Otherwise': Ada Russell in Amy Lowell's Life and Work." In *Amy Lowell, American Modern*, edited by Adrienne Munich and Melissa Bradshaw, 59–76. New Brunswick: Rutgers University Press, 2004.

Fahy, Thomas. "Unsilencing Lesbianism in the Early Fiction of Gayl Jones." In *After the Pain: Critical Essays on Gayl Jones*, edited by Fiona Mills and Keith B. Mitchell, 203–220. New York: Peter Lang, 2006.

Farley, Reynolds and Walter R. Allen. *The Color Line and the Quality of Life in America*. New York: Russell Sage Foundation, 1987.

Fass, Paula S. *The Damned and the Beautiful*. Oxford: Oxford University Press, 1977.

Faulkner, Anne Shaw. "Does Jazz Put the Sin in Syncopation?" *Ladies Home Journal* 38 (August 1921): 16, 34.

Feinstein, Elaine. *Bessie Smith: Empress of the Blues*. New York: Penguin, 1985.

Feinstein, Rachel A. *When Rape Was Legal: The Untold History of Sexual Violence during Slavery*. New York: Routledge, 2018. Accessed December 17, 2021. https://books.google.com.

Firestone, Shulamith. *The Dialectic of Sex: The Case for Feminist Revolution*. New York: Bantam, 1972.

Fischer, Lucy. Introduction to *American Cinema of the 1920s: Themes and Variations*. New Brunswick: Rutgers University Press, 2009.

Fisher, Dexter. Introduction to *Cogewea: The Half-Blood*. Lincoln: University of Nebraska Press, 1981.

Fishkin, Benjamin Hart. "F. Scott Fitzgerald and the Pain of Exclusion." In *Fears, Doubts and Joys of Not Belonging*, edited by Benjamin Hart Fishkin, Adaku T. Ankumah, and Bill F. Ndi. Bamenda: Langaa Research & Publishing Common Initiative Group, 2014.

Fitzgerald, F. Scott. "Echoes of the Jazz Age." *Scribner's Magazine* 90, no. 5 (1931): 459–465.

———. *The Great Gatsby*. New York: Charles Scribner's Sons, 1953.

Fitzpatrick, Kevin C. "Introduction: In the Aisle Seat with Dorothy Parker." In *Dorothy Parker: Complete Broadway, 1918–1923*, edited by Kevin C. Fitzpatrick, xiii–xxviii. Bloomington: iUniverse, 2014.

Fixico, Donald L. *Bureau of Indian Affairs*. Santa Barbara: ABC-CLIO, 2012.

Flash Lyrics. "Baby Doll." Accessed April 13, 2021. https://www.flashlyrics.com/lyrics/bessie-smith/baby-doll-41.

———. "Dinah." Accessed April 2, 2021. https://www.flashlyrics.com/lyrics/ethel-waters/dinah-84.

———. "Empty Bed Blues." Accessed April 5, 2021. https://www.flashlyrics.com/lyrics/bessie-smith/empty-bed-blues-56.

———. "I've Got What It Takes." Accessed April 2, 2021. https://www.flashlyrics.com/lyrics/bessie-smith/ive-got-what-it-takes-but-it-breaks-my-heart-to-give-it-away-61.

———. "My Man Blues." Accessed April 5, 2021. https://www.flashlyrics.com/lyrics/bessie-smith/my-man-blues-09.

———. "There'll Be a Hot Time in the Old Town Tonight." Accessed April 5, 2021. https://www.flashlyrics.com/lyrics/bessie-smith/therell-be-a-hot-time-in-the-old-town-tonight-98.

Fox, Meghan C. "'Vivid and Repulsive as the Truth': Hybridity and Sexual Difference in Djuna Barnes's *The Book of Repulsive Women*." *The Space Between: Literature and Culture 1914–1945* 12 (2016). Accessed December 17, 2021. https://scalar.usc.edu/works/the-space-between-literature-and-culture-1914-1945/vol12_2016_fox.

Francis, Elizabeth. *The Secret Treachery of Words: Feminism and Modernism in America*. Minneapolis: University of Minnesota Press, 2002.

Freeman, Susan K. *Sex Goes to School: Girls and Sex Education before the 1960s.* Champaign: University of Illinois Press, 2008.

Frei, Clifton. "Nella Larsen's Passing and the Tragedy of the Oppressed: Trauma, Race, Identity, and Reading Resistance," *NEIU 27th Annual Student Research and Creative Activities Symposium*, 2019.

Gall, Sandra J. "Seymour Barab's *Songs of Perfect Propriety Volumes I and II*: The Relationship between Barab's Music and Words by Dorothy Parker." PhD diss. University of Oklahoma, 2000.

Gerard, Jessica. "Lady Bountiful: Women of the Landed Classes and Rural Philanthropy." *Victorian Studies* 30, no. 2 (1987): 183–210.

Gilman, Charlotte Perkins. *Women and Economics: A Study of the Economic Relation Between Men and Women as a Factor in Social Evolution.* Boston: Small, Maynard & Co., 1898.

———. "The Yellow Wallpaper." In *Herland and Selected Stories*, edited by Barbara H. Solomon, 165–180. New York: Signet, 1992.

Gilman–Forlini, Quinn. "Erasing the Grotesque: An Analysis of Djuna Barnes' Detestation for *The Book of Repulsive Women*." *Apollon* 9 (2019): 33–37.

Gilmore, Leigh. *Autobiographics: A Feminist Theory of Women's Self-representation.* Ithaca: Cornell University Press, 1994.

Gioia, Ted. *The History of Jazz.* Oxford: Oxford University Press, 2011.

Goldberg, David Joseph. *Discontented America; The United States in the 1920s.* Baltimore: Johns Hopkins University Press, 1999.

Goodspeed-Chadwick, Julie. *Modernist Women Writers and War: Trauma and the Female Body in Djuna Barnes, H.D., and Gertrude Stein.* Baton Rouge: LSU Press, 2011.

Graydon, Lesley. "How Pink Is Your Melon, Joy? The Erotic, Sexual Language of Gertrude Stein." Accessed March 20, 2021. https://lesleygraydon.com.

Green, Barbara. "Spectacular Confessions: 'How It Feels to Be Forcibly Fed.'" *The Review of Contemporary Fiction* 13, no. 3 (1993): 70–88.

Greenberg, David. *Calvin Coolidge: The American Presidents Series: The 30th President, 1923–1929.* New York: Henry Holt and Company, 2006.

Griffin, Mary. "Novel of Race Consciousness." *The Detroit Free Press*, June 23, 1929.

Griffith, R. Marie. "Body Salvation: New Thoughts, Father Divine, and the Feast of Material Pleasures." *Religion and American Culture: A Journal of Interpretation* 11, no. 2 (2001): 119–153.

Hamilton, Marybeth. "SEX, The Drag, and 1920s Broadway." *The Drama Review* 36, no 4 (1992): 82–100.

———. *"When I'm Bad, I'm Better": Mae West, Sex, and American Entertainment.* Berkeley: University of California Press, 1997.

Hampshire, Audrey. "The Lavendar Lens: Lesbianism in the United States 1870–1969." *Nonviolent Social Change: the Bulletin of the Manchester College Peace Studies Institute* 35 (2008). Accessed December 17, 2021. http://ww2.manchester.edu/peacestudies/bulletin/2008/documents/Hampshire.pdf.

Harrison, Daphne Duval. *Black Pearls: Blues Queens of the 1920s*. New Brunswick: Rutgers University Press, 2000.

Haskell, Molly. *From Reverence to Rape: The Treatment of Women in the Movies*. Chicago: University of Chicago Press, 2016.

Hearne, Kimberly. "Fitzgerald's Rendering of a Dream." *The Explicator* 68, no. 3 (2010): 189–194.

Hegeman, Susan. "Taking Blondes Seriously." *American Literary History* 7, no. 3 (1995): 525–554.

Hinckley, James, Jim Hinckley, and Jon G. Robinson. *The Big Book of Car Culture*. St. Paul: Motorbooks, 2005.

Hine, Darlene Clark. "Rape and the Inner Lives of Black Women in the Middle West," *Signs* 14, no. 4 (1989): 912–920.

Historical Homos. "Ma and Bessie: Queens of the Bisexual Blues." Accessed April 2, 2021. https://www.historicalhomos.com/cumming-to-you-live/bisexual-blues.

Holton, Robert. "The Politics of Point of View: Representing History in Mourning Dove's Cogewea and D'Arcy McNickle's The Surrounded." *Studies in American Indian Literatures* 9, no. 2 (1997): 69–80.

Holzer, Lena. "Smashing the Binary? A New Era of Legal Gender Registration in the Yogyakarta Principles Plus 10." *International Journal of Gender, Sexuality and Law* 1, no. 1 (2020): 98–133.

Homestead, Melissa J. "Willa Cather, Sarah Orne Jewett, and the Historiography of Lesbian Sexuality." In *Willa Cather and the Nineteenth Century. Cather Studies 10*, edited by Richard Millington and Anne Kaufman, 3–37. Lincoln: University of Nebraska Press, 2015.

Horak, Laura. *Girls Will Be Boys: Cross–Dressed Women, Lesbians, and American Cinema, 1908–1934*. New Brunswick: Rutgers University Press, 2016.

Hostert, Anna Camaiti. *Passing: A Strategy to Dissolve Identities and Remap Differences*. Translated by Christine Marciasini. Plainsboro: Associated University Press, 2007.

Hovey, Jamie. "Lesbian Chivalry in Amy Lowell's *Sword Blades and Poppy Seed*." In *Amy Lowell, American Modern*, edited by Adrienne Munich and Melissa Bradshaw, 77–89. New Brunswick: Rutgers University Press, 2004.

Hughes, Langston. "The Negro Artist and the Racial Mountain." In *Within the Circle: An Anthology of African American Literary Criticism from the Harlem Renaissance to the Present*, edited by Angelyn Mitchell, 55–59. Durham: Duke University Press, 1994.

Hurston, Zora Neale. "How It Feels to Be Colored Me." *The World Tomorrow*, May 1928, 215–216.

———. *Their Eyes Were Watching God*. Champaign: University of Illinois Press, 1978.

Hutchinson, George. *In Search of Nella Larsen: A Biography of the Color Line*. Cambridge: Harvard University Press, 2006.

———. "Nella Larsen and the Veil of Race." *American Literary History* 9, no. 2 (1997): 329–349.

Hutchinson, Pamela. *Pandora's Box*. London: The British Film Institute, 2018.

Inness, Sherrie A. "Who's Afraid of Stephen Gordon?: The Lesbian in the United States Popular Imagination of the 1920s." *NWSA Journal* 4, no. 3 (1992): 303–320.

Jenainati, Cathia. *Feminism: A Graphic Guide*. London: Icon, 2019. Accessed December17, 2021. https://books.google.com.

Johnson, Ken. "Dorothy Parker's Perpetual Motion." In *American Women Short Story Writers: A Collection of Critical Essays*, edited by Julie Brown, 251–266. New York: Rutledge, 2000.

Johnson, Maria V. "'Jelly Jelly Jellyroll': Lesbian Sexuality and Identity in Women's Blues." *Women & Music* 7 (2003): 31–52.

Kaplan, Carla. "Introduction: Nella Larsen's Erotics of Race." In *Passing*, edited by Carla Kaplan. New York: Norton, 2007.

Karell, Linda K. *Writing Together, Writing Apart: Collaboration in Western American Literature*. Lincoln: University of Nebraska Press, 2002.

Katz, Jonathan Ned. *The Invention of Heterosexuality*. Chicago: University of Chicago Press, 2007.

Keats, John. *You Might as Well Live: The Life and Times of Dorothy Parker*. New York: Simon and Schuster, 1990. Accessed December 17, 2021. https://books.google .com.

Kent, Alicia. "Mourning Dove's Cogewea: Writing Her Way into Modernity." *MELUS* 24, no. 3 (1999): 39–66.

Kent, Kathryn R. "'Lullaby for a Lady's Lady': Lesbian Identity in *Ladies Almanack*." *Review of Contemporary Fiction* 13, no. 3 (1993): 89–96.

Kessler–Harris, Alice. Introduction to *Bread Givers*. New York: Persea, 2003.

Keyser, Catherine. *Playing Smart: New York Women Writers and Modern Magazine Culture*. New Brunswick: Rutgers University Press, 2010.

———. "The Macabre Magazine: Dorothy Parker, Humor, and the Female Body." In *Death Becomes Her: Cultural Narratives of Femininity and Death in Nineteenth–Century America*, edited by Elizabeth Dill and Sheri Weinstein, 131–156. Newcastle: Cambridge Scholars, 2008.

Knight, Oliver. *Following the Indian Wars: The Story of the Newspaper Correspondents among the Indian Campaigners*. Norman: University of Oklahoma Press, 1993.

Kwan, Samantha. "Navigating Public Spaces: Gender, Race, and Body Privilege in Everyday Life." In *The Politics of Women's Bodies: Sexuality, Appearance, and Behavior*, edited by Rose Weitz, 241–257. Oxford: Oxford University Press, 1998.

Larsen, Nella. *Passing*. New York: Norton, 2007.

Last FM. "'Taint Nobody's Business." Accessed April 5, 2021. https://www.last.fm/ music/Bessie+Smith/_/%27Tain%27t+Nobody%27s+Business+If+I+Do/+lyrics.

Latham, Angela. *Posing a Threat*. Middletown: Wesleyan University Press, 2000.

Lawrence, Bonita. "Gender, Race, and the Regulation of Native Identity in Canada and the United States: An Overview." *Hypatia* 18, no. 2 (2003): 3–31.

———. "Legislating Identity: Colonialism, Land and Indigenous Legacies." In *The SAGE Handbook of Identities*, edited by Margaret Wetherell and Chandra Talpade Mohanty, 508–528. Thousand Oaks: Sage, 2010.

Lawrence, Jane. "The Indian Health Service and the Sterilization of Native American Women." *American Indian Quarterly* 24, no. 3 (2000): 400–419.

Lee, Hermione. *Willa Cather: Double Lives*. New York: Vintage, 2017.

Lee, Shayne. *Erotic Revolutionaries: Black Women, Sexuality, and Popular Culture*. Lanham: Hamilton Books, 2010.

Leonard, Thomas C. "The Reluctant Conquerors: How the Generals Viewed the Indians." *American Heritage* 27, no. 5 (1976). Accessed December 17, 2021. https://www.americanheritage.com/reluctant–conquerors#1.

Linzie, Anna. *The True Story of Alice B. Toklas: A Study of Three Autobiographies*. Iowa City: University of Iowa Press, 2006.

Listerine advertisement. "The one true friend she has." *Delineator* 115, no. 1 (July 1929): 69.

Loos, Anita. *Gentlemen Prefer Blondes: The Illuminating Diary of a Professional Lady*. New York: Liveright, 1998.

Lorber, Judith. "Using Gender to Undo Gender: A Feminist Degendering Movement." *Feminist Theory* 1, no. 1 (2000): 79–95.

Louvish, Simon. *Mae West: It Ain't No Sin*. New York: St. Martin's Press, 2005.

Lovett, Josephine. *The Dancing Girl*. Original script, Binghamton University archives, 1928.

Lowell, Amy. *A Critical Fable*. New York: Houghton Mifflin, 1922.

———. *Ballads for Sale*. New York: Houghton Mifflin, 1927.

———. *The Complete Poetical Works of Amy Lowell*. New York: Houghton Mifflin, 1955.

———. *Pictures of the Floating World*. New York: Houghton Mifflin, 1921.

———. *Poetry and Poets: Essays*. New York: Biblo & Tannen, 1971.

———. *What's O'Clock*. New York: Houghton Mifflin, 1925.

Luhrs, Marie. "Fashionable Poetry." *Poetry* 30, no. 1 (1927): 52–54.

Lutes, Jean Marie. *Front Page Girls: Women Journalists in American Culture and Fiction, 1880–1930*. Ithaca: Cornell University Press, 2006.

Lyrics Mode. "Young Woman's Blues." Accessed April 5, 2021. https://www.lyricsmode.com/lyrics/b/bessie_smith/young_womans_blues.html.

Maillard, Kevin N. "The Pocahontas Exception: The Exemption of American Indian Ancestry from Racial Purity Law." *Michigan Journal of Race & Law* 12 (2007): 351–386.

Mark, Rebecca. Introduction to *Lifting Belly*. Tallahassee: The Naiad Press, 1995.

Marks, Patricia. *Bicycles, Bangs, and Bloomers: The New Woman in the Popular Press*. Lexington: University Press of Kentucky, 1990.

Martins, Susana S. "Gender Trouble and Lesbian Desire in Djuna Barnes's 'Nightwood.'" *Frontiers: A Journal of Women Studies* 20, no. 3 (1999): 108–126.

McCarthy, Ann. "Inside Stories: Stemteema's Histories of Early Contact in Mourning Dove's 'Cogewea: The Half–Blood.'" *Australasian Journal of American Studies* 25, no. 1 (2006): 32–48.

McGuire, John. "From the Courts to the State Legislatures: Social Justice Feminism, Labor Legislation, and the 1920s." *Labor History* 45, no. 2 (2004): 225–246.

McWhorter, Lucullus. "To the Reader." In *Cogewea: The Half–Blood*. Lincoln: University of Nebraska Press, 1981.

Meade, Marion. *Bobbed Hair and Bathtub Gin: Writers Running Wild in the Twenties*. Orlando: Houghton Mifflin Harcourt, 2004.

———. *Dorothy Parker: What Fresh Hell Is This?* New York: Penguin, 1989.

———. Introduction to *The Portable Dorothy Parker*. New York: Penguin, 2006.

Millay, Edna St. Vincent. *A Few Figs from Thistles*. New York: Harper and Brothers, 1922.

———. "I know my mind and I have made my choice." *Poetry: A Magazine of Verse*. 37, no. 1 (October 1930): 2.

Miller, Brett Candish. *Flawed Light: American Women Poets and Alcohol*. Champaign: University of Illinois Press, 2009.

Miller, Gwenn A. "Contact and Conquest in Colonial North America." In *A Companion to American Women's History*, edited by Nancy A. Hewitt, 35–48. Hoboken: John Wiley & Sons, 2005.

Milton, Emily. "Triangular Identities and Flourishing Sexualities: 1920s–'30s Harlem as a Positive Queer Space for the Formation of a Black Lesbian Identity." *Hard Wire: The Undergraduate Journal of Sexual Diversity Studies* (2013): 15–24.

Miquel-Baldellou, Marta. "The Beloved Purple of Their Eyes: Inheriting Bessie Smith's Politics of Sexuality." *Miscelanea: a Journal of English and American Studies* 36 (2007): 67–88.

Mondimore, Francis Mark. *A Natural History of Homosexuality*. Baltimore: The Johns Hopkins University Press, 1996.

Mulvey, Laura. "Unmasking the Gaze: Some Thoughts on New Feminist Film Theory and History." In *Reclaiming the Archive: Feminism and Film History*, edited by Vicki Callahan, 17–31. Detroit: Wayne State University Press, 2010.

Mumford, Kevin. *Interzones*. New York: Columbia University Press, 1997.

Munt, Sally. *Heroic Desire: Lesbian Identity and Cultural Space*. New York: New York University Press, 1998.

Naison, Mark. "Appropriating Black Music while Segregating Black People: The Paradox of 1920's American Culture." *DigitalResearch@Fordham*. Bronx African American History Project. 2020. Accessed December 17, 2021. https://fordham.bepress.com/cgi/viewcontent.cgi?article=1009&context=baahp_essays.

National Organization for Women. "History of Marches and Mass Actions." Accessed August 26, 2020. https://now.org.

Neatby, Nicole. "Preparing for the Working World: Women at Queen's during the 1920s." *Historical Studies in Education* 1, no. 1 (1989): 53–72.

Neilsen, Kim E. *Un–American Womanhood: Antiradicalism, Antifeminism, and the First Red Scare*. Columbus: The Ohio State University Press, 2001.

Noskin, David and Angela Marshalek. "Applying Multiculturalism to a High School American Literature Course: Changing Lenses and Crossing Borders." *The English Journal* 84, no. 6 (1995): 80–86.

Obourn, Milo. "Disabling Racial Economies: Albeism and the Reproduction of Racial Difference in Nella Larsen's Passing and Toni Morrison's 'Recitatif.'" In *Reading Contemporary Black British and African American Women Writers: Race, Ethics,*

Narrative Form, edited by Jean Wyatt and Sheldon George. New York: Routledge, 2020. Accessed December 17, 2021. https://books.google.com.

Orleck, Annelise. *Rethinking American Women's Activism*. New York: Routledge, 2015.

Outhistory. "Ma Rainey's 'Prove It on Me Blues.'" Accessed April 2, 2021. https://outhistory.org/exhibits/show/rainey/rainey2.

Owens, Louis. *Other Destinies: Understanding the American Indian Novel*. Norman: University of Oklahoma Press, 1994.

Parker, Dorothy. *Complete Stories*, edited by Colleen Breese. New York: Penguin, 1995. Accessed December 17, 2021. https://books.google.com.

———. *Dorothy Parker: Complete Broadway, 1918–1923*, edited by Kevin C. Fitzpatrick. Bloomington: iUniverse, 2014.

———. *Enough Rope*. New York: Boni and Liveright, 1926.

———. *Men I'm Not Married To*. New York: Doubleday, 1922.

———. *Not So Deep as a Well: Collected Poems*. London: Hamish Hamilton, 1937. Accessed December 17, 2021. https://books.google.com.

———. *The Portable Dorothy Parker*. New York: Penguin, 2006.

———. "Women: A Hate Song." *Vanity Fair*, August 1916. Accessed December 17, 2021. https://www.vanityfair.com/news/1916/08/women-a-hate-song.

Parker, Sarah. "Amy Lowell's Appetites: Food, Consumption and Homoerotic Desire in Amy Lowell's Poetry." In *Fat Sex: New Directions in Theory and Activism*, edited by Helen Hester and Caroline Walters, 159–180. New York: Routledge, 2015.

Parsons, Elsie Clews. "Sex." In *Civilization in the United States: An Inquiry by Thirty Americans*, edited by Harold E. Stearns, 309–318. New York: Harcourt, Brace, 1922.

Patterson, Martha H. Introduction to *The American New Woman Revisited: A Reader, 1894–1930*, edited by Martha H. Patterson, 1–28. New Brunswick: Rutgers University Press, 2008.

Pettit, Rhonda S. *A Gendered Collision: Sentimentalism and Modernism in Dorothy Parker's Poetry and Fiction*. Madison: Fairleigh Dickinson University Press, 2000.

Porter, Cole. "Just One of Those Things." *Poets.org*. Accessed April 7, 2021. https://poets.org/poem/just-one-those-things.

Protest Song Lyrics. "B.D. Woman's Blues, song lyrics." Accessed April 2, 2021. http://www.protestsonglyrics.net/LGBT_Songs/BD-Womans-Blues.phtml.

Rabinovitch-Fox, Einav. "[Re]Fashioning the New Woman: Women's Dress, the Oriental Style, and the Construction of American Feminist Imagery in the 1910s." *Journal of Women's History* 27, no. 2 (2015): 14–36.

Ramirez, Renya K. "Learning across Differences: Native and Ethnic Studies Feminisms." *American Quarterly* 60, no. 2 (2008): 303–307.

Reynolds, Jason and Ibram X. Kendi. *Stamped: Racism, Antiracism, and You*. New York: Little, Brown and Company 2020.

Roberts, Mary Louise. "True Womanhood Revisited." *Journal of Woman's History* 14, no. 1 (2002): 150–155.

Rowe, Kathleen. *The Unruly Woman: Gender and the Genres of Laughter*. Austin: University of Texas Press, 1995.

Russell, Paul. *The Gay 100: A Ranking of the Most Influential Gay Men and Lesbians, Past and Present*. New York: Kensington Books, 1995.

Russell, Thaddeus. *A Renegade History of the United States*. New York: Free Press, 2010.

Russo, Vito. *The Celloid Closet: Homosexuality in the Movies*. New York: HarperCollins, 1987.

Schlissel, Lillian. Introduction to *Three Plays by Mae West*. New York: Routledge, 1997.

Schreiner, Olive. *Woman and Labour*. Leipzig: Bernhard Tauchnitz, 1911.

Schwarz, A.B. Christa. *Gay Voices of the Harlem Renaissance*. Bloomington: Indiana University Press, 2003.

Seidler, Victor. *Jewish Philosophy and Western Culture: A Modern Introduction*. London: I.B. Tauris, 2007.

Sharp, Patrick B. *Savage Perils: Racial Frontiers and Nuclear Apocalypse in American Culture*. Norman: University of Oklahoma Press, 2007.

Shaw, Arnold. *The Jazz Age: Popular Music in the 1920s*. Oxford: Oxford University Press, 1987.

Sheets–Johnstone, Maxine. *The Roots of Power: Animate Form and Gendered Bodies*. Chicago: Open Court, 1994.

Shoemaker, Jeff. *Nella Larsen's Passing and Color Theory: Beyond Black & White*. Honors Thesis. Portland State University, 2014.

Silverman, Stephen M. *Funny Ladies*. Boston: New World City, 2018. Accessed December 17, 2021. https://books.google.com.

Silverstein, Stuart Y. Introduction to *Not Much Fun: The Lost Poems of Dorothy Parker*. New York: Scribner, 2009.

Simmons, Christina. *Making Marriage Modern*. Oxford: Oxford University Press, 2009.

Simon, Linda. *The Biography of Alice B. Toklas*. Lincoln: University of Nebraska Press, 1991.

Simpson, Amelia. "Black on Blonde: The Africanist Presence in Dorothy Parker's 'Big Blonde.'" *College Literature* 23, no. 3 (1996): 105–116.

———. "Premium Swift: Dorothy Parker's Iron Mask of Femininity (1996)." In *The Critical Waltz: Essays on the Work of Dorothy Parker*, edited by Rhonda S. Pettit. Madison: Fairleigh Dickinson University Press, 2005.

Six, Beverly G. "Mourning Dove (Hum–Ishu–Ma) [Christine Quintasket] (1882?–1936)." In *American Woman Writers, 1900–1945: A Bio–bibliographical Critical Sourcebook*, edited by Laurie Champion, 252–257. Westport: Greenwood, 2000.

Smith, Andrea. "American Indian Boarding Schools." In *Encyclopedia of Women and Religion in North America*, edited by Rosemary Skinner Keller, Rosemary Radford Ruether, and Marie Cantlon, 97–101. Bloomington: Indiana University Press, 2006.

Smith, Raymond A. and Donald P. Haider-Markel, *Gay and Lesbian Americans and Political Participation: A Reference Handbook*. Santa Barbara: ABC–CLIO, 2002.

Smith-Rosenberg, Carroll. "The New Woman as Androgyne: Social Disorder and Gender Crisis, 1870–1936." In *Feminism: Critical Concepts in Literary and Cultural Studies*, edited by Mary Evans, 156–208. New York: Routledge, 2001.

Song Lyrics. "I Need a Little Sugar in My Bowl." Accessed April 5, 2021. http:// www.songlyrics.com/Bessie-smith/need-a-little-sugar-in-my-bowl-lyrics.

———. "I Used to be Your Sweet Mama." Accessed April 2, 2021. http://www.song lyrics.com/Bessie-smith/i-used-to-be-your-sweet-mama-lyrics.

———. "It Won't Be You." Accessed April 5, 2021. http://www.songlyrics.com/ bessie-smith/it-won-t-be-you-lyrics.

———. "Pinchbacks—Take 'Em Away." Accessed April 2, 2021. http://www.songlyr ics.com/bessie-smith/pinchbacks-take-em-away-lyrics.

Sound Media. "I Want To Be Bad." Accessed April 2, 2021. http://www.songlyrics .com/helen–kane/i-want-to-be-bad-follow-thru-1929-show-lyrics.

Stein, Gertrude. *A Book Concluding with As a Wife Has a Cow: A Love Story*. New York: Ultramarine, 1992.

———. *A Stein Reader*. Evanston: Northwestern University Press, 1993.

———. "Before the Flowers of Friendship Faded." *Poetry Nook*. Accessed April 2, 2021. https://www.poetrynook.com/poem/flowers-friendship-faded-friendship -faded.

———. *Geography and Plays*. Mineola: Dover, 1999.

———. *Lifting Belly*. Tallahassee: The Naiad Press, 1995.

———. *Selected Writings of Gertrude Stein*. New York: Vintage Books, 1990.

Stein, Marc. *Rethinking the Gay and Lesbian Movement*. New York: Routledge, 2012.

Steinbeck, John. *Cannery Row*. New York: Penguin, 1994.

Stern, Alexandra Minna. "Forced Sterilization Policies in the US Targeted Minorities and Those with Disabilities—and Lasted into the 21st Century." *The Conversation*, August 26, 2020. https://theconversation.com/forced-sterilization-policies-in-the -us-targeted-Minorities-and-those-with-disabilities-and-lasted-into-the-21st-cen tury-143144.

Taft, Michael. *Talkin' To Myself: Blues Lyrics, 1921–1942*. New York: Rutledge, 2005.

Taggard, Genevieve. "You Might as Well Live." *New York Herald Tribune Books*, March 27, 1927.

Taylor, Melanie Benson. *Disturbing Calculations: The Economics of Identity in Postcolonial Southern, 1912–2002*. Athens: University of Georgia Press, 2008.

Toledo, Charlotte N. "She Would Not Be Silenced: Mae West's Struggle against Censorship." *The Downtown Review* 3, no. 2 (2016): 1–8.

Tolman, Deborah L. "Doing Desire: Adolescent Girls' Struggles for/with Sexuality." *Gender & Society* 8, no. 3 (1994): 324–342.

Trennert, Robert A. "Educating Indian Girls at Nonreservation Boarding Schools, 1878–1920." *Western Historical Quarterly* 13, no. 3 (1982): 271–290.

Utell, Janine. *Literary Couples and 20th–Century Life Writing: Narrative and Intimacy*. London: Bloomsbury Academic, 2020.

U.S. National Archives and Records Administration. "Photographs of the 369th Infantry and African Americans during World War I." *National Archives Educator Resources*, 2016. Accessed Dec. 17, 2021. https://www.archives.gov/education/ lessons/369th-infantry.

Valentiner, Dana-Sophia. "The Human Rights to Sexual Autonomy." *German Law Journal* 22, no. 5 (2021), 703–717.

Van Cleave, Kendra. "Fashioning the College Woman: Dress, Gender, and Sexuality at Smith College in the 1920s." *The Journal of American Culture* 32, no. 1 (2009): 4–15.

Veblen, Thorstein. *The Theory of the Leisure Class: An Economic Study of Institutions.* London: Macmillan, 1899.

Vieco, Francisco Jose Cortes. "'I hate Women. They get on my Nerves': Dorothy Parker's Poetry of Female Sympathy." *ES Review: Spanish Journal of English Studies* 38 (2017): 65–88.

———. "The (Mis)Education of 'The American Girl' in Europe in Anita Loos's *Gentlemen Prefer Blondes.*" *Revista de Estudios Norteamericanos* 19 (2015): 29–48.

Walby, Sylvia. "'Backlash' in Historical Context." In *Making Connections: Women's Studies, Women's Movements, Women's Lives,* edited by Mary Kennedy, Cathy Lubelska, and Val Walsh, 76–87. New York: Taylor and Francis, 2005.

Walker, Rafael. "Nella Larsen Reconsidered: The Trouble with Desire in 'Quicksand' and 'Passing.'" *MELUS* 41, no. 1 (2016): 165–192.

Waters, Michael. "A Pride Month Playlist, Brought to You by the Jazz Age." *Atlas Obscura*, June 9, 2017. https://www.atlasobscura.com/articles/queer-1920s-music-videos.

Webb, Joyce G. "The Evolution of Women's Roles within the University and the Workplace." *Forum on Public Policy* 5 (2010): 1–17. Accessed December 17, 2021. https://files.eric.ed.gov/fulltext/EJ913097.pdf.

Weeks, Jeffrey. *Sex, Politics and Society: The Regulation of Sexuality since 1800.* New York: Taylor and Francis, 2017.

Weitz, Rose. "A History of Women's Bodies." In *The Politics of Women's Bodies: Sexuality, Appearance, and Behavior,* edited by Rose Weitz, 3–12. Oxford: Oxford University Press, 1998.

West, Mae. *Three Plays by Mae West,* edited by Lillian Schlissel. New York: Routledge, 1997.

Wharton, Edith. *The House of Mirth.* Peterborough: Broadview, 2005.

Wight, Doris T. "Woman as Eros–Rose in Gertrude Stein's *Tender Buttons* and Contemporaneous Portraits," *Wisconsin Academy of Sciences, Arts and Letters* 74 (1986): 34–40.

Wilentz, Gay. "Cultural Mediation and the Immigrant's Daughter: Anzia Yezierska's *Bread Givers.*" *MELUS* 17, no. 3 (1991–1992): 33–41.

Williams, Sherley Anne. Foreword to *Their Eyes Were Watching God.* Champaign: University of Illinois Press, 1978.

Wilson, Edmund. *Classics and Commercials: A Literary Chronicle of the Forties.* New York: Macmillan, 1950. Accessed December 17, 2021. https://books.google.com.

———. "Dorothy Parker's Poems." *New Republic*, January 19, 1927.

Wing, Adrien Katherine. "Henry J. Richardson III: A Critical Race Man." *Temple International & Comparative Law Journal* 31, no. 1 (2017): 377–392.

Wollstonecraft, Mary. *A Vindication of the Rights of Woman.* Project Gutenberg, 2001. Accessed Dec. 17, 2021. http://www.gutenberg.org/ebooks/3420.

Wong, Elizabeth. "A Shameful History: Eugenics in Virginia." *ACLU Virginia*, January 11, 2013. Access December 17, 2021, https://acluva.org/en/news/shamful-history -Eugenics-virginia.

Woolf, Virginia. *A Room of One's Own*. Orlando: Harcourt, 1989.

Woolner, Cookie. "'Woman Slain in Queer Love Brawl': African American Women, Same-Sex Desire, and Violence in the Urban North, 1920–1929." *The Journal of African American History* 100, no. 3 (2015): 406–427.

Woyshner, Christine. "Teaching the Women's Club Movement in United States History." *The Social Studies* 93, no. 1 (2002): 11–17.

Yezierska, Anzia. *Bread Givers*. New York: Persea, 2003.

———. *How I Found America: Collected Stories of Anzia Yezierska*. New York: Persea, 1991.

Younging, Gregory. *Elements of Indigenous Style: A Guide for Writing By and About Indigenous Peoples*. Edmonton: Brush, 2018.

Zeitz, Joshua. *Flapper*. New York: Three Rivers Press, 2006.

Index

About the Author

Matthew Niven Teorey currently teaches in the English department at Peninsula College in Port Angeles, Washington. He earned his PhD at the University of New Mexico. This book was inspired by a humanities course he developed that takes an integrated look at the literature, music, dance, film, fashion, art/photography, drama, advertising, and popular culture of the 1920s.

CPSIA information can be obtained
at www.ICGtesting.com
Printed in the USA
LVHW100950081122
732643LV00002B/6

9 781793 628329